Intelligent Internal Control and Risk Management

T0313123

Intelligent Internal Control and Risk Management

Designing High-Performance Risk Control Systems

MATTHEW LEITCH

Routledge
Taylor & Francis Group

LONDON AND NEW YORK

First published in paperback 2024

First published 2008 by Gower Publishing

Published 2016 by Routledge
4 Park Square, Milton Park, Abingdon, Oxon OX14 4RN

and by Routledge
605 Third Avenue, New York, NY 10158

Routledge is an imprint of the Taylor & Francis Group, an informa business

British Library Cataloguing in Publication Data
Leitch, Matthew
Intelligent internal control and risk management :
designing high-performance risk control systems
1. Auditing, Internal 2. Risk management
I. Title
658.1′55′011

Library of Congress Cataloging-in-Publication Data
Leitch, Matthew.
Intelligent internal control and risk management : designing high-performance risk control systems / by Matthew Leitch.
p. cm.
Includes index.
ISBN 978-0-566-08799-8
1. Auditing, Internal. 2. Risk management. I. Title.

HF5668.25.L43 2008
658.15′5011--dc22

2007049170

ISBN 13: 978-0-566-08799-8 (hbk)
ISBN 13: 978-1-03-283800-7 (pbk)
ISBN 13: 978-1-315-58916-9 (ebk)

DOI: 10.4324/9781315589169

Contents

List of Tables

List of Figures

Introduction

What we have here is an opportunity to create value – actually a wagon-load of opportunities to create value. The rapidly merging fields of internal control and risk management often look established, standardized, and even dull. Experts in these fields cultivate that impression but the truth is that we're still at the Wild West stage. Most people working in this territory are pioneers trying to get by with a handful of crude tools. We're just getting started and many risk and control programmes are hanging on to survival by their fingernails. There are snake-oil salesmen who will sell you a cure for all your ills, and Coso is a barmaid at the Sarbanes-Oxley saloon.[1]

It's no surprise that many people today view internal control and risk management as dreary chores of little real value done only to placate regulators and auditors. Happily, it doesn't have to be that way, which is where the wagon-load of opportunities rumbles in.

The more we open our minds to new control techniques, and the harder we push ourselves to design better controls that give better results more easily, the greater the value will be.

A willingness to try new things is needed. There are many, many opportunities to improve internal control and risk management programmes, systems, tools, frameworks, and anything else that comes along in this area. Rarely have the value of risk management or internal control been measured and we should not, at this early stage, expect all new ideas to be promoted with quantified evidence of effectiveness and value. In time this will happen, but right now we already know a lot about what brings improvements and can quickly innovate our way to better results.

There are standards and widely quoted guides on how to do internal control and manage risk, but there are lots of them, they say different things, they lag behind leading practice, and many contain logical and practical flaws.

For example, even the biggest and most respected guides fail to mention the problem of *designing* controls. Yet this is where most people have the greatest difficulty and the scope is greatest for increasing value.

So, not only must we be willing to try new techniques but sometimes they will be techniques the official guidance hasn't yet recognized.

These are fields where we need to focus on design, innovation, and value, so they are what this book is about.

Note

1 COSO is the usual name for the Committee of Sponsoring Organizations of the Treadway Commission. COSO has published some of the most influential documents on internal control.

The Bigger Picture

1 *How Much Improvement is Possible?*

There's a lot of scope for getting greater business value from risk control. Evidence that risk and control programmes add value is patchy. This may be because many don't provide value but it's also because little attention has been paid to assessing or improving the value they provide.

Here are two examples to illustrate the scope for improvement and some of the main reasons why the opportunities still exist. Both examples contrast two approaches to a similar problem to highlight the room for improvement.

Example 1: Sarbanes-Oxley versus Revenue Assurance

The driving force behind risk and control over the last few decades has not been value. More often what people want is 'assurance' – a feeling of comfort, some protection from losses or just from embarrassment. Most often it is external demands that cause action. Regulators demand improvements and auditors nag for them.

When an auditor, especially an external auditor, recommends an improvement to controls it is usually with little concern for the cost of implementing or operating that control. The auditor wants to feel 'covered' by having recommended doing something in the face of a risk that exists, at least in theory. It is then for executives to decide whether the control is worthwhile or not, or just go along with it so that they themselves are also 'covered' from criticism should anything go wrong. Things go wrong often in organizations large and small but failure to act on the recommendations of a respected independent expert could make those problems more damaging personally for the executives concerned.

SECTION 404 OF THE SARBANES-OXLEY ACT 2002

The way Section 404 of the Sarbanes-Oxley Act of 2002 has been implemented has made this all painfully clear. The fiasco started with a flurry of financial reporting scandals at Enron, Worldcom, and elsewhere in the USA, that gave the impetus needed for the Sarbanes-Oxley Act to be passed into law. The Act included sections on internal controls over financial reporting. Section 404 required an external audit to attest to the statement top management had to make about the effectiveness of its controls.

At the time this was thought of by politicians and officials as a small extension to existing external audits and the average cost to companies listed in the USA was estimated at $91,000.[1]

The Act itself said very little in detail about controls or this new audit. The details were to be worked out by the Securities Exchange Commission (SEC) and a new body, the Public Companies Accounting Oversight Board (PCAOB).

The SEC decided that attesting to the statement on controls effectiveness made by top management could only be done if the external auditors did their own audit of internal controls in the company. Just looking at how management had gone about their assessment was not enough. They also decided that management should express their assessment of internal controls effectiveness as a black-and-white statement. Either the controls are effective or they are not. Even PricewaterhouseCoopers, the audit firm that has gained the most from Section 404, had not been promoting such an aggressive approach.

This, however, was just the first stage of interpretation to inflate the cost of compliance.

The PCAOB took their time deciding what audit standards to impose on external auditors. While they drafted their own proposals the gap was filled by guidance from the AICPA (American Institute of Certified Public Accountants) which was lobbying hard.

When the PCAOB's key guidance, Auditing Standard No. 2, was issued it painted a picture of a highly detailed and dismally old-fashioned audit. Examples of tests made it clear that they imagined many more tests and much higher audit test sample sizes than external auditors had relied on in the past.

This crucial standard also missed great opportunities to promote cost-effective audits using some of the techniques in Chapter 7 of this book.

Next it was the turn of external audit firms to pump up the costs of compliance. The PCAOB's guidance applied to external audit firms, not to companies. In fact there was little detail governing what companies did and this left many people asking for more 'guidance'. The big firms were only too happy to meet this need and did so by issuing their own guidance documents, usually based on the idea that companies would do basically the same as external auditors were required to do, but more of it. PricewaterhouseCoopers issued what was probably the most comprehensive guide,[2] containing among other things tables of required test sample sizes and required coverage levels.

Nor was this the last stage of cost magnification because now the paranoia spread to companies. Desperate to comply and unsure about what was required to do so, many decided to give themselves a big safety margin and simply do a vast amount of work. They asked their auditors what would be enough, but auditors could not say for sure and if pressed for guidance they certainly weren't going to suggest taking it easy. Consultants employed to help companies naturally reinforced these fears and quickly spread word of the rules laid down by the external audit firms. For internal controls specialists it was a feeding frenzy and the external audit firms roughly doubled their audit fees. Until early 2005 the dominant idea was to *comply* whatever the cost. Then the SEC asked companies for feedback.

Suddenly the floodgates opened and people began to feel empowered to speak out in public against what was happening. The big audit firms gave their view that things were working well, the requirements were sensible, companies and markets were seeing benefits, and things should be left as they were. They pointed to the large numbers of 'remediation' actions triggered by Section 404 audits as evidence that benefits were being enjoyed, though in practice many of these remediation actions were trivial or unnecessary. They pointed to benefits like improved understanding, documentation, and increased assurance.

But, with almost no exceptions, everyone else said the implementation of Section 404 had been too costly for the benefits gained.

The SEC and PCAOB reacted by blaming the external audit firms for taking an overly mechanical approach to the audits and in documents issued in May 2005 they countered various rules contained in the PricewaterhouseCoopers guide and others of its kind.

A year later and the SEC again sought feedback on the implementation of Section 404. This time respondents commented in even stronger language (e.g. 'staggering costs', 'unreasonably high', 'extreme conservatism on the part of the auditor community'). In response the SEC repeated its messages from a year earlier and began to criticize the PCAOB as well.

The story is still running, but at this stage it is clear that the costs of Section 404 were too high. The benefits are less clear since most people have avoided serious debate about them. The usual formula for comments is to say how much you support the aims of the Act before launching into criticisms of its implementation.

It is also clear that auditors, and especially the big external audit firms, have had a huge influence on the thinking behind internal controls and business risk management. They have written most of the guidance, though rarely published it themselves.[3]

Thanks to the Sarbanes-Oxley Act, and Section 404 in particular, the reputation of internal control and business risk management has been damaged severely.

All this is now quite well known in the world of risk and control, but fewer people have a clear idea of just how different things could be. Once you have the contrast it is easier to see the full extent of the value opportunity.

HOW IT COULD AND SHOULD BE: REVENUE ASSURANCE

Here's an unforgettable example of risk control that delivered measured financial benefits, among others, far in excess of its costs.

In the 1990s telecommunications was a huge growth industry with national markets being opened up to competition, with new technology, the Internet, and high expectations. Such was the pace of change that most companies in this sector, the 'telcos', found it difficult to keep their billing systems up to date with their products, prices, and customer requirements.

At some point people began to realize that many bills sent to customers were incomplete. Customers who were prepared to pay for the services they had used weren't even being asked to pay. How much money was involved? Nobody knew for certain but early examples included figures of over 10 per cent of revenue. In at least one case a new mobile service was launched before any billing capability existed, so it was given away free. More typically most people thought the lost revenue was usually somewhere between 2 per cent and 5 per cent of total revenue.

Notice that we're talking about percentages of *revenue*, not profit. As a percentage of typical profits it was a much larger amount and the problem quickly got a lot of attention.

Teams were formed in most telcos to tackle this problem and the euphemistic name given to their activities was 'revenue assurance'. In theory, the goal of revenue assurance was to provide assurance to management that all services provided were billed completely and accurately. In reality, everyone knew they were not being billed completely and accurately so the real goal was to reduce the size of the losses.

Very soon there were conferences on revenue assurance and dozens of software and hardware tools on sale to help do it.

Although the big audit firms quickly joined in, the main ideas on how to do revenue assurance tended to reflect quality management and engineering more than accountancy. This is because many people doing revenue assurance, being telecommunications people, had that kind of background and this helped them deal with the complex systems issues involved.

In the UK, the industry regulator, Oftel, introduced rules requiring the big operators in the UK to measure the accuracy of their 'metering' (i.e. the initial measurement of call durations and other details used in billing). Many years later this was extended to measuring the accuracy of bills themselves.[4]

Measurement could be done in various ways, but the most popular was to use electronic boxes that could make telephone calls automatically according to a pre-specified schedule of times and durations and then compare calls made with the call records provided for billing. Many millions of calls were made this way every month.

As so often, regulation was driving internal control but this time telcos were doing revenue assurance for their own reasons. The UK regulations did no more than push them to an even higher level of accuracy than most thought worthwhile, and revenue assurance also thrived in countries without such regulations.

The direct savings and money recovered by back-billing customers could easily be calculated, even if the total benefits of the work could not be, and typically revenue assurance projects generated several times the money they cost.

New projects were justified on crude cost-benefit grounds without even trying to consider the impact on customers or work saved internally. Consultants offered to work on a commission basis, taking a percentage of the money saved or recovered.

Most revenue assurance projects relied heavily on software tools to make detailed comparisons between databases and search huge files for anomalies that indicated lost money. This combination of technology and money proved highly effective, even though the projects were often difficult to manage due to the high levels of uncertainty involved.

Was this gold rush something that could only happen in telecoms? Perhaps few other industries will ever find such rich pickings from control improvements, and even in telecoms things are harder now, but telecoms is not unique.

True, the pace of change at telcos had been a factor, the complex technology had contributed, and it was difficult to detect incomplete billing without the opportunity to reconcile against physical stocks. On the other hand, these characteristics are not unique to telecoms billing.

Telcos found that the bills they received from other telcos contained an element of over-billing as well, so it was possible to save a lot of money by checking bills and challenging suspected errors. Internet sites turned out to have similar problems. Billing for engineering work proved unreliable.

Perhaps most frightening, or inspiring, is the fact that most of us involved in this work found many more problems with data and systems than their users imagined possible. People would think errors of a particular type were rare or even impossible, and be stunned when shown thousands of examples revealed by software interrogation.

If you are working in another industry and feel that it couldn't happen where you work, don't be so sure. Until you've looked, effectively and comprehensively, it is unsafe to be relaxed. A worthwhile number of errors may be only a tiny percentage of the total and so just checking a sample of 100 items, say, is of little use.

For example, one UK building society in the 1990s was considering changing its status to become a bank. The change required a vote by all 'members' of the society, which meant all account holders. Work to check this revealed that a number of accounts did not have customers associated with them. There was money, but no owner.

Detecting overpayment and double payment of invoices received is a traditional way for auditors to demonstrate their value and experts in this field say that certain types of invoice are a particular problem. It is sometimes called 'recovery auditing'.

In 1998 the United States General Accounting Office made a report[5] to Congress on trials of recovery auditing carried out within the Department of Defense, with the help of external specialists. Overall the report gives encouraging information about the value of recovery audits, but also reveals some of the difficulties. At the time of the report the auditors had audited 80 per cent of the $7.2 bn of payments and found $19.1 mn of recoveries. This is a rate of 0.33 per cent, which is typical.

The $19.1 mn in overpayments included $12.4 mn of cash discounts missed or taken at the wrong rate, $2.2 mn from most favoured customer terms not being received, $1.3 mn because of duplicate payments made, and $1.2 mn from credits for returned merchandise not being taken.

The auditors were required to audit invoices paid some years earlier and were handicapped by lack of certain records. Consequently, although they identified $19.1 mn that could be recovered, less than 10 per cent of this had actually been recovered at the time of the report and the project had stalled for eight months because vendors disputed the recovery claims and the Department of Defense decided to double check everything for itself.

The external specialists doing the audit were paid a percentage of net recoveries so, presumably, they were extremely frustrated by this and by their client's failure to act on potential recoveries they found outside the year they were asked to study and others affecting other departments. Nevertheless, money was recovered even in this mature payment process.

Recovery auditing seems to have grown in the Department of Defense because in 2005 a financial management regulation was introduced that required a cost-effective recovery audit process be in place in every DoD Component with contracts totalling over $500m. In 2006 it reported that well over $100 mn of potential recoveries had been found with yet more expected from an audit of the Navy's telecommunication payments. This progress is despite continued problems in managing recovery audits and recovery audit contracts.[6]

In financial institutions errors happen that can be far more costly than an incorrect telecoms bill. In the city it is possible to lose millions by a simple slip. Easy come, easy go.

Clearly, not every industry has such opportunities to gain clear cut financial benefits from controls work as telecoms in the 1990s, but if we apply methods of similar efficiency there is more to be found than most people realize.

Furthermore, if we factor in other gains, such as the impact on customers and work saved internally, the benefits stack up.

THE CONTRAST

Consider the differences between the abysmal implementation of Section 404 of the Sarbanes-Oxley Act and the clearly beneficial contribution of revenue assurance. Both were aimed at financial processes, but while one generated millions of hours of audit work the other focused on value, then achieved it by improving controls and by using effective tools, including computers and statistics.

Risk control can provide major, measurable value. It is much more than a comfort blanket, if we make the effort to pursue that value and use the right techniques and tools.

Example 2: Bureaucratic controls versus intelligent controls

Another reason that risk management and internal control projects have often delivered less value than they could have is a tendency to draw from a limited repertoire of controls. This again may be a legacy from the world of financial auditing, which has tended to focus on documentation and signatures above all else.

Getting familiar with a wider range of more interesting control mechanisms helps us see and realise the value in risk control.

Here's a fictitious illustration inspired by two contrasting, real-life training organizations.

A FICTITIOUS TRAINING ORGANIZATION

Imagine that the Institute of ABC (IABC), a membership organization, offers a range of training courses to its members and the general public. The courses are promoted and administered by the IABC but presented by trainers from various companies.

A printed catalogue of courses is produced each calendar year and a great deal of thought goes into deciding what courses to offer in it. (No other public courses are run.)

Companies wanting to present courses submit course proposals for consideration in May the preceding year. The submissions are then sifted by a committee that meets several times before final decisions are made about what to include, when, and how many times.

The IABC's course selection committee uses its accumulated experience of past courses, knowledge of trends, and a points system for evaluating submissions. It is clear that the right people are on the committee, that they consider each course carefully and consistently, and the financial commitment the catalogue represents is well understood.

By normal standards of internal control this is squeaky clean. The major risks taken when selecting courses are carefully considered by the right people, and their agreement is recorded formally through meeting minutes and sign-offs.

But, can you think of a worse way to manage a training programme?

The quickest they can react to a topical issue arising is seven months, and that is only possible if the issue happens to arise in May and someone immediately proposes a relevant course. If something happens in June, just after the deadline for submissions, it will be at least 18 months before any response is possible.

The long cycle time means that learning from experience takes years when it should take just weeks or a few months. It is very difficult for the IABC to experiment with new ideas. Consequently, their training catalogue is likely to remain devoid of topical and leading-edge courses, instead featuring old favourites, year after year, with falling returns. There is also the risk that they will fail to adapt to unexpected changes in customer requirements and be displaced by competitors who have.

POSSIBLE IMPROVEMENTS

This is an imaginary scenario (though based on reality), so imagine you are a risk control expert sent to review the activity and make suggestions. Your first step is to learn how things are done now and why. You need to know all this to have a chance of making useful suggestions, and anyway the managers won't listen unless they feel you really understand how good they are and what constraints they face.

Human nature being what it is the managers concerned quickly dive into their rationale for doing what they do. They say that the reasons for printing an annual catalogue include customers who like it, a track record of sales using it, higher compilation, printing, and postage costs if more editions are printed, and the extra work that would be created by having to manage more than one catalogue a year. Furthermore, they point out that their track record of choosing courses is good, as evidenced by the consistently acceptable sales of the courses offered.

You calmly acknowledge all this and move them on to how they could increase sales and service to members by discovering new courses that might sell even better, including topical courses. Besides, who said anything about printing more editions of the catalogue?

You want to help them think of better ways to manage the risk and uncertainty that affects their training business, so you ask 'Is there any way to learn more about what people want and might buy through actual experience or at least contact with them?' A bit more conversation leads to the discovery that they occasionally present tailored in-house courses based on those in the catalogue. They have quite a good database of past and potential customers and the ability to email most of them. There's even a website, though it just shows what is in the catalogue. Now you're getting somewhere.

After more discussion the team decides to take forward the following ideas:

- Changing the course feedback form to ask people about other things they would like to learn about.
- Holding quarterly meetings to review the tailored courses requested during the year, concentrating on what people wanted that was different from the standard course, and why.
- Shortening the lead time for the annual catalogue from over six months to around two, with the proviso that they will still encourage course proposals early in the year to allow the consideration to be spread out over time as usual.
- Adding short modules to existing courses to try out new themes. The feedback form can ask if people would like to know more about topics in the course.
- Offering a limited number of courses that are not in the catalogue on a trial basis, sharing the risk with the presenters, and concentrating on short events. These are to be promoted by email and on the website, with feedback scrutinized intensively.

THE CONTRAST

Again there is a huge contrast between high- and low-value approaches to risk control. This time it is the type of controls used that makes the difference. While bureaucratic, defensive controls can be a route to stagnation and eventual failure, controls based on intelligence, learning, and adaptiveness offer a way to more opportunities and improved performance. Clearly the best recommendations may not be the traditional favourite control mechanisms of checking and restriction.

Used well these controls are more interesting to managers. Instead of inwardly groaning at being asked to produce another document, sign their names somewhere, or fill in another checklist, the control ideas coming forward seem more like clever management techniques than dreary controls.

What this book does and does not provide

This book is not a comprehensive textbook on internal control and risk management. There are topics I don't discuss at all. There are many important documents from regulators that don't get mentioned. Auditing gets only limited coverage.

What this book provides is an arsenal of powerful ideas and techniques for increasing the value of business risk control. It only discusses topics where there are opportunities to improve value greatly by doing something other than following received wisdom.

The keys to getting more value from business control include:

- focusing on value;
- clever design of high-performing control mechanisms; and
- a good understanding of the psychology of risk and control.

How this book is organized

This first part, 'The bigger picture', continues with a look at the history of risk management and internal controls to highlight where the main improvements in value will come from. One of these improvements arises from integrating the thinking behind the two disciplines into one, simpler, more realistic view of risk control, which is what happens in Chapter 3. To focus attention further on the things that really make a positive impact Chapter 4 looks at the psychology of behaviour in the face of risk and uncertainty and argues that if we point risk control at two key objectives from day to day this will translate into wider benefits.

Part II is a collection of 60 high-performance control mechanisms presented as a 'pattern language' so that it is clear when to use each mechanism and why. Most organizations will benefit from implementing more of these mechanisms to upgrade existing control systems.

If you do nothing else, please read Part II and refer back to it whenever you want ideas for control mechanisms. The value of risk control projects is limited by the value of the best controls we can think of at the time. Better ideas will mean more value.

Finally, Part III looks at the challenge of getting improvement to happen, approaching it from a variety of angles. Chapter 11 surveys techniques for changing behaviour, especially techniques that provide people with triggers for new behaviours, something that training and procedure manuals usually do not.

Chapter 12 suggests how individual skill at handling risk and uncertainty can be understood and improved. Whether you are a chief executive or an accounts clerk there are barriers to overcome and the big ones are described in Chapter 13. The following chapters suggest ways to overcome or sidestep the barriers.

One of these barriers is the 'gridlock' that happens when everyone feels that other people are blocking change. Chapter 14 suggests what people in different roles in an organization can each press for and shows why they are desirable for that role as well as the organization overall. Chapter 15 develops this further with the Friendly Expansion strategy and some ideas on the level of innovation typical in risk control projects and how to manage it.

Another source of friction is common but unhelpful ideas that are believed by some people in most organizations and that tend to limit the role of risk control and block the use of good techniques. Chapter 16 goes through these unhelpful ideas and has suggestions on how to deal with them. The final chapter looks to the future and predicts the frontiers on which risk control will make progress over the next ten years or so.

Notes

1 This excluded fees paid to audit firms and was an average across a large number of SEC-registered companies, many of which are relatively small. The details are in the final rule 'Management's Reports on Internal Control Over Financial Reporting and Certification of Disclosure in Exchange Act Periodic Reports', effective from 14 August 2003.

2 PricewaterhouseCoopers (2004) *Sarbanes-Oxley Act: Section 404 – Practical Guidance for Management.*

3 Documents published by the Committee of Sponsoring Organizations of the Treadway Commission ('COSO') are usually written by an audit firm. Crucially, Coopers & Lybrand wrote the internal control framework, whose ideas were imported into the SEC's documents on Section 404 of the Sarbanes-Oxley Act and into the PCAOB's Auditing Standard 2.

4 The most recent version of the standard is 'Office of Telecommunications Standard for Telecommunications Metering Systems and Billing Systems – OTR 003: 2001', now available from the Ofcom website.

5 United States General Accounting Office (1998) *GAO/NSIAD-99-12 Contract Management: Recovery Auditing offers Potential to Identify Overpayments.* Washington DC: United States General Accounting Office.

6 Inspector General of the United States Department of Defense (2007) *Report D-2007-110: Identification and Reporting of Improper Payments through Recovery Auditing.* Arlington, VA: Inspector General, Department of Defense.

2 Risk Management and Internal Control: Poised for Progress

If we trace the development of the ideas behind risk management and internal control some exciting possibilities emerge. There are opportunities to borrow ideas and techniques from competing approaches and fuse them into one. There are opportunities to combine specialist risk control teams in large organizations. And there are opportunities to combine and rationalize the thinking behind internal control and risk management to create one simpler perspective.

The origins of internal control

Many years ago internal controls were purely concerned with bookkeeping. They were checks that bookkeepers did to detect errors and fraud. Indeed, the English word 'control' derives from an ancient bookkeeping control that involved keeping two records of transactions and checking one against the other, the 'roll'. The Latin for this is 'contra rotulus'. However, in recent decades the phrase 'internal control' has become ambitious and now claims to include much more than bookkeeping and to include things that are not checks.

During the second half of the twentieth century internal control became firmly established in thinking about financial audits, particularly those carried out on companies by independent audit firms acting for shareholders.

Since internal controls were there to detect and reduce errors and fraud an auditor who established that the controls were working well would need less evidence from other sources to assess the reliability of a company's financial statements. Sometimes an internal controls approach to audit was less costly and, therefore, more profitable for the auditor.

As companies got larger, more complicated, and more computerized the importance of the internal control element of external audits increased. Each time there was a major scandal involving a large company that had falsified its accounts people thought of internal controls and wondered how they could be made more effective. At the same time external audit firms gradually grew and merged creating an ever smaller group of ever larger and more powerful organizations with huge influence.

In 1992 the Committee of Sponsoring Organizations of the Treadway Committee, known simply as COSO, published a landmark document called their internal control framework which contained an influential definition of internal control. This definition said internal control was a process designed to provide reasonable assurance as to achievement of controls in three areas:

- effectiveness and efficiency of operations;
- reliability of financial reporting; and
- compliance with applicable laws and regulations.

Can you think of something that happens in a company that is *not*, arguably, part of internal control? It's not easy, is it? Even setting the objectives in the first place quickly gets sucked into internal control in COSO's framework.

The definition reflected the expanding concept of internal control, but may also have been influenced by the commercial interests of its authors, Coopers & Lybrand, at the time one of the largest external audit firms in the world.

Some partners at Coopers & Lybrand were thrilled to be involved in drafting the framework and felt it was a great commercial opportunity. In a way it justified advice by their control consultants on almost any aspect of management.

How long they had to wait for those commercial hopes to be realized is unknown but, over a decade later, the Sarbanes-Oxley gravy train pulled in, making the framework look like one of the best marketing investments in the history of auditing.

Another important innovation in COSO's internal controls framework was the inclusion of risk assessment. Previous texts on internal controls had tended to produce long checklists of controls, but the COSO framework turned control into a working machine. It had elements that *did things* and exchanged information.

Risk assessment was seen as the means by which investment in controls was directed. Although the framework failed to follow up the risk assessment with explicit references to controls design, a full risk management process of some kind was implied.

In this model, risk management became *part of* internal control.

The long war with quality management

All this time internal control had been gaining ground. It had growing credibility in board rooms, with financial market regulators, and with governments. The audit firms regarded it as *the* way to manage the health of business and financial processes as well as manage businesses generally.

However, theirs was not the only view. Process health already had a long-established management approach: quality management. This had been tremendously successful in manufacturing, where the repetitive processes and opportunities for measurement were perfect for statistical process control techniques. Quality also had a less technical side concerning customer requirements and was popularized far beyond its manufacturing base, even being seen as applicable to bookkeeping in finance departments.

A slow war has been going on between the quality movement and internal control to be the dominant approach to process health and gradually internal control is winning. Technically there seems little to choose between them. While internal control has the advantage of being explicitly risk-focused and covering deliberate fraud as well as accidental error, quality management is better at quantification and puts greater emphasis on engineering and implementing solutions.

In the 1990s the quality movement became closely identified with quality management systems based on having documented procedures and checking that people followed them at all times. This unattractive approach may have helped create an opening for internal control, but Six Sigma, the current incarnation of quality management, has gone back to the best of quality thinking.

Perhaps the true basis of internal control's success is that in developed Western economies there are more and more accountants and financiers and fewer and fewer engineers and manufacturers.

An opportunity for progress

Quality management has a lot of good ideas that internal control practitioners should learn and incorporate in their work. Measurement and statistical process control are well developed and useful. The methods of implementing improvements are better developed than those typically used in internal control projects.

The origins of risk management

The need to manage risk has arisen in many fields and the approaches used in each reflect the skills and interests of the people involved and the availability of relevant data.

Search the Internet for 'risk management' and you will find that some material is mathematically influenced and some is not. The mathematical influence is evident in the following areas:

- The decision science approach to risk and uncertainty, which is heavily influenced by expected values, utility theory, and Bayesian approaches to combining information.
- Operational research, for example using mathematical models and simulation to optimize operations in large businesses and other organizations.
- Scientific risk analysis, such as work to assess health risks from drugs, chemicals, radio waves, and so on.
- Scientific approaches to measurement uncertainty.
- Financial risk management, including market and credit risk, which has long been mathematically driven and benefits from vast databases of information about historical prices and loan defaults.
- Actuarial work for insurance purposes, which is notoriously mathematical and also benefits from vast amounts of data about past risk occurrences and their costs.

- Operational risk management in leading banks, where measurement of operational risk is being attempted in a mathematical way thanks to the requirements of Basel II.
- Statistical Process Control, which has arisen as part of quality management, particularly in manufacturing, and is now a core part of Six Sigma.
- Some project risk management, where simulation and quantitative methods are gradually gaining ground.
- Forecasting, where much of the best work has been in connection with weather forecasts and economic forecasting.
- Medicine, where the profession has become more sophisticated at finding out and weighing risks, and increasingly sees a responsibility to explain risks effectively to patients.

Extensive scientific literature exists for many of these topics and in associated areas like psychology and artificial intelligence.

Typically, risk is understood in terms of explicit models in which variables are linked. At first it seems that there are no 'risks' as such because the word 'risk' is not always used, but in fact most of the risks are represented by the uncertain future values of variables in these models.

Applying these ideas usually requires skilled work over a period of time to build and test models.

In contrast, there is a lot of material with little mathematical basis, even where numbers are used:

- Accounting controls and auditing, where the emphasis tends to be on 'professional judgement' but often reduced to categories like 'High', 'Medium', and 'Low' or to traffic-light colours.
- Governance, where risk and control are usually mentioned only in high-level summary.
- Safety at work, where the emphasis is on simple judgements and categories, and a lot of the effort goes into trying to persuade workers to take more care of themselves.
- IT security, which also tends to keep away from mathematics although some approaches aim for financial calculations of the cost and value of counter-measures against risks.
- Most project risk management, which relies on making a list of risk items called a 'risk register' and rating each item individually.
- Risk management standards, which also tend to follow the risk register approach, with individual ratings.
- Enterprise Risk Management, which aims to apply the risk register approach to everything in an organization.

Here the thinking is very different. Risks are seen as separate entities and usually represented as lists of items treated as if unconnected with each other.

Working with these methods usually involves workshops and flip charts.

Conceptual differences between risk management traditions

If only the non-mathematical approaches were just a more convenient, more approximate version of the mathematical. Sadly, they are not.

The conceptual bases of the mathematical and non-mathematical approaches differ radically. It is not a matter of whether the approach uses numbers or not. The fundamental beliefs implied by the different approaches are so different that people in the different camps find it hard to agree on much.

Before I present a detailed comparison of the two, here is an example to show how differently the two approaches go about understanding and managing risk in the same situation.

Imagine that we are working in a government-funded organization whose goal is to reduce teenage smoking using advertising methods.

In the mathematically based approach modelling begins immediately because it is tackling the whole problem, not just the uncertainty. We want to think through what causes smoking and what can be done about it. At its simplest the key variable in the model could just be the percentage of teenagers who smoke, but more elaborate versions might look at the number and percentage of smokers of different ages, and perhaps also represent how often they smoke. There might even be distinctions between heavy, daily smokers and people who only smoke occasionally, such as at parties. Perhaps different persuasive methods would work with these different groups.

To the model might then be added likely causal influences on teenage smoking, such as attitudes towards smoking, parental behaviour, legal restrictions, the cost of cigarettes, smoking behaviour earlier in life, alcohol abuse, and the example set by friends. These would be represented by other variables and linked to the level of smoking by relationships whose properties are likely to be uncertain.

Since the job of the organization is to reduce teenage smoking by using advertising methods, the model also needs variables to represent things like the amount and quality of advertising, the number of teenagers and pre-teens exposed to it, and the number of times they see it. Again, the links between these variables and other related variables, mainly attitudes towards smoking, would need to be considered and made part of the model.

Nobody expects perfect predictions. The goal of modelling in this way is to clarify beliefs and compute their implications, including the implications of our various uncertainties.

Consequently, modelling would typically represent links between variables, and future levels of each variable, using probability distributions of various kinds. This is where uncertainty comes in. Various measures of risk/uncertainty have been devised.

Models that include uncertainty explicitly do not have to be complex or hard to understand, though sometimes they are.

More work would go into estimating the strength and any timing delays in the relationships between variables in this model so that the effect of investments in different forms and extents of advertising using different messages could be estimated. This would lead, almost inevitably, to the idea of doing experiments with potential advertisements to study attitude changes (if any) on a small scale and so improve the reliability of the model.

In summary, in this approach the uncertainties about future levels of smoking and the effectiveness of various advertising approaches are the 'risks' that need to be managed, but are rarely given that name. There is an explicit model that links variables and informs all planning, not just planning to do with risk; the modelling starts before a plan exists.

What would a non-mathematically inspired approach look like by contrast? At first there would be no serious consideration of risks or uncertainty. After some debate a plan of action would emerge and only then would risk-thinking kick in. A workshop might be held at which people begin by restating the objective, which of course is to cut teenage smoking by using advertising methods. The group would then suggest things that could happen that might mean they fail to cut teenage smoking, such as 'Advertisements have an ineffective message', 'Advertisements are not seen by enough teenagers', and 'Advertisements backfire'. These suggestions would often be generated by looking at each step in the initial plan of action and thinking about what could stop it being done or stop it producing the desired results.

These ideas would be described as 'risks' and listed. Most risks would be expressed relative to some desired outcome. For example, 'Insufficient viewing of advertising' rather than the more neutral 'Level of viewing of advertising' which the mathematical approach would usually prefer.

Against the risks the team would then try to write actions they could take to manage those risks, such as testing advertisements before they are used widely.

Table 2.1 compares the two approaches side by side, picking out some of the less obvious but fundamental conceptual differences implied by their language and preferred practices. Of course to do this I've ignored some occasional exceptions. Sometimes mathematicians try to use ideas from the non-mathematical world, like targets for example, and already some progressive risk managers are making more use of mathematical concepts. However, the differences in practice are still real and stark.

With hundreds of years of development and science behind it the conceptual basis of the mathematically influenced work is far more rigorous, accurate, consistent, realistic, better researched, less commercially manipulated, and more reliable than the non-mathematical work. The non-mathematical approach is based on some conceptual errors that have led to serious practical problems. However, this doesn't mean that the mathematical approach is always more useful.

The mathematical approaches have done well where data are plentiful and there are people, such as scientists, engineers, and financial 'quants' to do the clever stuff and use the results. The non-mathematical approaches have developed among groups who typically lack, or at least do not reward, mathematical skill and where data are hard to come by. When nearly all risk assessments feel like guesswork people seem to think they don't matter and are less concerned about getting the thinking right.

Table 2.1   Mathematical and non-mathematical approaches to risk management

Mathematical	Non-mathematical
Often does not use the word 'risk'.	Almost always uses the word 'risk'.
Part of the same thought process that generates the plan of action.	Usually begins once a basic plan of action is already in mind.
The models used are explicit.	The models used are implicit.
Risk is seen as a lack of knowledge (perhaps arising from unpredictable variability) that makes it hard or impossible to know the future exactly.	Risks are treated as real things that exist outside our minds.
The thinker is responsible for defining the models.	Often no effort is made to define models used.
Variables need to be defined, especially if they are to be measured. Also, events in probability theory are seen as sets of atomic outcomes. These sets need to be defined.	Risks and events are named and given descriptions, but not usually with the intention of defining them.
Models have variables in them whose values are uncertain and usually represented using probabilities or probability densities. These variables represent the behaviour of a system and are usually closest in intent to measures of performance. 'Risks' are usually just uncertainties about future values of performance/behaviour measures.	Risks are separate things that rub shoulders with objectives, critical success factors, measures of performance, and so on, but are different from them.
Most models are concerned with all possible outcomes.	Risk thinking is almost always concerned only with bad potential outcomes.
Risk and uncertainty change as information arrives, which it can at any time.	Risks are often seen as things that can be completely understood with sufficient effort and, once this is done, there is nothing more to be learned from experience.
Variables in a model are linked by mathematical relationships representing causal or statistical connections.	In practice, risks are usually treated as if unconnected even though people often know this is not the case.
Decision-making usually focuses on finding optimal decisions within the model given a way to value different outcomes e.g. in money terms or with an explicit objective function.	Decision-making usually focuses on reaching targets that are considered givens.
Comparisons of 'better' and 'worse' are made between explicitly identified alternatives.	'Good' and 'bad' are rarely defined explicitly but play a big role in thinking because, usually, only bad potential outcomes are considered.
Numerical measurement using real numbers (i.e. not just whole numbers) is preferred.	Categories with verbal descriptions or defined by number ranges are usually preferred.

The non-mathematical approaches typically do not provide a true analysis of risk; instead they provide a worry-driven 'to do' list; but such a list is useful. Very often people feel that a session discussing the risks they have listed has been a helpful one, even if technically the output is indefensible.

Risk workshops are sometimes a much needed opportunity for people to speak more openly about their concerns and provide a helpful mandate for risk responses that otherwise people might view as unnecessary or time wasting. As explained in Chapter 4, the psychological impact of risk control activities is crucial.

Another opportunity for progress

The opportunity here is to take the clear thinking of the mathematical tradition and put it into tools and techniques that are so easy to understand and use that they can become universal.

The fact that mathematical, scientific ideas on risk have often failed to penetrate corporate risk management does not mean they should not or never will.

If you are working in corporate or project risk management then the existence of more logical and better-researched methods is a huge opportunity, provided you can introduce them in a way that fits the skills and available data of your organization. That's the challenge.

People often think that, because most of the literature on a technique (e.g. something for mathematically modelling risks) is written using impenetrable mathematics, the technique cannot be useful to anyone who is not an advanced mathematician. This is not always correct. Simple interpretations are often possible and methods can be explained in terms many people can understand, if we make the effort.

Computer software has made sophisticated simulations easy, multivariable statistical model fitting can be done in the most common spreadsheet software, and as time goes by more and more people are learning the basics of more sophisticated risk-thinking. We've never been in a better position to make progress.

The mathematical tradition offers a fantastic range of techniques and concepts. With some effort we can make those applicable to more situations.

Internal control and risk management collide

Internal control has been expanding and has claimed to include risk management. Ironically, risk management has also been expanding and claims to include internal controls.

The final opportunity highlighted by the history of internal control and risk management is to integrate the two. The time has come to take the best thinking about how to manage risk and combine it with the grinding power of control systems. There is also scope to simplify and improve the thinking behind each and to merge the activities and teams involved.

The next chapter offers a perspective that achieves this.

3 *Integrated Risk Control is Simpler*

This chapter presents a simple, logical, common sense way of looking at internal control and risk management that integrates them conceptually and so opens the door to integrating them in practical ways too. I use the phrase 'risk control' to refer to this integrated perspective. (Practical integration is a matter of design and design is the main focus of Part II.)

Making rapid progress towards worthwhile risk control is hard if your mental models of how it works are unclear. Happily, the integrated view of risk management and internal control offered in this chapter is simpler and more grounded in reality than most models of internal control or of risk management have been.

A mental picture of risk control

The literature on risk and control is littered with diagrams of cubes, circles, triangles, pyramids, trees, and so on, but of course none of these exist physically. They are attempts to make sense of patterns of human behaviour and computer processing spread out over time and space, and mixed with other behaviour so that they are hard to see.

Sometimes the abstract diagrams carry subtle assumptions that are misleading or idealistic. For example, a process diagram drawn as a sequence of numbered boxes joined by lines may suggest that the activities in each box are carried out in chronological order, when in reality they are carried out in parallel or with considerable backtracking. A pyramid may suggest that the people or activities at the top of the pyramid are somehow centralized or more important than those lower down, when in reality the 'lowest' level is the largest and most important and the activities at the 'top' are widely distributed.

Many of these models are abstract, with individual elements unclear and relationships even fuzzier. If we just took the geometric abstractions of internal control and put them in the same picture as the geometric abstractions of risk management, the result would be too many shapes!

What we need in order to make practical progress is a mental model of risk control that is grounded in *reality*. The perspective offered in this book begins with some observations on reality today then suggests two immediate objectives through which many other good things can be achieved. Everything else about risk control is a matter for creative design and choice. Here is a summary.

OBSERVATIONS

- Some activities we do because the world is uncertain. In this perspective these are called 'controls' though this slightly differs from common usage.
- Some controls generate other controls i.e. they involve inventing controls and deciding to do them at a later time or when something happens. Control systems are self-generating and self-perpetuating.
- Some controls involve explicit thinking about risk and uncertainty, and some of these generate other controls.
- Controls, including controls that generate other controls, occur throughout organizations.
- How all this is done is a matter for creative design and choice.

OBJECTIVES

Because of the importance of human behaviour in the face of uncertainty there are two objectives through which much else – saved money, reduced shocks, more good opportunities, increased shareholder value, whatever you want – can be achieved. They are these:

1. To help people take off their mental blinkers and see the true range of possibilities they face.
2. To help people behave competently in a way that is consistent with that wider view.

The rest of this chapter explains the observations in more detail then gives some other useful background on the state of risk control today and how things really work. The objectives, however, are so important they are covered in the next chapter.

RISK CONTROL DISTINGUISHED FROM OTHER ACTIVITIES

Imagine the people and computer systems in a large organization, at work, busy typing memos, loading vans, mending machinery, sending letters, selling food, planting crops, and so on.

Each person, team, or system has jobs to do. There are activities they perform that directly do those jobs. For example, a farmer ploughs a field. A sales assistant takes money for a pair of shoes sold in a shop. A shelf-stacker puts tins of baked beans onto a supermarket shelf. A bookkeeper records how much money a customer owes. These activities are the essential jobs of the organization.

These essential jobs would need to be done even in a world without uncertainty. However, there are other things people do because the world is uncertain. These are *controls*.

Most obviously, there are things those people, teams, and systems do that are to make sure the main jobs are done correctly every time. The farmer checks the tractor is in good working order. The sales assistant gets authorization to take payment via the customer's credit card. A shelf-stacker's supervisor walks past to make sure the shelves look neat and the goods are in the correct locations. A bookkeeper checks that the sales ledger agrees with the nominal ledger.

In a certain, reliable world controls like this would not be necessary. In our real world they are essential, though we can get away with not doing some of them for a while before bad luck catches up with us.

Less obviously, there also things that people do because there is uncertainty but that are done to create or take better advantage of opportunities that may arise in future. For example, a farmer experiments with a new type of grain to see if it gives better profits on his land. A sales assistant asks if the customer needs any spare laces with the new shoes, just in case. A shelf-stacker piles up a heavily promoted brand of beans in the hope of selling many tins.

These activities are responses to risk and uncertainty and should also be in our minds when we think of controls, even though conventionally they are not part of internal control thinking and frequently are ignored by risk managers too.

In a certain world these controls would not be needed either, but in our real world they are essential if we are to keep up with competition or make progress, though we can cope without them for a short while.

Incidentally, what counts as the essential job and what is a control depend on your perspective. Most of the time they are clear enough, but if your whole job is to perform stock checks then you might well consider stock-checking the essential job and your controls include the things you do to make sure stock-checking is done correctly.

In summary, work can be divided between the core job and controls done to improve results in the face of uncertainty. Some controls need to be kept up all the time or things come crashing to a halt almost immediately, but many can be set aside for a short while and we may even mistake this for improved efficiency.

This perspective lays the foundation for integrating risk management and internal control by marking out a territory that both can reasonably be seen as occupying.

CONTROLS THAT INVOLVE THINKING ABOUT RISK AND/OR GENERATING CONTROLS

Controls can be carried out repetitively either according to a fixed schedule or when some trigger occurs. For example, a bank reconciliation might be done daily, according to a fixed schedule. A project approval might be done whenever there is a project to be considered.

Controls can also be one-offs, triggered by a date and time or by some event. These are common on projects.

The way controls are planned is particularly interesting and it is through the idea of *dynamic generation* (i.e. controls generating other controls over time) that we can begin to integrate internal control and risk management into one.

The actions that put controls in place are themselves controls, and may involve explicit thinking about risk. For example, a company might have a policy that every IT project has to have an initial security assessment performed that identifies further security work needed before new systems can be made live. That initial

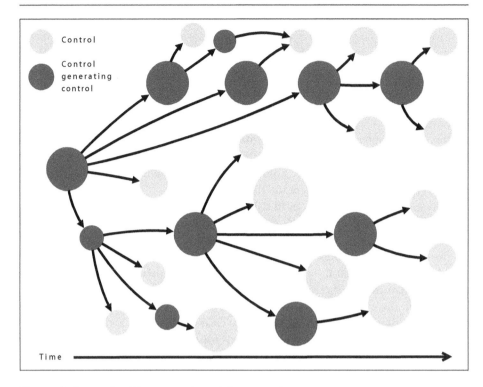

Figure 3.1   A self-generating risk control system

assessment is a control and it generates more controls, some of which will also generate yet more controls, ultimately resulting in routine security procedures for the new system and the people using and supporting it.

Figure 3.1 may help you imagine this self-generating, self-perpetuating aspect of a control system. The circles represent controls happening in different parts of an organization at different times. The darker circles are the special ones that generate other controls. In this picture, a single control at the start (on the left) generates five controls, four of which generate more controls themselves and so on. In a large organization this would be just a tiny part of the full system.

When you are designing a control system there are some control requirements that are predictable long in advance but others that cannot be determined until things start happening. For the latter you will need to design controls that generate other controls.

Controls that are one-off actions are usually set up by other controls that generate those controls and are themselves usually repeating controls.

A well-designed control system should be self-sustaining – generating the actions that will keep it going and keep it up to date. One can envisage a single, central control activity that operates regularly and generates all the others, but this is only one design option and may not be the most robust.

Table 3.1   The characteristics of intelligent controls

Other controls	Intelligent controls
View of outcomes Things are either right (what we wanted/planned) or wrong. Our objectives are fixed.	**View of outcomes** There may be different levels of performance and outcomes may be evaluated in more ways than just right versus wrong. Our objectives may change.
Main mechanisms Preventing things from happening at all. Checking before something is done and giving a go-ahead if appropriate. Checking something after it is done and correcting if it is wrong.	**Main mechanisms** Cause-effect interventions Doing things to learn, learning, and adapting in future actions. Assessing uncertainty. Exploiting statistical laws. Adapting internal control plans dynamically (especially in projects).

Controls that generate other controls often involve some explicit thinking about risk and uncertainty, but not always. They don't necessarily look like the typical, theoretical risk management process seen in COSO's Enterprise Risk Management (ERM) framework and elsewhere, which is an inefficient and ineffective choice in many situations. (Other controls that generate controls are described later in this book in Chapter 6.)

A complementary idea that helps to highlight many of the more interesting but less familiar controls is the idea of *intelligent internal controls*.

I don't know if it is possible to draw a clean line between 'intelligent' controls and other controls. However, intelligent controls can be characterized on the basis of who carries them out and the mechanisms used.

First, intelligent controls are much more likely to be carried out by people with management roles (at any level), though they may be helped by computer systems and other people.

Second, intelligent controls rely on a different set of control mechanisms. Table 3.1 presents a comparison.

In summary, the integrated view of risk control is that the control system includes controls that generate other controls, and many of these are intelligent controls featuring risk-related thinking.

CONTROLS ARE EVERYWHERE

Controls occur everywhere. They are at every level of every organization, in some form. Sometimes they look the same in different places but usually they do not. Consistency can be helpful but uniformity can have serious drawbacks. This is true for all controls including intelligent controls and controls that generate other controls.

Control systems are highly distributed and can be decentralized. Often it is possible to harness this to make progress happen more quickly than would be possible with one grinding, centralized, perhaps annual process.

CREATIVE DESIGN AND CHOICE

Controls get put in place by a variety of people at different times for different reasons and using *different methods*. The defining characteristic of effective risk control is that risk is controlled effectively, not that one particular mental process is used to do it. For example, just listing risks and writing controls against them will not design a control system worthy of the name, not because it is a useless thing to do but because it is not enough and does not work well in many common situations.

We need to get people to do their jobs a little differently so that they manage risk and uncertainty better. There are lots of ways to do that.

An example based on a large organization would be too long for this simple introduction, so here are two examples on a small scale. Although these examples are laid out as tables, with areas of uncertainty linked to improvement ideas, this is not the only way you can do it, and usually not the best for large scale design. Any design method that works counts as risk control.

Example 1   After taking some good advice and getting suggestions from its employees and volunteers a charity working to help women at risk from their partners might find that its important areas of uncertainty and ideas for improvement include those shown in Table 3.2.

Example 2   After talking to a friend he plays golf with, a local builder might decide that his areas of uncertainty and ideas for improvement include those shown in Table 3.3.

Other observations on risk control today

THE NATURAL EVOLUTION OF CONTROL SYSTEMS

Internal controls that are systematically designed, implemented, and maintained by focused internal control specialists with great skill are a small minority of controls. Most controls happened for other reasons. For example:

- A software package had them built in.
- After a costly or embarrassing incident or near miss people thought about how to prevent its recurrence.
- A manager was appointed who had had an embarrassing incident in a previous role and wanted the controls he or she was used to.
- An internal or external auditor recommended the control and it was put on a list and followed up until done.

Table 3.2   Illustrative responses to uncertainty in a charity

Areas of uncertainty	Ideas for improvement management
The risks around individual cases involving women.	Review the information collected about risk factors in each case. Experiment with a checklist of risk factors.
Funding. Uncertainty about income from one year to the next and also uncertainty about the cost of programmes under consideration.	New forecasting and commitment planning approach based on Adrian Poffley's book,[1] which is excellent on this.
Effectiveness of programmes. The true impact of programmes is sometimes hard to measure or even judge, and the effects of proposed programmes are even more difficult to predict.	We've tended to argue about what to do until we reach some kind of consensus but then commit to programmes as if we know what they will achieve. Time to look at how we can gather more information through trials and develop our programmes in an evolutionary way, dynamically adjusting priorities as we learn quickly.
The reactions of volunteers. We rely on volunteers and major changes to the way things are done can affect their willingness to continue supporting.	New programme of consultation with volunteers on various ideas for improving programmes and the way the charity is run.
Reliability of bookkeeping and accounting.	Get the accounting controls documentation reviewed. Time to consider a full time bookkeeper.

1   Poffley, A. (2002) *Financial Stewardship of Charities*. London: Directory of Social Change.

- Some special event like a listing on a stock exchange triggered a one-off internal controls upgrade programme – most likely focused on financial reporting.

Controls tend to fall away again not because of deliberate optimization but because of events such as these:

- The person responsible for carrying out a control retires, is transferred, resigns, or is laid off.
- Work pressure from other priorities leads to a control gradually being neglected and then forgotten about altogether.
- The way work is done changes so that the old control cannot be performed or is no longer relevant.
- Software is replaced with new software.

Table 3.3   Illustrative responses to uncertainty for a builder

Areas of uncertainty	Ideas for improved management
The health and safety of the team.	Get the protective clothing I've been meaning to buy for months. Discuss the risk factors of each job with the lads before starting, and give them reminders relevant to each job.
Unexpected problems on jobs, especially what we find when we start digging and the results of using unfamiliar tools or materials.	Most of the warning signs are obvious so I'll start checking through a list of potential problem areas and spend a bit more time on design and planning. It would be worth discussing major uncertainties with customers because some will be prepared to pay for work unexpectedly required, particularly if they have been warned of the possibilities. I'll look at equipment that might allow me to check what is underground or behind a wall before I give a quote.
Our schedule through the year, particularly the effects of cancellations, sickness, weather, and project problems.	Stop promising dates to customers so far in advance. Start giving indications of start dates where the customer can be flexible. Update the customer closer to the start time. Look back over typical drift over the last few years so I can give customers a realistic range.
Whether customers will pay.	Stage payments through the job. Can't think why I've never asked for more than the cost of materials until now.
The uncertainty in the customer's mind about what they want. They seem particularly vague on materials, but some customers find everything difficult to decide.	Increase my range of samples of materials so I can show people the real colour and texture. Offer a drawing service including 3D/perspective drawings of projects.

In many ways this evolution works well. Controls tend to grow where there is pain and fall away where there is little or no pain but plenty of pressure to do more important things.

However, there are some predictable weaknesses in natural evolution of control systems. These include the following:

- Controls are rarely implemented in good time. Remediation is the norm. Often, something has to go wrong before action is taken.
- Controls to generate and make the most of future opportunities are not as common as they should be because the link to the pain this causes is not obvious.
- The strength of each type of control implemented initially depends on the enthusiasm of the person who thought of it, not actual need. There are usually large gaps in some areas, especially when a business sets up an entirely new process and this is done by young people with limited practical experience of operating such processes (e.g. many business analysts employed by large IT companies).
- Controls against rare but serious risks can fall away due to lack of pain even though the risk is still there, as threatening as ever. It may be that the event has never happened to the organization so it feels rather theoretical to most people.
- Routine errors are tolerated. People seem to accept low but persistent levels of error and other losses as inevitable and acceptable, even when they are not. Losses of revenue in telecoms are small as a percentage of total revenue and many are persistent problems that have been there since the beginning. By contrast, losses due to dramatic events tend to get more attention.
- Controls sometimes live on long after their usefulness has ended because people are not under enough pressure or are very dedicated to following laid down policies. Large inefficiencies can build up.

Controls designed as an integrated system rather than piecemeal can be more efficient and effective. This is particularly so if special skill is applied and the focus is on value rather than just risk coverage.

THE CONTRIBUTION OF DELIBERATE INVENTION AND IMPLEMENTATION

Specialist controls designers are still rare individuals but there are more of them now than ever before. Often they have very deep knowledge of a narrow range of controls, but even the generalists are becoming more common. Examples are listed in Table 3.4.

In addition, there are many specialists employed by companies that create business software.

In large companies the problem is sometimes not just the lack of specialists but the profusion of different groups with similar objectives but different approaches, sometimes vying with each other for control of improvement projects. For example, if a particular business unit is seen as having control problems it can expect to be pounded by internal and external auditors, and offered help by managers of internal control, quality, processes, security, business continuity, and so on.

This profusion is also seen in multiple audits. Some people in very large organizations face potential annual visits from quality auditors, compliance

Table 3.4   **Risk control specialists**

Credit-scoring specialists and credit-risk managers generally. Market risk managers. Insurance managers. Health and safety officers. Corporate risk managers. Compliance officers. Lawyers. Internal auditors acting in design roles	Quality managers. Revenue assurance managers. Operational risk managers. Internal control managers (often focused on internal controls over financial reporting). ERP software security configuration specialists. ERP parameterization specialists.	IT security specialists in a range of things: virus protection, security, firewalls. Disaster recovery and business continuity specialists. Security officers. Fraud managers. Money-laundering officers.

auditors, health and safety auditors, internal auditors, external auditors, and the Sarbanes-Oxley testing team.

At the other end of the scale, most organizations with fewer than 1,000 employees have no internal auditors and no internal controls designers or managers.

Controls specialists divide their time between carrying out controls themselves and encouraging and helping others to insert them in their work.

ALTERNATIVE MEANINGS OF COMMON RISK RELATED WORDS

The perspective on risk control described above is only one way of looking at things. There are others. Bearing in mind the many areas where people try to manage risk and exercise control, and the differing conceptual roots of their approaches, it is not surprising that the jargon is confusing. We have words with multiple meanings, common words with surprising technical redefinitions, vague words, controversial definitions – all the usual problems of specialist language.

Formal definitions exist for most of the key phrases, but they are not always good definitions and besides that they are not used by most people and not likely to be. To communicate effectively we need to understand the range of meanings people have for words and phrases, and understand which meanings work well and which can lead to mistakes. Here are some key phrases discussed from that point of view.

RISK

What a minefield. First, there is a big difference between 'some risks' and 'some risk'. One letter is all that separates two quite different meanings.

1. *'Some risks'*: We say this when we are thinking of risks as countable entities. Usually we have in mind some kind of event that might happen and that we care about for some reason. The idea of an event is itself a difficult one. It is best

to think of an event as a set of alternative states of the world grouped together and given a name or description.

2. *'Some risk'*: We say this when we are thinking of some kind of measure of the extent to which we are exposed to uncertainty that we care about. Our measure of risk might just be some ill-defined feeling of its extent or a well-defined measurement (e.g. the standard deviation of a distribution or a Value at Risk number).

When someone says 'We need to estimate the risk arising from these risks' they are saying something meaningful even though it seems bizarre.

Second, there is the issue of whether risks and uncertainties are the same thing or different. One school of thought says that a risk is a potential outcome whose probability is known, whereas an uncertainty is a potential outcome whose probability is not known. Another, more common approach is to recognize no meaningful difference between risk and uncertainty, and this too can be justified by diving into the philosophy of probability. I often say 'risk and uncertainty' to make sure everyone knows I have a broad view in mind.

Third, there is the question of whether a risk can be a good thing or not. In common language almost everyone thinks of risks as *bad* things that might happen. However, many risk managers and authors have realized that some uncertainties that we care about concern good things that might happen, and managing these with the same process can be useful and occasionally unavoidable. Moreover, there are events whose consequences include some bad effects and some good ones, making separation even more awkward.

UPSIDE AND DOWNSIDE

Different interpretations of these terms also exist. There are people for whom the upside of risk is not part of risk itself but the returns that they hope to gain by taking risk. For others the upside and downside are features of risk but here there are different views on what separates upside from downside. Presumably there is a neutral level between good and bad. Where is that line drawn? Do we have a choice?

A few examples will show that we *do* have a choice but we usually make it almost unconsciously and sometimes we would be better off being more deliberate. I call this level that separates good from bad the 'benchmark level' and it can be set according to what we expect, plan, think is morally right, or for other reasons.

For example, suppose you are in a large building company and considering the risk of injury from accidents on building sites and records of accidents over the last 20 years show that on average two people are killed and ten are injured each year. You may have a plan to reduce this to one killed and seven injured each year, but would you put it that way to people working on your building sites? Saying you *plan* to kill one person and injure seven is not good communication and also it would be wrong to be pleasantly surprised if only five people were injured. Similarly, if you did some calculations and decided that the mathematical expected outcomes (i.e. probability weighted averages) were two deaths and eight injuries it would be wrong to be happy if only one person died. One death is still too many. For this risk the natural benchmark is zero deaths and zero injuries. Anything else seems callous.

In contrast, if you were considering the risky returns from an investment in shares in a large company the traditional benchmark level is the mathematical 'expected' return, so anything better than that is upside and anything worse is downside. Alternatively, if you were not a city professional you might think that what you paid for the shares is your benchmark and any profit is upside while a loss is downside. Or you could decide that your benchmark is some target level, quite possibly higher than the expected returns but equal to the amount you need to pay off the last of your mortgage before you retire.

Project risk management usually takes some version of the project plan as the benchmark, but here again there are exceptions and I suspect that often this is not recognized when risks are weighed.

Sometimes we do not know if the impact of some potential event would be good or bad, even though we know it matters to us.

The somewhat arbitrary nature of the benchmark level, combined with the fact that risks often have a mixture of good and bad effects, and that sometimes we just don't know, should persuade most people that the current fashion among specialists for thinking of risks as either good or bad is here to stay. Practical risk control needs to cover everything in one process.

INTERNAL CONTROL

Despite being quoted hundreds of times as the true definition of 'internal control' the COSO version provides little practical help. What the phrase really means depends on who is using it.

If an internal control specialist is using it then he or she probably means just about all aspects of management, but probably with an emphasis on bookkeeping. If a non-specialist uses it she or she probably means checks on bookkeeping.

RISK CONTROL

In this book I'm using the phrase 'risk control' to refer to the discipline created by integrating risk management and internal control.

4 Goals from People and Behaviour

In this chapter it's time to take a look at human behaviour in the face of uncertainty and see how powerful social forces can derail even technically brilliant risk-control schemes. These 'people problems' are so powerful that, at the end of the chapter, it will be clear that tackling them is the main job of risk control and I will restate the two objectives that risk control should work on from day to day.

Guidance from the psychology of risk and control

In the last few decades psychologists have documented an amazing variety of irrational human behaviours linked to risk and uncertainty. Our mental capacity is not unlimited, we cannot remember everything, and we succumb to a number of biases that we are rarely aware of. We rely heavily on mental short cuts that work well most of the time but sometimes lead us to large errors. There are also social pressures and problems generated by our management systems.

From all these effects one tendency seems to me particularly important for risk control. It is the tendency to see the future too narrowly. We don't always see the future too narrowly and, when we do, it seems to be for a number of different reasons. However, narrowness is typical.

For example, suppose you ask someone to tell you what they can about the future value of some uncertain amount, such as next month's sales, or the value of the FTSE 100 index in a week's time, or the temperature at midday tomorrow. Ask them to give a range of numbers so that they are 80 per cent certain the actual value will be in that range. Typically the range they give will be too narrow and the actual value will fall outside their range more than 20 per cent of the time.

Why this happens is not clear, but it does.

The subtle cognitive errors that psychologists have studied in so much detail are probably weak forces compared to the influence of other people. You can probably recognize the most common mechanisms. To introduce them, let's follow an imaginary business idea from birth to death.

MENTAL BLINKERS ON A BUSINESS PROJECT

Imagine someone has an idea for a business project. They develop that idea, trying it out on colleagues to see what they think. Gradually, getting feedback from friends turns into advocacy. The person with the idea begins to talk up the benefits, play down the costs, and feign more certainty about both benefits and costs than is reasonable.

The next stage might be to submit a written business case to win more senior support for the idea. Perhaps the business case has to conform to a document template that calls for a list of the risks involved with some suggestions on how they can be managed. In theory this should lead the proponent to think carefully about the risks and uncertainties, and give an honest account of them.

In practice it is far too late to expect such honesty. The proponent knows that getting his or her idea accepted is part of career progression and behaves as a committed advocate, continuing to make bold predictions about outcomes and providing the minimum analysis of risks that seems permissible.

The proponent knows that the benefits need to be great enough to get approval, but is wary of raising expectations too high and being set a tough target. Consequently, he or she aims to communicate the lowest expectations capable of winning backing. This means that the range of outcomes mentioned and discussed tends to be much too narrow.

However, this is only the beginning. Suppose the project gets approval to start and a team is assembled. Now the project's leader wants to keep people motivated. Once again it seems a bad idea to mention really bad things that might happen in case it harms morale, while there is no sense in raising expectations too high. It might lead to frustration later on.

After a time things start to work out differently from expectations. If that means better than expected then the project leader will be tempted to keep this information back, for a time at least, in case things start to get sticky later on and some slack is needed. On the other hand, if things start to look bad the project leader has to decide what to say to his or her boss. If things have yet to fall behind schedule or go over budget many people prefer to say nothing for the time being. After all, they may still find a way to deal with the potential problems that are looming. Besides, their boss will expect to be presented with solutions not problems, so the project leader will often decide to say nothing for now while seeking a solution.

The boss's situation is a little different. Most people want to know what is going on, but some prefer not to be told about potential problems. They reason that if they haven't been told then they are less liable for blame than if they had been told about a nasty potential situation but did nothing. When it comes to personal liability for death or injury it may or may not be safer to remain ignorant of the risks; in the UK at least this legal point has not been settled. Consequently, some bosses don't try very hard to find out about potential problems and may even give off signals that discourage subordinates from revealing them.

As things go from bad to slightly worse the project leader revisits the question of what to tell his or her boss. Having held back bad news earlier, open discussion of the potential problems now seems even less attractive than before. Many people in this situation prefer to take a risk to avoid loss of face and, like rogue trader Nick Leeson who brought down Barings bank, they carry on, hoping to get lucky and never have to admit to their problems.

Clearly, these are powerful forces. Not talking about risks and uncertainties leads to not managing them and even to genuine belief that they do not exist.

Many technically excellent risk management initiatives have had disappointing results because people are strongly motivated to avoid talking about alternative outcomes.

MORE MENTAL BLINKERS

Having begun with some examples around an imaginary project, let's consider some more of the perspective-narrowing thoughts that prevent us from managing risk and uncertainty as well as we could.

People in very senior leadership positions often feel under pressure to provide a kind of visionary leadership based on imagining an ideal future for their organization and inspiring everyone in the organization to work to get to that ideal future. The pressure is often intense when the leader comes to write about strategy. Phrases like 'hard choices' and 'clear strategy' seem to push the leader towards setting out one path to one destination.

At the same time, common sense says that this is a fool's game. Predictions about the future are often wrong so making predictions in public often leads to embarrassment. Publicly stating a strategy can destroy options that should have been left open.

Credibility is at stake, which is one of the reasons that people make narrow predictions. For example, when people are asked how long it will take to complete phases of a project they usually give ranges that are too narrow as well as being optimistic. They feel, correctly it seems, that people judge their competence from the width of the ranges they give. Narrow ranges are taken as evidence of competence, even though they should be evidence of the opposite.

Another common reason for being blind to alternative outcomes is a focus on targets. Asked how much something will cost, people sometimes answer 'Well, the budget is…' which is not the same thing at all. The idea is that somehow the actual cost will be made to match a figure guesstimated some time earlier.

We also struggle to predict the impact of vicious and virtuous circles, and to see the combined effect of many small risks.

One of the unpredictable factors in the future that we struggle to understand is our own actions. What will we do if various things happen? We tend to imagine only the actions we can think of now, not the actions we or others might think of in future.

Even highly quantitative and mathematical risk modelling is not immune from these effects. Experts frequently provide detailed information from their models as to what risk probabilities are without mentioning the additional 'model risk' arising from the possibility that their models are wrong. In finance, the usual starting point is to imagine that price changes are normally distributed, but they are not. The actual distribution, in some timescales at least, has fatter tails, meaning that most modelling in finance has blinkers.

And what happens if we do open our minds to the full range of reasonable possibilities? Then we hit the next challenge, which is knowing how to act in the face of what can seem overwhelming complexity.

Cases of uncertainty suppression

People often behave as if they are more certain than they really are or should be. However, publicly available information about this very subtle and personal failing can be hard to find. The journalists and authors who write about the cases are not looking for uncertainty suppression and do not give the details that would reveal it. However, there are exceptions.

BOO.COM

One of the most outrageous failures of the dot com era was boo.com. Boo was an Internet clothing retailer that aimed to launch simultaneously in several countries, using a website that let you try clothes on a pert 3D model. Internet nerds flocked to the site to wonder at the technology and experiment with the lingerie section.

The chief executive and a founder of the company, Ernst Malmsten, later wrote a book[1] about the experience. In it he explained that he wanted to put the record straight and correct the popular myth that he and his fellow directors had burned through $135 mn by high living and baseless optimism. His account is remarkably detailed, even explaining the company drink (vodka and grapefruit juice), the extensive business travel, and the various bars they visited.

After a number of delays on the all-important website Ernst commissioned a review by outside consultants to report on what the problems were and what could be done. The report detailed a large number of control weaknesses, though nothing that would surprise an IT auditor. The launch would have to be delayed even longer than expected.

Ernst came to a chilling realization. He realized first of all that responsibility for the problems ultimately rested with him. He was the one who had wanted to do so much from the start. Instead of just getting something small working in one country and then expanding, he had wanted to make everything happen in one giant launch. Having created this enormous pressure he had then *banned* talk of problems and delays as defeatist. So, instead of sharing and managing their concerns, people had preferred to ride blindly into the guns.

Sadly, this realization came too late to save the company. The damage was already too serious. However, it does give us a remarkably clear example of uncertainty suppression, driven from the top of a company. Ernst had spent a long time persuading backers to part with their money and eventually had come to believe his own hype and exaggerated confidence of success. He had gone for an insanely risky plan and prevented others from managing the risks of that plan by forcing them to ignore those risks.

WEAPONS OF MASS DESTRUCTION IN IRAQ

Salesmanship, such as when trying to raise money, is one of the major problems and it manifests itself in many ways.

When Tony Blair became prime minister of the United Kingdom on 2 May 1997 most people thought things could only get better. Blair was seen by many as a good communicator. Even when his opponents pointed out that, for example, Blair spoke with a slightly different accent when talking to people in different parts of the UK, this just seemed like more evidence of what a good communicator and politician he was.

As the years went by this view gradually changed and people began to trust him less and less. The war in Iraq, which still drags on with little prospect of a happy ending, was one of the major factors to damage his popularity and in the build-up to that war something happened that perfectly illustrates our cultural difficulties with uncertainty.

We expect a salesperson to be 'confident' and this often translates into making statements about costs and benefits of something that are confident statements. People trying to be confident replace timid words like 'might' and 'could' with their confident alternative, 'will.' It's a communication skill.

It is also lying. It is pretending that something is more certain than it really is.

As part of his justification for joining the war against Saddam Hussein, Tony Blair promised the British public a dossier of intelligence information. When it was published the dossier included the statement that Saddam could deploy weapons of mass destruction (WMDs) within 45 minutes if he wanted to.

No WMDs were ever found.

Later, an enquiry into intelligence on WMDs around the world, including Iraq, was conducted by a committee led by Lord Butler of Brockwell. The report[2] published as a result included a long section on Iraq that looked at the dossier. The report gives sections of the dossier side by side with sections from the original intelligence documents on which they were based. They are remarkably similar, but the consistent difference between the two is that the original documents contained strong statements about the limitations of the evidence and the difficulty of drawing firm conclusions, while the dossier did not.

The lie was simply about the level of certainty in the intelligence.

THE HOLYROOD BUILDING PROJECT

Most of the clearest published examples of uncertainty suppression come from public sector fiascos because they often give rise to public enquiries and these make detailed information public.

In 1998 the Secretary of State at the time, Donald Dewar, initiated a project to build accommodation for the new Scottish Parliament in Edinburgh. Early thinking had been that an existing building might be adapted for use but this was rejected in favour of something new that Scottish people could be proud of.

The initial cost was estimated at around £10 mn to £40 mn, but by the time the building work was nearly complete the actual cost had grown to around £435 mn. It was outrageous and a public inquiry, chaired by Lord Fraser of Carmyllie, followed. The documents and testimonies that provided the evidence for this inquiry were made public on a website[3] and include various versions of the risk registers, for example.

During one period between 1998 and 1999, before construction had begun, successive designs were being produced by the architect Enric Miralles, in response to changes in the estimated amount of accommodation required. Each design was then costed by the quantity surveyors appointed to the project. At the time the total budget for the building was £50 mn but none of the designs was within the budget and in fact things were getting worse rather than better. This meant that they faced an enormous potential problem.

Apparently the senior civil servants in charge of the project did not explain this to the responsible minister. When asked at the public inquiry why they hadn't done so they gave these answers:[4]

> *Mrs Doig: 'I certainly would not have felt comfortable going to Ministers one day and saying, "Well, I think I need an extra budget of such-and-such", and then going back the next day and saying, "Oh, no, the design's changed a bit; it's down again, it's up again." That would not be a good use of Ministers' time, and we had to wait and see.'*

> *Mr Thomson: 'If all you can do by going to Ministers is to share your anxiety with them, there is not much point in going to Ministers. You just need to get on with it. When there is a decision point, that is when you go to Ministers.'*

With hindsight these seem weak justifications. Mrs Doig seemed to think she would be expected to know exactly how much money was required and did not want to discuss the matter with Ministers until she knew. Mr Thomson did not want to discuss the matter with Ministers until he had found some kind of solution to the cost problem. Costs continued to rise unpredictably and they never found a solution. Both preferred to carry on, presumably hoping that they would find some way out of their difficulties and never have to break bad news to their superiors.

Had these two known how to discuss uncertainties without loss of credibility, for example by simply giving Ministers regular briefings on all major areas of risk and uncertainty on the project, they would have been able to talk about and better manage the situation they were in.

Another aspect of uncertainty blindness illustrated by the Holyrood fiasco is the tendency to think that goals are enough for delegation. At the outset there was a brief, a budget, and a deadline for the project. In effect, these said 'If you deliver this combination then we'll be happy customers.' As long as these seemed achievable they told people working on the project what was valued and gave them a basis for trading off timeliness against cost, cost against quality, and so on.

However, as it became clear that the original combination of cost, quality, and deadline was not achievable people wondered what to deliver instead. In the absence of clear guidance people picked up on the strong though unquantified language about quality and decided that quality should not be sacrificed but costs would have to rise, which they did.

Had the authors of the original brief been more open minded about possible alternative futures they might have thought to say more about how they would value different levels of quality, cost, and timeliness, so that if the preferred combination became unfeasible there would still be guidance to work with. Better still, such value guidance could have been provided and continually updated through the life of the project in light of the latest information.

Another aspect of the Holyrood building project that is worth noting is that it relied on all the usual risk management procedures and tools. Most people in the industry, if asked to look at the formal procedures that were operated to manage risk, would have agreed that they were all standard practice but we know now that they were totally inadequate for the job and human factors easily overcame their puny resistance.

This is common. Many famously uncontrolled projects had 'best practice' risk management procedures, which indicates how powerful the human factors are.

SHELL'S OIL RESERVES

On 9 January 2004 Shell announced that 3.9 bn barrels of oil and gas were being moved from the 'proved' category to the less certain 'scope for recovery' category. In accounting terms, their oil and gas 'reserves' were to drop by 20 per cent. Two months later this figure was revised to around 25 per cent, and by the following January a string of announcements had cut reserves by about a third in total. In terms of the key performance indicators used by analysts to compare oil companies, Shell went from leading BP and Exxon to lagging behind them. It was a disaster.

The company paid out fines and compensation totalling around $700 mn. The chairman, Phil Watts, and exploration and product chief, Walter van der Vijver, departed, followed later by the chief financial officer for oil and gas exploration, Frank Coopman, and the group chief financial officer, Judy Boynton. The settlement with shareholders amounted to between 10 per cent and 13 per cent of their damages, unusually high for this kind of action.

Detailed analyses were done by the Financial Services Authority in support of their £17 mn fine of Shell and by law firm Davis Polk & Wardwell at the request of Shell's board. These reports reveal a catalogue of optimistic misjudgements, fuelled in part by personal bonuses for increasing reserves and the existence of political fiefdoms in the group. Problems and errors had been raised internally on many occasions down the years only to be watered down before they reached the Board or ignored.

In July 2002 the strategy was to play for time and hope that reserves that had been optimistically booked would indeed become proven. It didn't happen.

The reserves revelation was finally prompted by a hard hitting internal report by Coopman that recommended immediate correction of reserves, saying it was a legal obligation. In response, van der Vijver, then head of exploration and product, replied saying in an email 'This is absolute dynamite, not at all what I expected and needs to be destroyed.' Ironically, van der Vijver was actively suppressing the truth in large part because his predecessor, Watts, had done so in the past.

It looks as if overstatement of reserves had been going on for years and involved many people putting up overstated figures that were welcomed by senior executives, who then went to great lengths to keep things secret for as long as possible from the outside world.

Facts can be inconvenient but expectations, being uncertain, are far more pliable. This is why it is so often uncertainty that is distorted.

Thanks to the detail revealed about these cases it is not hard to see how people ignored and hid potential problems. Not all cases of blinkered thinking about the future are as clear cut.

MURKIER CASES

The pension company Equitable Life Assurance Society closed to new business in 2000 and was sold to Halifax in 2001 after past decisions caught up with it. Prior to 1988, in pursuit of rapid growth, it enticed customers with a guaranteed minimum annuity percentage. At the time, with high inflation and interest rates, this must have seemed a risky but not unsustainable practice. Faced with low interest rates and increasingly long-lived customers they began to realize, too late, that it was going to cost them a lot to make good on their promises. Some customers complained. Management decided to control the costs by simply cutting back on one of the other benefits promised to pensioners if they decided to claim their guaranteed annuity rate.

Mathematically, it worked, but when a pensioner and his lawyers challenged the approach the case eventually went to the House of Lords who agreed it was wrong.

It is possible that, even in the 1970s, when guaranteed annuity rates were being developed, the board knew exactly what they were doing and simply felt that their decision would take so long to turn into a crisis that they would be long retired themselves by then. In short, this could have been an example of an agency problem, not underestimation of uncertainty.

On the other hand, it may well have been that management underestimated the likelihood of interest rates and mortality changing as much as they did, and underestimated the potential impact for Equitable Life. Then, when problems started to develop, they may well have been too narrow in thinking that they could control public reaction by sticking to their argument that their calculation approach was in some way fair.

Similarly, Metronet's Public Private Partnership (PPP) contract with London Underground to modernize London's tube system may well have been reached after thorough and realistic assessment of risk and they may have managed their operations subsequently with expertise that the world has yet to appreciate.

However, as I write, the company is in administration and it looks very much as if its business plan was founded on the usual mixture of optimism and overconfidence, and that subsequent management of the work was poor. The official report by the PPP Arbiter that plunged Metronet into crisis cites their poor management of risk among other things.

The big message for risk control

How does this dismal catalogue help us? It helps because these factors are so strong, so fundamental to getting value from risk control programmes, that tackling them becomes the core of the work.

The scope of risk control is not 'all management', as COSO would have it. The scope of risk control is the things we do, or should do, because the world is uncertain. If something would have to be done even in a certain world, such as making a plan or allocating resources, then it is not risk control.

The objectives of risk control I suggest are simply these:

1. To help people take off their mental blinkers and see the true range of possibilities they face.
2. To help people behave competently in a way that is consistent with that wider view.

Whether it is reminding an accounts clerk that bank mistakes can happen so a bank reconciliation is necessary, or encouraging the chairman of the board to use scenario planning to create more flexible, realistic plans, the fundamental objectives are the same.

A major goal for designers of controls is to find controls that are effective at addressing uncertainty suppression. What these are is still a research subject but all the control ideas presented in this book are aimed at doing this in some way.

Notes

1   Malmsten, E., Portanger, E., and Drazin, C. (2002) *boo hoo*. Arrow.
2   'Review of Intelligence on Weapons of Mass Destruction.' 14 July 2004, available from its own website at www.butlerreview.org.uk.
3   A fascinating resource: www.holyroodinquiry.org.
4   Paragraphs 8.18 and 8.19 of the Holyrood Inquiry final report.

High Value Control Mechanisms

5 A Summary of Control Patterns for More Value

You have now reached the heart of this book: a collection of 60 ideas for internal controls that will give more value at less cost, ranging from planning techniques to analytics, and from ideas on computerized edit checks to ideas on audit methods.

This is not a comprehensive collection of controls, which would be an enormous tome. Instead, it's a collection of ideas that are likely to add value if used. Many are highly efficient and effective control mechanisms. Some will be new to you and some may be familiar but with new refinements.

You may also find some familiar ideas are suggested for a narrower range of situations than you expect. For example, control through fixed targets is widely used in organizations today and it has its place. It's just that in many situations there are better alternatives. I present fixed target control but explain the narrow set of situations where it is a good choice and also explain alternatives that work better in other situations.

You can add value by shifting from one type of control to another that is more suited to the circumstances.

How to benefit from this collection

The corollary of 'garbage in; garbage out' is 'great stuff in; great stuff out'. If you feed your mind with good ideas for controls then, when you need to design a control system, good, creative ideas will flow more easily.

The control ideas in this part are organized into bite-sized chunks so that you can dip in where you like, or just cram everything in, whichever you prefer. Doing so will change the ideas you consider first in a design situation, almost certainly towards higher-value mechanisms.

Each idea is presented in a standard format called a design pattern that links the solutions presented with the situations where they are useful and the reasons why. The ideas are also grouped and linked together to make it easier to combine the ideas to solve specific problems.

Format of presentation

The design pattern format is based on a book called *A Pattern Language* written by architect Christopher Alexander and co-workers about how to design regions, towns, buildings, and interiors.[1] This is the book that launched design patterns and is still arguably the best set of design patterns ever written – better than those in computing that followed. I've followed Alexander's format as closely as possible.

Every design pattern has the following:

- A reference number and a name.
- An example that is as archetypal as possible. All the examples are fictitious unless otherwise stated.
- An introductory paragraph explaining where the idea can be used and what larger design patterns it helps to create.
- Three diamonds to mark the beginning of the core of the pattern.
- A statement, in italics, of the issue, problem, or some related insight that begins the rationale for the solution to be presented.
- The body of the problem (often the longest section) that gives the empirical background to the problem, evidence for the validity of the solution, and the range of ways that the solution can be manifested. It ends with a summary of the value of the solution.
- A summary statement of the solution in italics, stated as an instruction.
- Occasionally, a diagram or other illustration further explaining the parts of the solution.
- Three more diamonds to mark the end of the core of the pattern.
- A paragraph that ties the pattern to subsidiary patterns that help to complete it, embellish it, or fill it out.

A summary of the ideas

Put in place a self-generating system of controls by including controls that generate, refine, replace, and manage other controls.

1. SELF-GENERATING CONTROL SYSTEM
2. CONTROLS DEVELOPMENT RESOURCE DIRECTION
3. CONTROLS GENERATION APPLICATIONS
4. DOUBLE LOOP DESIGN
5. TOP-DOWN DESIGN WITH SCHEMES
6. POST-IMPLEMENTATION REFINEMENT
7. FACTOR-DRIVEN DESIGN
8. CAUSE-EFFECT INTERVENTION
9. EVOLVING UNCERTAINTY LISTS
10. RISK REGISTERS
11. MATRIX MAPPING OF RISKS AND CONTROLS
12. PROCESS STEP ANALYSIS
13. CAUSAL MODELS
14. MONTE CARLO SIMULATION
15. FAULT AND EVENT TREE ANALYSIS
16. STORY-TELLING ABOUT THE FUTURE
17. GENERIC CONTROL DESIGN LIBRARY

18. CONTROL PATTERNS
19. PROCESS CONTROL FRAMEWORK
20. PROJECT CONTROL FRAMEWORK

Keep controls whose only function is to provide assurance to a minimum. Rely more on routine monitoring that is primarily done to improve process performance and drive projects. Make audit activities as refined and as efficient as possible.

21. CONTROLS SUPERVISION HIERARCHY
22. PROCESS MANAGEMENT CONTROL
23. PROCESS STATS PACK
24. PERSONAL COMPARATIVES
25. STATISTICAL PROCESS CONTROL
26. RISK-FACTOR MONITORING
27. HEALTHY CONVERSATIONS ABOUT CONTROL PERFORMANCE
28. CONTROL INTERVIEW QUESTIONS
29. REPORTING WITH UNCERTAINTY
30. EXPLANATION FIRST ANALYTICS
31. GRAPHICAL BUSINESS ANALYTICS
32. RANDOM FRAUD AUDITS
33. ADAPTIVE AUDIT
34. AUDIT AGAINST CONTROLS DESIGNED
35. ALL EVIDENCE AUDIT
36. AGILE DOCUMENTATION REVIEWS

Stay in control using alertness, learning, and agility rather than heavy, rigid defences.

37. FLEXIBLE REQUIREMENTS
38. RISK WEIGHTING
39. FLEXIBLE AGREEMENTS
40. FLEXIBLE PLANS
41. THE CRITICAL CHAIN METHOD
42. EVOLUTIONARY PROJECT MANAGEMENT
43. PORTFOLIO MANAGEMENT
44. NEGATIVE FEEDBACK CONTROL LOOPS
45. ACCELERATED TARGETS
46. REFORECASTING TO COMPLETION
47. FORECASTING WITH STATISTICAL EXTRAPOLATION

Keep driving towards higher inherent reliability so that checking and correction are less burdensome.

48. MULTI-LAYERED ACCESS RESTRICTION
49. SEGREGATION RULES ON ROLES
50. COGNITIVE ERGONOMICS

Use automation to make checking and correction as efficient as possible and use this power to go after lost money.

51. SPREADSHEET TIGHTENING OR REPLACEMENT
52. COMPUTER SUPPORTED AUTHORIZATIONS
53. EXTENDED EDIT CHECKS
54. SHIFT FROM PRE TO POST
55. RECOVERY/CLEANSING PROJECT
56. DISCREPANCY SEARCH
57. ANOMALY SEARCH
58. END-TO-END RECONCILIATION
59. MASS CORRECTION TOOL
60. ERROR FILE REDUCTION BY CLUSTER

Note

1   Alexander, C., Ishikawa, S., and Silverstein, M. with Jacobson, M., Fiksdahl-King, I., and Angel, S. (1977) *A Pattern Language*. Oxford: Oxford University Press.

6 *Controls that Generate Other Controls*

Of all the controls everyone should know about it is controls that generate other controls that need to come first. There are two reasons.

First, controls that generate other controls are the key to understanding how risk management and internal control integrate into one thing. The reality is that, in an organization of any size, there are people all over the place at different times thinking of control activities and planning to do them. Sometimes they are prompted to do this by their calendars and sometimes by things that have happened or are planned.

They generate those control ideas and plan their implementation in a number of different ways. It certainly is not the case that all controls are generated by one universal corporate process.

Risk registers and their usual attendant processes are one example of a control that generates other controls but they are not the only way of doing it and there are better alternatives in most situations.

If you want to design an efficient, effective control system then you should understand a wide range of alternative techniques and when to apply them.

Second, controls that generate other controls are usually intelligent controls. To get more value from risk control initiatives it makes sense to concentrate on the people and activities whose decisions and actions can have the most impact on value. In theory, at least, that means people in management positions, especially senior management positions, and the major decisions they take.

The controls involved at this level are largely what I call intelligent internal controls. This idea was introduced in Chapter 3. It means controls that involve some thinking, knowledge, usually judgement, and that are typically carried out by managers. It includes most controls that generate other controls.

This chapter and the next two chapters focus on various types of intelligent internal control.

The control patterns start now.

1   Self-generating control system

Example: A typical consulting company works to win and complete projects with its clients. It designs a self-generating control system with regular, calendarized controls, controls linked to triggering events, and controls that generate extra controls of all types. For example, its system includes quarterly reviews of control improvement requirements, a bid review procedure that is used for every bid, and a project risk management planning procedure that is used for every client project and generates many project controls when used, some of which are one-offs while others are regular or triggered.

Every organization needs a SELF-GENERATING CONTROL SYSTEM and most already have one, though not necessarily well designed.

Controls need to be designed and implemented, but what causes this? Other controls, of course.

Self-generating risk control systems are the norm today, even if they aren't seen that way by many people and often could be better designed. Many controls are scheduled to repeat regularly, for example every day, month, quarter, or year. Many more controls repeat when triggered by some event, such as the receipt of an invoice, a complaint by an angry customer, or the acquisition of another company. Still other risk controls happen once only, either at a planned date and time, or when triggered in response to an event. These controls are more common on projects.

It is obvious that controls need to be devised and revised, and most of the activities that do that are themselves repeated regularly or repeated when triggered. They are often seen as a layer separate and 'above' controls that operates to manage them, but for me it is simpler to see them all as controls. The activities that generate controls are widespread, varied, and often not coordinated. The theoretical idea of a single corporate process of monitoring that manages controls has unrealistic implications.

The language, concepts, and techniques of internal control and risk management have tended to focus differently. Internal control language talks about controls that 'operate', i.e. continue doing their thing over and over during a period of time. Risk management language is more often about 'responses' to risk that are one-offs, though they may be things that happen very slowly over a period of time. In fact some are exactly the same activities that an internal control person would say were 'operating.'

As discussed in Chapter 2, internal control and risk management have increasingly overlapped and begun to merge. The simple integration of these approaches means working with both ongoing and one-off actions in mind. It also means combining the grinding persistence of internal control thinking with the risk responsiveness of risk management thinking.

Putting the two together highlights an important design opportunity.

The health of control systems rises and falls, at times falling dangerously low as a result of other pressures, rapid change, resource shortages, and so on. We can think of the regularly repeating and frequently triggered controls as a resistant core that continues to sustain the others. It also makes sense to build in some redundancy in this core so that if one control, such as a regular meeting, stops or is missed a few times then something else will notice the problem, compensate, and stimulate the failing control to recover.

Therefore:

Design a control system with a bedrock of regular, calendar-driven controls and controls triggered by frequently occurring events, and ensure that these include controls that, when appropriate, generate, adapt, refine, and replace other controls.

A SELF-GENERATING CONTROL SYSTEM needs to include appropriate controls for generating controls such as TOP-DOWN DESIGN WITH SCHEMES and for refining controls such as POST-IMPLEMENTATION REFINEMENT. It will normally need to be decentralized and use the concept of CONTROLS GENERATION APPLICATIONS. When used at large scale it will also need CONTROLS DEVELOPMENT RESOURCE DIRECTION.

2   Controls development resource direction

Example: A company that makes personal loans had always outsourced the loan processing work to a large bank but then decided to implement its own systems and begin doing the loan processing in house. The project was the biggest the company had ever attempted and would need to design and implement hundreds of new controls to make the processes and systems work reliably and efficiently. A controls designer worked with others to establish some basics about the controls needed and deduce the specialist work needed to design and implement them during the project. The resources needed were estimated, identified, and directed to get on with the work.

CONTROLS DEVELOPMENT RESOURCE DIRECTION is an important part of a SELF-GENERATING CONTROL SYSTEM and relevant at all times but especially when major change is planned or anticipated.

It is obvious that controls should be designed and implemented in good time rather than after they are needed, and it is obvious that this means identifying the expertise needed to do that and making sure that expertise is available and directed to do the work. This is easier said than done.

A disturbingly high proportion of work to design and implement internal controls is done to correct weaknesses that already exist. An unknown but quite possibly lower proportion is done in advance of being needed so that a weakness will never exist.

We could call this the remediation syndrome. Countless actions are generated by internal audit and Sarbanes-Oxley reviews to fix perceived weaknesses. Explicit controls development activities in projects are rare but even when controls development is planned in good time it often doesn't get done because project plans fall behind and resources are claimed for other priorities. On other occasions controls development is simply inept.

In some ways the situation is worse still for gradual change because it often goes unnoticed. For example, growing complexity is common and has important implications for the design of control systems, but people rarely notice the gradual growth of baffling, stifling complexity in their organizations.

The first challenge is to identify change in advance. The second is to deduce what work is needed in sufficient time to get it done. The key to doing this is to make deductions from the distinctive characteristics of changes to their implications for the control mechanisms that are needed.

A lot of controls theory focuses on control objectives but to anticipate the amount of work involved and who is best equipped to do it we need to get beyond that stage and think about the specific types of *mechanism* that will need more work, and the special skills required to do it. This does not have to be done in detail. A high-level scheme is all that is needed.

In summary, directing controls development resources in good time maintains effective control and cuts remediation.

Therefore:

Scan the future looking for trends, anticipated or potential changes, and plans that imply a change to controls is required. Deduce the implications for the control mechanisms used and so the types of expertise needed to put them in place, and the quantity of work involved. In good time, direct the right people to do the work.

CONTROLS DEVELOPMENT RESOURCE DIRECTION makes use of TOP-DOWN DESIGN WITH SCHEMES.

3   Controls generation applications

Example: A large organization will usually have some kind of risk-control process to generate controls operating in every significant project, programme, and business unit, plus something at group level, and other variations aimed at specific categories of risk such as insurable risks, health and safety, and certain legal compliance risks.

CONTROLS GENERATION APPLICATIONS are the usual way organizations arrange their risk control, by default, and are a key part of a SELF-GENERATING CONTROL SYSTEM.

A variety of controls that generate other controls is needed to meet different situations.

When a control is put in place to generate other controls its scope is rarely 'all controls and all risks everywhere in our organization'. The total job is usually divided into separate (though linked) applications such as individual projects, programmes, sets of investments, organizational units, types of asset, and categories of risk.

In the usual jargon of risk management these are 'applications' of risk management. Often in the risk management literature it is unclear whether the writer envisages one process that covers everything or multiple applications of the same process. Part of the confusion arises because people see different applications as being standardized at the 'process' level but the word process means different things to different people.

For anything other than the smallest organizations a single control that generates all other controls is not a practical alternative, nor is it sensible to address each application using exactly the same approach.

Figure 6.1 illustrates multiple applications in one organization.

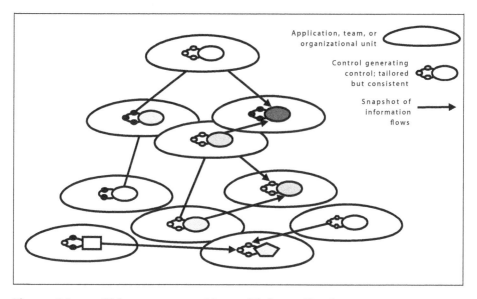

Figure 6.1   Risk management in multiple applications

For example, an electricity supply company might use advanced probabilistic modelling to design and manage its distribution network and purchase electricity from generators, but very simple and unquantified methods for controls over financial reporting. It makes no sense to tell the engineers to stop doing such clever things for the sake of consistency with the accountants, or to ask the accountants to raise their game to match the engineers. Both groups are doing what works for them.

Some degree of consistency is helpful if information about risk and controls is to be exchanged but this does not require all risk-thinking to be done in the same way. A satisfactory method of exchanging risk- and control-related information that accommodates the full variety of risk analysis and controls design methods in use today does not exist but would be very useful.

A high-level control can be designed and implemented to recognize applications and initiate a suitable control for each one.

In summary, thinking in terms of multiple applications of control generating controls is realistic and helps to counter the tendency to think of risk control as something that is done only at a very high level. Therefore:

Think of controls that generate other controls as being allocated to applications, and communicating with each other.

Key design techniques for generating controls include TOP-DOWN DESIGN WITH SCHEMES, POST-IMPLEMENTATION REFINEMENT, CAUSE-EFFECT INTERVENTION, and FACTOR-DRIVEN DESIGN. Continued improvement can be achieved using DOUBLE LOOP DESIGN.

4   Double loop design

Example: A large project where a risk-register-based process for generating controls has been chosen will need to monitor continually the effectiveness of that process, looking for signs that more quantification or causal analysis is needed, for example.

DOUBLE LOOP DESIGN is applicable to any intelligent control that generates other controls, in any CONTROLS GENERATION APPLICATION.

No controls design is perfect, or perfectly adapted for where it is used.

There are many alternative ways to approach risk analysis and controls design, with many tools, techniques, models, formulae, frameworks, and so on. No approach should be considered perfect and all should be under review.

Double loop design is illustrated by the example in Figure 6.2 which shows a fairly typical risk management process with an extra learning/design loop added to monitor and improve the main process.

In summary, DOUBLE LOOP DESIGN aims to keep control generation controls effective and make use of improving ideas. Therefore:

Add a second loop to risk analysis and controls design processes to monitor their performance and make improvements and adaptations.

There are no subsidiary control patterns to this one in this book.

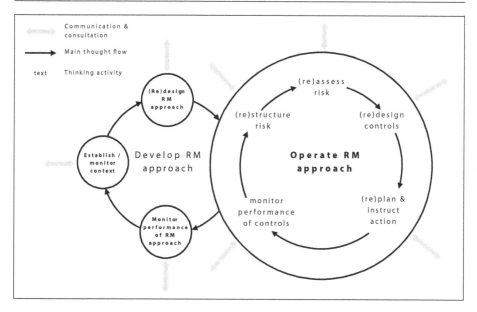

Figure 6.2   DOUBLE LOOP DESIGN, **illustrated by a typical risk management control**

5   Top-down design with schemes

Example: Suppose an insurance claims processing system is to be implemented and controls development is part of the project. The controls designers begin with a survey of the distinctive characteristics of the company, its business, its customers, competitive strategy, systems, people, the project, and so on. From this they deduce things about the shape of the control system and capture them in a high-level design called a scheme. This gives management an early view of what is to be built and why.

TOP-DOWN DESIGN WITH SCHEMES is a part of CONTROLS DEVELOPMENT RESOURCE DIRECTION and one of the most efficient ways to generate controls.

When there's a lot of controls work to do it is easy to lose sight of the overall design in a mass of detail.

When I first joined a team of control specialists trying to design controls as part of a large project I found that our methods were based on audit techniques. The idea was to get hold of process designs and information about systems and turn them into risk control matrices using control objectives. It was a fiasco. The business analysts continued until the deadline just working out the system and process designs, leaving the controls team with virtually no time to do the matrices. Before that we could say very little and missed many opportunities to input requirements to various teams in the project. Nobody had any idea of what we would design, and when they finally got our input it was a mass of detail with no overall shape or rationale.

Various frustrating experiences taught me that controls designers need to start designing before details of processes and systems are available and influence them along the way as well as responding to them.

Clients of the design activity need to be shown high-level designs early on, with a solid rationale, and need to see plans for detailed development that are realistic. The detailed work should then expand on, and revise, the initial, high-level scheme.

The high-level scheme should include any specific control mechanisms that are obvious from an early stage plus information about which types of control mechanism will be most important and which will need most work.

These decisions should be explained in terms of distinctive characteristics and their implications for controls, or be based on a risk model. Usually risk registers are not suitable for this because of the difficulty of controlling the level of detail.

Aim to have a good idea of what you are building after just 10 per cent of the design work is done.

In summary, working top down enables controls development to be better managed, gives a much earlier view of what is to be built, and gives better designs. Therefore:

Use no more than the first 10 per cent of design time to design a high level scheme of controls showing key controls and the emphasis on different types of control mechanism, with a solid rationale. Then do the detailed work and revise the scheme as necessary.

The design of the high-level scheme is usually best done using FACTOR-DRIVEN DESIGN and may use a GENERIC CONTROL DESIGN LIBRARY or CONTROL PATTERNS. Other useful subsidiary control patterns are CAUSE-EFFECT INTERVENTION, EVOLVING UNCERTAINTY LISTS, and RISK REGISTERS.

6   Post-implementation refinement

Example: An organization that has just gone live with a suite of new systems should expect several particularly tough weeks and plan to refine controls rapidly during this period. If no difficulties are experienced this may mean that insufficient checking is being done and problems are piling up without being noticed.

POST-IMPLEMENTATION REFINEMENT is a vital part of a SELF-GENERATING CONTROL SYSTEM and applies when significant system, process, or control changes are implemented.

Most controls can be made better once there is some experience to go on, and after a major implementation changes are often needed urgently.

Even the best analyses of risk, and designs for controls, are unlikely to produce perfect control systems so it is important to expect some problems, watch out for them, and be ready to make changes and refinements quickly.

For new systems and processes it is hard to estimate error rates to within an order of magnitude, let alone accurately. In addition, people usually perform controls less effectively when they are unfamiliar with them.

Therefore:

Plan to continue working on controls post-implementation.

POST-IMPLEMENTATION REFINEMENT can be managed using PROCESS MANAGEMENT CONTROL.

7   Factor-driven design

Example: Imagine a new government department needs to overhaul the controls over financial accounting and does it by looking at the distinctive characteristics of its activities, systems, environment, strategy, and other things that might influence the design of the controls. By thinking about the distinctive characteristics the designers are able to deduce things about the scheme of controls that will be needed. These are used to modify and detail an existing, generic scheme of controls to fit it to their requirements.

FACTOR-DRIVEN DESIGN is one of the most practical ways to design control systems, especially within TOP-DOWN DESIGN WITH SCHEMES.

Most controls design has to be done quickly, with a shortage of information, and on the basis of weak information about the real risks faced.

In the last two decades increasing attention has been paid to using perceptions of risk as an input to design of control systems. This is appropriate, but of course risk is not the only consideration. We also care about costs, the time needed to implement controls, and even strategic and cultural fit. Moreover, most risk assessments are unavoidably unreliable.

Combine the complexity of the issues involved, the flaky risk information, and the lack of time usually available to make design decisions and we face a very tough challenge. Reinventing control schemes each time is not practical.

On the other hand, just using some standard design regardless of circumstances is not attractive either.

What we need to do is make use of a repertoire of existing designs of high quality and fit them carefully to new situations, modifying, combining, and detailing them as necessary.

The circumstances that most need to be taken into consideration when modifying a generic design are the *distinctive characteristics* of the situation. These could relate to anything potentially relevant. *Distinctive* means 'important and different from usual' while *characteristic* refers to any factor (i.e. something known or likely) that may be relevant.

Here are some examples of typical distinctive characteristics and some possible implications for controls:

CONTROL PERFORMANCE REQUIREMENTS (DERIVED FROM COMPETITIVE STRATEGY)

- Very quick processing is required, so ...
    - Need controls to catch delayed items.
    - Try to get controls off the critical path. Replace pre-transaction checks with post-transaction reviews where possible.
    - Automated controls preferred.

- Very flexible processing is required, so ...
    - It is probably complex and allows easy adjustments, so easier to defraud.
    - Probably more parts of the process are manual.
    - Control mechanisms also need to be flexible.

- Low hassle to the customer is crucial, so ...
    - There are fewer opportunities to impose controls on the customer.
    - Try to avoid errors affecting the customer.

- Exact timing is needed, so ...
    - Controls are needed to catch delayed items, manage fluctuating workload, etc.

- Reliable service to the customer is essential, so ...
    - Mistakes affecting customers must be reduced.

- Very economical processing is required, so ...
    - Probably need automated controls if the processing is on a large scale.

- Highly regulated activity (e.g. selling pensions), so ...
  - Covering compliance risk will take more work. Need to monitor forthcoming regulations/laws and start changing processes in good time.

CULTURAL FEATURES

- Behavioural norms encourage fraud/theft. Patterns of crime already established, so ...
  - High risk of fraud/theft. Collusion a possibility. Could be social/staffing problems if established fiddles are tackled strongly without supporting action by top management.

- Organization wishes to empower its people, so ...
  - Old-fashioned controls undermine empowerment. Try to make teams work and give people the information they need to make good decisions themselves for the company. Talk of quality rather than control.

- There are functional silos, so ...
  - Functional silos are a problem for process-level monitoring controls so a cross-functional committee is needed.

- Weak control environment, so ...
  - Undermines manual controls and may hinder controls design activity. Monitoring is unlikely to work well unless the control environment is improved. Expect control weaknesses at all levels.

DATA FEATURES

- Data are standing data, so ...
  - Data errors accumulate unless cleared.
  - Individual data items are typically more sensitive.
  - Data entry workload is probably uneven with few users trained to do it, so may need to pre-book work to ensure staff available.

- Data is transaction data, so ...
  - Data errors probably will not accumulate.
  - Individual items typically less sensitive.
  - Data entry workload typically more even but much higher.

- Data very complex, so ...
  - Difficult to enter correctly because of complex data entry screens. Will require more emphasis on usability engineering.
  - Harder to write software correctly so more software quality assurance needed.

- Very high volumes of transactions, so ...
  - Tiny error percentages still produce many exceptions to be corrected. Often need system tools to prioritize, investigate, and clear errors.
  - Manual controls unlikely to be efficient.

- Highly predictable data values, so ...
  - Easier to control and to monitor. Favours computer filtering and assisted review.

- Transactions can be divided into sub-populations which are highly predictable or at least have very common characteristics, so ...
  - Look to split transactions into separate streams, each with their own controls.

- Population contains some very high-value and high-risk items, so ...
  - Requires either a very reliable process or a special approach to controlling the bigger items.

- Data about individuals is held, so ...
  - Privacy legislation applies and confidentiality breaches could seriously damage customer confidence.

- Very abstract business based on rules, definitions, possibilities (e.g. insurance, derivatives), so ...
  - Higher error risks. Trouble can arise through not understanding the business clearly.
  - Small actions can have big effects, perhaps not immediately visible to those involved.

PROCESS FEATURES

- The process is highly complex, so ...
  - This has different implications depending on whether the process is automated or manual. Complexity is one of the top drivers of controls development effort.

- Customers capture data (e.g. type them into a website), so ...
  - Error prone, especially if the product is complex e.g. insurance, mortgages. Companies assume their customers are interested in, and understand, their products; often this is wrong.
  - Rarely possible to provide training to customers. Usability is key, as are edit checks.
  - Customers could include professional fraudsters.

- Suppliers capture data (e.g. type it into a website), so ...
  - Again, you can rarely train so the software must be usability tested with lots of edit checks.

- Process is highly automated, so ...
  - Probably more reliable, but risk of systematic errors. More stress on IT controls.

- Process is highly manual, so ...
  - Probably less reliable, especially if work is boring, flexible, complex, or under time pressure.
  - Manual controls are vulnerable to boredom and fatigue.

- The assets are easy to dispose of if stolen, so ...
  - Raises risk of theft/fraud.

- High values of money are paid out, so ...
  - High fraud risk including sophisticated computer attacks, and also risk of interest from money launderers.

- Multilingual, so ...
  - Communication difficulties. Multiple versions of software perhaps. Particularly high risk of misleading field names on data input screens and forms so usability testing needed.

- International or geographically distributed, so ...
  - Different sets of regulations to comply with. Harder to control small, distant offices. Nationalist distrust is possible.
  - Cultural differences in attitudes to fraud. Potential for misunderstandings.

- Many separate databases and interfaces, so ...
  - More places for interface failures and opportunities for databases to get out of agreement. More chances to mis-map fields in one database to fields in another. Recoverability is more complex.

- Existing business process controls are very good or very poor/there is no existing process, so ...
  - If existing process and at least some controls are good, many people will be doing the right thing already. Otherwise, there will be more work on controls to do.

- Immediate environment of the process is inside the organization, so ...
  - Look to protect the process from messy inputs.

WORKLOAD FEATURES

*   Workload is rapidly rising/falling, so ...
    *   Staffing problems because many staff are new, or because they are insecure and disgruntled.

*   Workload is highly variable/constant, so ...
    *   High or low proportion of temporary staff affecting error risks and IT security.

*   Continuous work is required/periodic work only/slow response only is required, so ...
    *   Need for business continuity, among other things, is determined.

*   Environment is very fast changing or very stable, so ...
    *   Choice between very refined, automated controls and quick and dirty manual controls is affected.

*   Many changes in processes, systems, or people, so ...
    *   Lower inherent reliability is to be expected, so error rates will be greater and controls and monitoring are more important than ever.

*   Very high/very low proportion of work in the existing process is controls, so ...
    *   Decision over how much effort to invest in refining controls in detail is affected.

PROJECT FEATURES

*   Poor project health (e.g. uncertain sponsorship, politics, unclear or shifting requirements, over-ambitious objectives and impossible timetables), so ...
    *   Expect delays, frantic efforts to meet deadlines, and pressure to ignore controls. Expect low-reliability software and lack of adequate training of staff. Compensate with powerful monitoring controls from go-live onwards.

Inferences such as these may seem insignificant individually but soon build up to shape the control system. Observations at a more detailed level lead to inferences that are more detailed too.

In summary, FACTOR-DRIVEN DESIGN uses generic controls designs or control patterns but tailors them on the basis of factors without an explicit risk analysis phase. Even when done poorly it tends to produce control systems that resemble the high-quality generic starting point and it can be done quickly. Therefore:

Build a library of good-quality designs for controls and controls schemes and apply them by assessing new situations to identify their distinctive characteristics. Deduce from these characteristics the changes that need to be made to fit generic designs to the specific situation. Modify the generic designs to produce the final design.

FACTOR-DRIVEN DESIGN can make use of a GENERIC CONTROL DESIGN LIBRARY or CONTROL PATTERNS.

8 Cause-effect intervention

Example: Mobile telephone network companies have competed with each other for years to keep hold of subscribers. They have learned a lot about why customers leave them for a competitor and try to manage the causes of defection.

CAUSE-EFFECT INTERVENTION is a natural response to uncertainty and a common thought pattern in TOP-DOWN DESIGN WITH SCHEMES.

Manipulating cause and effect is a common part of planning of all kinds, but what part of it manages risk and uncertainty?

When we are thinking of how to achieve something we often look for ways to manipulate cause and effect to get the effects we want and prevent the effects we don't want. Much of this is not really managing risk and uncertainty. The causal relationships may be so certain and our interventions so decisive that we think in terms of making something happen, or blocking it. There is little or no doubt involved.

However, there are also many cause-effect relationships, and interventions, where significant uncertainty exists. The message of risk control is that we should extend our thinking to cover these too.

There are many possible interventions. We often think of the world as operating by cause and effect, often with the details of how cause leads to effect being unknown to us. We could imagine a vast network of cause-and-effect links, but in practice we usually only think of a very few at a time. If we put our microscope over one event in the network its situation looks like Figure 6.3, and of course any of those causes or effects could be put in the centre and would have their own causes and effects.

Since events include things that we could do we have various ways to influence the world shown:

- Add events (i.e. our actions) that will change the cause events, directly or indirectly.
- Add events that will change the central event, directly or indirectly.
- Add events that will change the effect events, directly or indirectly.
- Learn more about the unknown causal links and then reconsider our options.

The idea is simply to think about the possible causes and effects of something and then think of ways to manage them to advantage. It may be that some event is

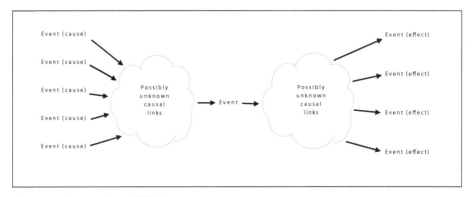

Figure 6.3   Causal links

desirable, so you want to increase the likelihood of it happening and magnify the resulting benefits if it does. Alternatively, the event may be undesirable, so you want to decrease the likelihood of it happening and reduce the impact if it does.

This is one of the most commonly described approaches to managing risk, but is surprisingly difficult to separate from other planning. We tend to see acts as managing risk only when the probability of a relevant event is not close to zero or one either before or after including the intervention. For example, we see something as risk management if it:

- changes the likelihood of something happening, but only slightly;
- changes the knock-on impact of something that is unlikely to occur; or
- influences something that is only a loose probabilistic cause of something we are interested in.

In each of these examples there are interventions that look very similar but are something more definite than risk management:

1. If we take an act that radically changes the likelihood of something happening we would say we were making it happen (or not happen), not managing the risk of it happening (or not happening).
2. If we take an act that changes the effects of something that we are expecting to happen we would say we were just managing the impact, not managing the impact of a risk.
3. If we take an act that changes a cause that strongly determines the event of concern we would just say we were managing, not managing risk.

> *Hiking example*: Imagine you are planning to go hiking in the countryside at the weekend. You will need to wear your walking boots when hiking so your objective is to be wearing them. To reduce the risk of hiking without your walking boots on you plan to find and put on your walking boots. Is this managing risk or just an odd way of justifying putting your boots on? Obviously this is not risk management. Finding and putting on your boots is an action that takes you from not having boots on, with near certainty, to having boots on, again with

near certainty. It makes a radical difference to the probability of your having boots on. This is the main action you plan to take, not risk management for it.

Now imagine you suddenly remember that the last time you used your walking boots was months ago before you moved to a new flat and you're not sure where they are or even if you kept them. In the light of that you decide to have a look for the boots before the weekend so you have time to buy some more if you can't find them. Now, that's risk management!

There are two practical reasons for being clear about this distinction. First, it is easier to consider weaker influences and unexpected outcomes as part of initial planning than do it separately later. (The same point could be made about most intelligent controls.) Second, risk management sessions are too often wasted writing down actions that are not risk management.

Hiking example continued: Suppose I wrote out a 'risk register' for your hiking trip and on there I wrote in the objective column 'Wear walking boots', and in the risk column 'Failure to wear walking boots', and then in the action column 'Find and put on walking boots'. On the face of it I seem to have fulfilled the requirements of the risk register template. There is no tip off in the wording that reveals I kept my mental blinkers on the whole time and have done no risk management whatsoever.

Here are some examples of simple patterns of cause-effect intervention.

Compensating contracts: This is where we set up a contract with another party so that, if some event happens, they will exchange something of value with us which tends to compensate for the impact of the event. Usually we think of this as compensation for something bad that happens to us but it could also be something good that happens, leading to us paying the other party. Examples of this include taking out insurance, reinsurance, laying off bets by placing opposite bets, hedging contracts, penalty clauses, choosing to deal with organizations who compensate, and profit sharing (i.e. sharing our profit with others).

Fixed price contracts: Here, we make a contract with another party for them to deliver some result to us for a price that is fixed to us. If the cost of achieving the result is more or less than the price we pay that is the other party's concern, not ours. Examples include subcontracting at a fixed price and factoring debt.

Dependencies, contingency plans, and incrementalism: Imagine there are two actions we need to take and the outcome overall depends on whether those actions are effective. Three of the possible connections between effectiveness and overall success are:

1. IF (action 1 is effective AND action 2 is effective) THEN result is success.
2. IF (action 1 is effective) THEN result is success.
3. IF (action 1 is effective OR action 2 is effective) THEN result is success.

Clearly if we have a choice our least favourite rule will be the first one. Both action 1 and action 2 have to be effective for us to reach success. In the second rule action 2 is irrelevant to success, which is helpful, but we only have one chance to succeed, and that is by making action 1 effective. The final rule gives us two chances for success, albeit at the cost of potentially having to attempt both actions.

This analysis gives a number of techniques for making plans that cope with uncertainty better.

Once you recognize that there is a chance of some actions not being as effective as you had imagined the value of reducing dependencies is clear. Sometimes an existing plan includes unnecessary dependencies and it is possible to change rule 1 into rule 2 and still achieve the same result. However, more often it is only by slightly modifying our view of success that we can make it dependent on fewer effective actions. In other words, by *reducing dependencies* we can go from:

IF (action 1 is effective AND action 2 is effective) THEN result is success.

to:

IF (action 1 is effective) THEN result is success.

One way of getting from rule 1 to rule 2 is to break success into two or more parts (i.e. *increments*), each of which is dependent on fewer effective actions. Sometimes achievement of each increment of success is dependent on achieving previous increments, but sometimes it is not, giving two variants on this technique. In other words, from the all-or-nothing:

IF (action 1 is effective AND action 2 is effective) THEN result is success.

to the incremental:

IF (action 1 is effective) THEN result is part of success.
IF (action 2 is effective AND action 1 was effective) THEN result is the other part of success.

to the fully independent:

IF (action 1 is effective) THEN result is part of success.
IF (action 2 is effective) THEN result is the other part of success.

If you can find other actions that achieve the success desired this opens up two other tactics, based on changing rule 2 to rule 3. If there is scope for trying one action and then using the second only if the first fails, then the second action is a *contingency* plan. If this is not possible it may still be possible to try both actions in *parallel*. Acting in parallel is more costly but may still be worthwhile.

It may be that you need to take other actions in order to put in place resources needed for a contingency action, in the form of contingency funds, redundant systems, and so on.

In all these situations it may be that there are many actions and many increments of success, not just two.

Buffers: Consider the humble inbox of your email program. It is a buffer between events and your actions. It gives you time to respond. Another example is the store room of a corner shop. When a product has sold out in the shop the shopkeeper can get some more from the store room and perhaps order more from a supplier. Again, the buffer stock gives the shopkeeper time to respond, but in this case it is by taking a rapid response first (refilling the shelf from stock in the store room) that he has the ability to take the slower response of ordering more from the supplier.

In principle, a buffer is an action we can take quickly, in response to some event, to gain time to take some other action. You could have a sequence of buffer actions, each gaining time to take the next one.

Safety margins: This is something we look for when our actions could give rise to a variety of outcomes and some are particularly unpleasant. Under the circumstances we will try to plan towards outcomes comfortably dissimilar from the unpleasant ones.

> *Example*: Imagine you are preparing to take a professional examination that is important to you and that failure would be a very serious outcome indeed. Would you do just enough preparation to pass, provided nothing untoward happened, or would you aim to pass comfortably? When I was in this situation many years ago it surprised me that there were people I studied with who aimed to do 'just enough'. I would imagine coming down with a bad cold the day before the exam, misreading my watch and doing a question too few, then having a page of my answers lost by the examiner. I was relieved to pass every time (though I once came within one mark of failure) but many people failed.

Demand management: The situation here is that we are operating some process that must respond to events, but the process has its limits. To keep within those limits we may be able to take actions that influence the events and use them to manage that demand.

Risk-factor management: Lack of exercise is thought to be a risk factor driving many ailments, so taking exercise is a way to manage the risk of those ailments. Notice that if the connection between a cause and the effect is a close one (e.g. if you do not exercise you are virtually guaranteed to get the ailment, but will not get it otherwise) we would not say this was managing the *risk*. There isn't enough uncertainty involved.

In summary, thinking through causes and effects and considering ways to intervene is a natural approach and constantly in use. Therefore:

When thinking in terms of chains of cause and effect and looking for good places to intervene, include weak, probabilistic effects too.

CAUSE-EFFECT INTERVENTION is easier with explicit CAUSAL MODELS.

9 Evolving uncertainty lists

Example: Imagine a team needs to develop a marketing strategy for a business. They decide to follow a systematic thought process adapted from a book, but add their own twist, which is to end each marketing strategy meeting by listing the areas of uncertainty that concern them most and planning research and other activities to be done before the next strategy meeting. The initial, rather muddled lists gradually evolve into a more structured list and then into a causal model while their actions change from being mostly research actions to being a risk plan for the marketing strategy as it is carried out.

EVOLVING UNCERTAINTY LISTS are one of the best ways to generate controls, especially in project-like situations and may be used within TOP-DOWN DESIGN WITH SCHEMES.

The best way to think through uncertainty is often unclear at first but it is vital to begin early before uncertainty starts to disappear from view.

Most ideas and plans that develop in an organization have to be 'sold' internally to get wider support and this leads the people with the plan to be advocates. Very soon this need for advocacy starts to drive uncertainty suppression and it is hard even to concede that there are risks connected with the idea, let alone discuss what to do in response.

To intercept this dangerous syndrome it is vital to start early. Perhaps the idea comes first, but then immediately it is possible to start considering the many areas of uncertainty around it and what their significance might be, and how they can be resolved. Or it might be that considering uncertainty leads to the idea. Perhaps the idea is in response to a request from a customer or leader, in which case it helps if that person takes the lead by outlining areas of uncertainty, thereby showing that this is expected.

Unfortunately, at an early stage our ideas tend to be muddled and unclear. That extends to our ideas about uncertainty and its importance. We may have little more than some disconnected thoughts and gut feelings. It is often unrealistic to try to jump straight to a well-structured model of the situation and our uncertainties.

An iterative approach of gradually evolving sophistication helps overcome this. It also means that actions to resolve the uncertainties around the idea are generated with a focus on the ones thought to be most important. Other actions to manage the uncertainties cannot be taken immediately and will develop to become the controls that are part of the idea being developed. For example, a consultant developing a bid to win work from a client may go through three or four loops of uncertainties, each time identifying more information that would help win the work, and also ideas for the project plan and contract that will manage risk. The end result of this is a bid document that incorporates ideas for managing risk. Along the way, actions that were to find out more, or work out solutions, were also completed.

In summary, EVOLVING UNCERTAINTY LISTS reduce the risk of uncertainty suppression in the development of business ideas and begin generating controls quickly, leading to efficient development of ideas/plans that incorporate controls. Therefore:

Starting from the earliest possible point in time list 'areas of uncertainty' and consider their significance before planning what to do about them. Repeat this frequently, evolving the list into a more sophisticated structure if possible, completing what control actions you can, and adding or improving others.

Table 6.1   Example of an item from an initial list of areas of uncertainty

Area of uncertainty	Significance	Actions to find out more	Other actions	Other details
Size of this market.	Initial estimates vary by a factor of 100. Critical.	Check trade journals and Internet.	Can we monitor sales better than usual and create a more flexible roll-out plan?	ML by Monday.

EVOLVING UNCERTAINTY LISTS can lead to different forms of risk analysis and controls design including CAUSAL MODELS and RISK REGISTERS. Another control pattern that is often useful is STORY-TELLING ABOUT THE FUTURE. The lists may be populated using PROCESS STEP ANALYSIS and laid out using MATRIX MAPPING OF RISKS AND CONTROLS.

10   Risk registers

Example: The managers of a harbour could list the main types of accident that can happen and actions to reduce the likelihood of such accidents and minimize their impact. These would be listed against the risks and assigned owners.

RISK REGISTERS are another way to generate controls but should be used only when the conditions are ideal, or as a stepping stone to more robust methods such as CAUSAL MODELS. Usually EVOLVING UNCERTAINTY LISTS are a better choice in this role.

Actions often need to be identified and allocated to manage potential accidents and other events that tend to be separate from each other.

A risk register is simply a list of potential problems, to which information can be attached, and against which controls are usually written. Risk registers do not demand much thinking about structure and inter-relationships, making them suitable when inter-relationships are not important and the people doing the risk analysis do not have much skill or time.

The use of the word 'risk' almost always triggers people to think exclusively of bad things that may happen. Another name for most risk registers that describes them accurately is 'Worry-Driven Action Lists'.

Although many different styles of risk register, and many different processes for using them, have been devised they share common characteristics. Risks tend to be grouped into types, they tend to be rated in some way to highlight those felt to be most important, and there are usually 'owners' for risks and their related controls.

In summary, RISK REGISTERS are a simple way to organize information about worries. Therefore:

Provided the risks of concern are thought to be largely unrelated, list them, rate them in some way, and decide what more, if anything, to do about them.

Table 6.2 shows a typical line from a risk register.

Table 6.2   Example from a risk register

Risk	Risk rating	Actions	Owner	Deadline
Insufficient market size.	Medium.	Check trade journals and Internet.	ML.	By Monday.

RISK REGISTERS are common and may be unavoidable but usually better results come from EVOLVING UNCERTAINTY LISTS, CAUSAL MODELS, and FACTOR-DRIVEN DESIGN. They can be laid out using MATRIX MAPPING OF RISKS AND CONTROLS and can be populated using PROCESS STEP ANALYSIS. Ideas for controls can be generated using some other design method and drawing on a GENERIC CONTROL DESIGN LIBRARY or CONTROL PATTERNS.

11 Matrix mapping of risks and controls

Example: Documenting the relationship between risks and controls over financial reporting can be done compactly and conveniently using matrices.

MATRIX MAPPING OF RISKS AND CONTROLS is a useful format in any situation that requires the coverage provided by controls to be shown against risks.

It is common to map risks and controls to test the coverage of the controls, but risks and controls usually map in a many-to-many way making the layout crucial.

The most common type of risk-to-control mapping at the moment is one that goes through accounting processes (e.g. sales from sales order through to collection of cash) looking at controls that help ensure the accounts are correct, or at least acceptably accurate. In this analysis it is not important whether the company is trading successfully, so long as the accounts accurately reflect performance.

As corporate governance rules have developed in various countries it is these matrices that are usually among the first requirements, directly or indirectly.

However, other types of analysis are also possible. For example:

* *Revenue and cost assurance*: Mistakes and system flaws cost businesses dear through incomplete billing and over-payment for goods and services received. Systematic mapping of internal controls is one way to identify where this might be happening and find ways to reduce it.
* *Data conversion*: When data are moved from an old computer system to a new one a set of checks is needed to ensure that data are not lost or damaged in the process.
* *Profitable trading*: This kind of analysis is concerned with objectives like selling the right goods at a good price and getting paid for them.
* *Compliance with laws and regulations*: This can be quite a lengthy analysis, even in overview.
* *Support processes*: For example, people in a company's computer department carry out processes that support others. The computer department's processes can also be analysed for error and fraud risks.
* *IT security risks*: e-business processes need careful security design and a detailed analysis is needed to confirm that the design is adequate, in principle at least.
* *Business unit overview*: This is the level at which top-level analyses are usually pitched for compliance with corporate governance regulations such as the UK's Turnbull guidance.

Risks and controls map in a many-to-many way. In other words, many risks may be addressed by one control, and one risk may be addressed by the combination of more than one control.

One common format for writing down these mappings is to make a list of risks then write all relevant controls against each risk. (Examples abound in COSO's internal controls framework, especially in the evaluation tools volume.) The format is some variation on Table 6.3.

Table 6.3   Risk control table in common format

Risk/control objective	Controls
Risk A	Control 1 Control 2 Control 3
Risk B	Control 1 Control 4
Risk C	Control 2 Control 3
Risk D	Control 5
etc.	etc.

With this format all the controls relevant to each risk are written next to the risk, which means that some controls are listed more than once. People find this annoyingly repetitive and it makes the documentation larger than it needs to be. It also means that a list of controls cannot be produced from the mapping without removing duplicates.

In an effort to reduce the duplication people often write in only enough controls to show that coverage is adequate and do not show the full mapping. For example, if a risk is covered adequately by the first control written against it then other relevant controls may be left out. This means that control coverage is usually understated and it is hard to see the multiple layers of defence that make up the system. Control systems should be multi-layered and usually are.

Another approach to the problem of duplication is to choose a breakdown of the risks that maps fairly neatly to the controls in place. People sometimes do this without realizing that they have. A risk is simply suggested because someone thinks of the control first and this prompts the idea of the risk.

These behaviours undermine the value of the mapping. The coverage is not clear and complete. The controls are not tested against a fully independent analysis of risk. Documentation is needlessly long and a list of controls cannot be produced without removing duplicates. Furthermore, the controls are in no particular order or structure making it hard to use control frameworks directly. Multiply these irritations across hundreds of people doing mappings in a large organization and you can see that the simple choice of format has big implications for the value of the mapping. They create vast quantities of nearly useless documentation.

Fortunately, a much better solution exists that avoids all these problems: matrix mapping.

In MATRIX MAPPING OF RISKS AND CONTROLS the controls are listed on the left as row headings and the risks are listed along the top of a matrix as column headings. Each cell of the matrix is used to show whether the control on that line is linked to the risk in the column.

Table 6.4   Risk control table matrix layout

Control	Risk A	Risk B	Risk C	Risk D	etc.
Control 1		1	1		
Control 2			1		1
Control 3	1				1
Control 4			1	1	1
etc.					

In the example in Table 6.4, Risk A is covered by Control 3 only. Risk B is covered by Control 1 only. Risk C is covered by Controls 1, 2, and 4. And so on.

At first glance this seems unpromising. Surely there will be lots of wasted space? Won't the column headings be difficult to read? What if there are too many risks to fit across the page?

All these are minor issues whose impact can be minimized, and they are insignificant next to the drawbacks of the risk list approach.

With this design it is easy to mark off the links and the multi-layered nature of the control system is much easier to see. The controls can be grouped under subheadings from a controls scheme that help to keep all types of control in mind.

If the matrices are on a spreadsheet and the controls are listed vertically as recommended it is easy to add columns to capture useful information about each control (in addition to its profile of coverage of control objectives). This information can be sorted and reported to meet various needs. But what information is useful? Here are some suggestions:

- *Design and implementation information:* e.g. name of the developer, whether software needs to be written, whether the control already exists or not. This is relevant if controls are still being developed.
- *Manager responsible for operation of the control:* This is useful for various review and confirmation exercises. Processes almost always cut across departments but people naturally want to know what they are responsible for.
- *Frequency of operation of the control:* This can sometimes be useful where there is a choice and you want to make the most economic set of decisions about frequencies.

If you are designing controls within a project to implement a new system, or set of systems, expect to be asked to specify requirements for software (e.g. access controls, reports, interface checks) months before other decisions about control have to be taken, and probably a bit before you are ready.

The matrix mapping format was developed from my experiences in this kind of project. It makes it easier to identify controls with an implication for software, while high-level design of control systems makes it possible to respond to even the most demanding software developers. The technique of marking off controls against risks makes it easier to make changes to the matrices as the software and process people change their minds about how things will work, which is another major practical advantage.

Most matrix spreadsheets will not fit onto one sheet of paper without some trickery. Compared to risk listing the matrix format is far more compact, but it can be difficult to fit to the width of a page even in landscape format.

The following techniques reduce the problem:

- *Stay electronic:* Avoid hardcopy altogether if possible. You can get more text on a spreadsheet if you use comments for extended descriptions and comments. These cannot be printed at all.
- *Turn the risks through 90 degrees:* This allows the columns to be narrower.
- *Hide columns:* Hide any columns not needed by the person who wants the hardcopy.
- *Set column and row headings so every page has them:* This is possible on some spreadsheet programs. If not, split the matrix by splitting the set of risks/steps.

A summary of advantages of matrix mapping over risk lists is given in Table 6.5.

Therefore:

Map controls to risks by listing risks as column headings and controls as row headings, then mark where controls address risks in the matrix resulting.

There are no subsidiary control patterns to this one in this book.

12   Process step analysis

Example: A company needing to check the coverage of its controls over financial reporting for a particular accounting cycle might draw that cycle in a diagram showing every data flow, data store, and process, then generate from this diagram and list of the steps involved. Each process, each store, and each flow is a step.

PROCESS STEP ANALYSIS is a rigorous way to structure risk around processes and can be used to populate EVOLVING UNCERTAINTY LISTS and RISK REGISTERS.

Table 6.5   Advantages of matrix mapping

Risk-list format	Matrix mapping format
Does not conveniently represent many-to-many relations between risks and controls, leading to distortion and repetition of control descriptions.	Very easy to show many-to-many relations. Avoids distortion. Controls are described only once, saving space.
Does not provide a list of controls.	Provides a list of controls, which can be neatly organized into control types.
Repetition of controls makes it hard to record extra information about controls, while their disorganized distribution through the matrix makes specific controls hard to find quickly.	Extra information can be put against each control and the controls can be grouped meaningfully. For example, it is easy to give each manager a list of the controls he/she is responsible for, or produce a list of all control reports needed from a new system, or pull out the rules for segregation of duties.
Hard to automate.	Easily automated on a spreadsheet giving dramatically smaller matrices and the ability to sort controls.
Does not prompt people to think of controls.	Provides ideas for controls.
Almost useless for designing controls.	Ideal for designing controls.

In a complex sequence of information processing it is easy to miss important activities and the risk that goes with them.

The ideal framework of risks to use as column headings in a control matrix is one that omits nothing significant within the scope of the analysis and matches conveniently with the effects of the internal controls. If the risks are too broad it is difficult to show coverage accurately. (A control has to be put against the risk but it is not clear that the control only covers part of that particular risk.) On the other hand, if the risks are too fine the matrix becomes large unnecessarily.

One way to create a breakdown of process-related risks systematically is to draw out the process and then cut it into steps to which a short, standard list of control objectives is applied. Each combination of step and objective is a risk (i.e. the implied risk of not achieving the objective).

Here's how that works in the context of financial accounting, an ideal place to use the technique due to the long established use of fixed sets of control objectives.

* *If many accounting cycles are being analysed, decide how to divide up the cycles* e.g. 'purchases' or 'purchases and payables'? It is usually best to go with the longest, most inclusive processes possible. Do not forget to include processes

like returns and adjustments that may be infrequent and low value, typically, because these are often weakly controlled areas.

- *Identify the underlying information processing*, excluding internal control steps. Most people find it helps to draw diagrams but with practice this can be omitted. Look for the physical stores of data (e.g. paper forms, computer databases, and computer files), physical transfers of data, data capture steps, and calculations. Exclude internal control steps such as checks and authorizations, which are things done to ensure that the underlying information processing is done correctly. It is not usually necessary to identify every data movement that happens within a single database used by a single computer application, though this can sometimes be helpful. Be sure to list all the data capture steps including things like bad debt provision entry, and obscure reference data edits.

- *Carve up the underlying processing into steps*. Typically there will be data capture steps, data transfer steps, and calculation (including summary) steps. It is not necessary to list the steps in any particular order but it is clearer to work in the order of processing transactions, with reference data done last or interleaved with transaction processing steps. There are choices in selecting the steps but aim to minimize the number of steps while maximizing the precision of the mapping.

- *Apply a standard set of 'control objectives' to every step*. The traditional control objectives are Completeness, Accuracy, and Validity, to which Uniqueness should be added. (See below for an explanation.) The effect of this is to divide up all possible errors at each step into a small number of standard categories.

Control objectives are just the flip side of risks. If the risk is 'incomplete posting of sales to the sales ledger', then the objective is 'complete posting of sales to the sales ledger.' The traditional trio of Completeness, Accuracy, and Validity is based on the idea that accounting processes mainly involve copying information from one place to another, item by item (e.g. sale by sale). 'Complete' means that all items that should have been copied across have been. 'Accurate' means that all items copied across kept their value or any calculation is correct. 'Valid' means no items are inserted without having been copied from the previous stage i.e. nothing has been made up. There is one further error that could occur, which is for an item to be copied across more than once. Traditionally, this is included under either Completeness or Validity, but neither approach is satisfactory as many controls confirm Completeness or Validity without helping on duplication. It is best to introduce a fourth control objective, 'Uniqueness'.

These control objectives are always with respect to the previous stage of processing, rather than to original truth. For example, controls often ensure that some data have been copied *completely* from one database to another, but not that the data are a complete record of the business activities they represent. So, Complete, Accurate, Valid, and Unique always mean compared with the data at the previous step.

Some data flows are 'structured' in the sense that they are made of units, each of which is itself composed of smaller units. For example, the data flow may be made of a series of files, each of which is composed of a number of records, each of which is made up of a number of fields of data.

If some of the controls apply to one or more levels but not all it is possible to show this distinction on the control matrix by using multiple steps (i.e. columns) for the data flow, one for each level of the structure you want to analyse separately.

Debt management is often included as an extra control objective. Strictly this is not directly an issue for financial reporting, provided bad debt provisions are accurate. However, it is comforting to know that doubtful debts are not taken on as this reduces the risk of provisions turning out to be incorrect.

Three other control objectives that might be used are confidentiality, auditability, and non-repudiation. (Non-repudiation relates to electronic records of contracts. Suppose a customer places an order but later claims not to have done. If you provide an ordinary computer record of the order the customer could say you made it up. However, modern cryptographic techniques allow you to retain a record of an order received electronically from a customer in such a way that you could not have made it up, and so the customer cannot 'repudiate' the order.)

A control should be shown as applying to a step if it increases the probability that any of the control objectives will be met for that step. The set of steps a control applies to can be called the 'span' of the control. Here are some examples to show the principle:

- A hash total is used to check that a file of data has been copied without alteration from one computer to another. (Let's assume the interface is one step in the process breakdown.) The control should be shown as applying to that interface step only.
- A reconciliation is performed between data at one point in the processing and another point, three steps later. The control should be shown as applying to all three steps.
- A control is used to ensure that software programs within an application are not changed by accident. This slightly reduces the risk of error and fraud of various types for all steps performed using that application.
- A computer checks data to see that they match a business rule, such as that customer ages should be between 0 and 150 years old. Some mistyped dates of birth will be caught by this check. The assurance applies to all steps prior to this point, because an error at any of these steps could be caught by the check (unless of course exactly the same check is also performed earlier on).

If the risk framework uses a small set of standardized control objectives as discussed above it is possible to produce a rigorous but extraordinarily compact mapping of risks to controls using a matrix.

The control objectives addressed by an internal control are a property of the control, and do not change depending on where it is applied. Therefore, it is enough to provide a column for each step in the processing cycle and show in the matrix which steps each control provides assurance over. To capture the analysis at the more detailed level of control objectives, use the spreadsheet to record the control objectives addressed by each control and then summarize the overall assurance on each step for each control objective.

Table 6.6 shows the basic format. The spreadsheet formulae are simple, using nothing more sophisticated than the sumif( ) function in the summary cells. The elements added to a basic risk control matrix have grey borders.

Table 6.6   Matrix mapping with standard control objectives

	C	A	V	U	Step A	Step B	Step C	Step D	etc.
Control 1	1	1				1	1		
Control 2	1	1	1				1		1
Control 3				1	1				1
Control 4		1	1				1	1	1
etc									
Summary									
Completeness					0	1	2	0	1
Accuracy					0	1	3	1	2
Validity					0	0	2	1	2
Uniqueness					1	0	0	0	1

In practice it is better to put the summary cells at the top of the page so they can be frozen on-screen as you scroll around the matrix. This way you can always see the summarized position as you work.

It is also helpful to set up rows to show the perceived risk of each type of error for each step; think of it as a target for the total coverage score. In the example above the assurance provided by each control for each control objective is shown as all or nothing i.e. 1 or 0. However, controls vary greatly in their effectiveness and this can be shown by using factors other than one.

In theory at least the difference between the coverage target and the coverage achieved can be calculated by the spreadsheet and on some spreadsheet programs it is possible to colour code the differences automatically using conditional formatting to show where weaknesses lie.

Table 6.7 shows these techniques.

In this example there are obviously some problems with the coverage. There are many gaps but also some over-controlled steps where it may be possible to cut out some work and complexity from the controls.

These numbers are all subjective judgements, but this is still better than unquantified judgement. In some cases it may be possible to support judgements with data and calculations based on data, but this is unlikely to be worthwhile except with the most costly processes.

One challenge with the fully quantified variant is to calibrate the targets correctly. You can get a feel for targets by scoring actual controls on a process that is thought to be well controlled and where performance has been good (i.e. errors

Table 6.7   Matrix mapping calculations

Targets					Step A	Step B	Step C	Step D	etc.
Completeness					0.5	1.0	0.2	0.6	1.0
Accuracy					1.0	0.5	0.2	2.0	1.0
Validity					1.0	1.0	0.2	0.2	1.0
Uniqueness					0.5	1.0	1.0	2.0	1.5
Differences					Step A	Step B	Step C	Step D	etc.
Completeness					-0.5	-0.5	0.5	-0.6	-0.8
Accuracy					-1.0	0.5	2.8	-1.0	1.0
Validity					-1.0	-1.0	0.6	-0.1	-0.2
Uniqueness					0.0	-1.0	-1.0	-2.0	-1.0
	C	A	V	U	Step A	Step B	Step C	Step D	etc.
Control 1	0.5	1.0				1	1		
Control 2	0.2	1.0	0.7				1		1
Control 3				0.5	1				1
Control 4		1.0	0.1				1	1	1
etc.									

known and tolerably low). These scores provide a guide for setting targets on other processes.

This kind of sophistication is helpful if you can do it but not essential. Even without targets and coverage factors the spreadsheet analysis is still far more precise than it would be with the conventional approach.

Another enhancement to the basic spreadsheet is to add another worksheet to show a coloured version of the original matrix, for each control objective individually. This can be done using a sheet for each control objective or a single sheet with a cell into which you type the one letter abbreviation of the objective whose analysis is to be displayed.

In summary, this is a systematic way to produce an analysis of risk around a process and in conjunction with MATRIX MAPPING OF RISKS AND CONTROLS can produce extremely compact documentation that is easy to analyse. Therefore:

Map out the information processing in physical terms and generate a list of steps with risks, each step being a data flow, store, or process in the model.

There are no subsidiary control patterns to this one in this book.

13   Causal models

Example: Suppose a local authority is making plans to deal with municipal solid waste over the coming decades and needs to look at all its options. They develop a model of the waste creation and disposal showing the causal links they believe are relevant to them. The model is drawn using boxes and arrows and is partly quantified. They use it to understand what they are still uncertain of and how important it is, and also to explore alternative strategies. This includes actions they can take to learn more about how waste works so that they can manage it better.

CAUSAL MODELS are one of the most rigorous and informative ways to understand uncertainty and examine the impact of alternative controls. They support CAUSE-EFFECT INTERVENTION and should often be the ultimate form reached through EVOLVING UNCERTAINTY LISTS.

Uncertainties are not separate from each other or from other thinking.

Suppose a business strategist is thinking deep, strategic thoughts about products, markets, and returns. Future growth in potential markets is almost certain to be one of the important factors to consider. It will be listed in documents, perhaps shown as a bubble on a 'strategy map' or other drawing of the planning problem. If the strategist is using a numerical model there will be a spreadsheet with cells for market growth rates and formulae to combine those rates with other information and provide projections of business results.

But, of course, those market growth rates are uncertain. They are uncertainties that matter, which makes them the same as risks in most interpretations. In non-mathematically-based approaches to risk management risks like this would be described as something like 'Risk of insufficient market growth' but the idea on which this is based is simply the uncertainty about market growth. Similarly, a risk register item like 'Risk of competition' comes from uncertainty about the 'Intensity of competition' and 'Risk of being hit by a meteor' is from the uncertain variable 'Meteor impacts'.

In this way 'risks' are necessarily linked to our mental models of how things work and what would happen if we took alternative actions. Risks are the uncertainties around those models.

Not surprisingly 'risks' are also connected to each other via the mental models. You can experiment with existing risk registers to understand how this works.

The items on a typical risk register are linked to one or more consequences that may or may not have found their way onto the register. Often many register items have at least one link to another item on the register. Some are within loops and some of those loops are vicious/virtuous circles.

Situations where the risk register items are largely separate from each other are rare. Connections are much more common.

For example, a typical group risk register I examined recently gave the usual high-level survey of risks across the business. (A project risk register would have seemed more closely linked even without diagramming.)

The original register contained 31 rows. From the text I identified a total of 41 nodes (i.e. variables in a mental model of the business and its environment) and designated 30 of these as being the direct counterpart of a risk register item.

The remaining 11 nodes were causes or effects also referred to in the risk register item text. I added all the causal links between nodes directly implied by the text or obvious from general knowledge.

Using this procedure I identified 107 links, of which 100 involved at least 1 risk register item and 51 had a risk register item at both ends. All the risk register items were linked into the network. The picture of the network shows the nodes to be massively linked to each other.

Of the 30 risk register items on the causal network, 22 had a direct causal impact on one or more other risk register items and 17 were directly caused by another risk register item (at least in part). Also, 17 of the risk register items had other risk register items as both causes and effects.

Fourteen of the 30 risk register items were part of at least one loop, while 21 of all 41 nodes were involved in at least one loop.

In summary, the risk register items were highly interlinked, with around half involved in causal links with other risk register items, most of these being part of loops. There were about three times as many links as risk register items.

Experiments like this suggest that directly estimating impact on results of interest is very difficult because:

- links between variables are common;
- the properties of these links are often highly uncertain – we don't know how strong they are or what time delays may be involved;
- many things that might happen are linked to impacts we care about by one or more steps of causality whose strength is uncertain; and
- many links create loops that either amplify or reduce the impact of some unexpected event, making impact estimation particularly difficult.

This implies that we should try to model these links and carefully assess our uncertainties. This is not always simple to do and it is easy to end up with a lot of boxes and arrows on a diagram and no time to do anything with them.

Therefore it is important do work iteratively, starting with the variables we regard as the results we value and want to influence, and working back little by little to the variables that influence them and that we might be able to control.

The reward for this effort is a much more complete and controllable view of risk with scope for moving towards greater detail and quantification over time. Alternative controls can be added to the model to consider their potential impact.[1]

If there are important connections between uncertainties – and there usually are – then it is easier to put them on a picture than to list 'risks' and pretend the connections and the underlying mental models do not exist.

In summary, models explicitly showing causal links define one possible analysis of risk and provide outstanding insight into risky situations. The apparent complexity compared to risk registers just reflects the fact that the links are made explicit and can be controlled by working iteratively. Therefore:

Capture knowledge about how things work in a causal map (diagram). Add knowledge about areas of uncertainty derived from the map: current values of variables, future values of variables, properties of links, the structure of the model itself, and which variables to put value on and how. Develop actions from these and other sources and consider including them within the model. Do all this iteratively based on insights from each version of the model.

CAUSAL MODELS do not create the controls so need to be combined with CAUSE-EFFECT INTERVENTIONS, GENERIC CONTROL DESIGN LIBRARIES, or CONTROL PATTERNS. They can also support RISK REGISTERS. When CAUSAL MODELS can be quantified it is possible to use MONTE CARLO SIMULATION to understand the combined impact of uncertainties. A specific style of CAUSAL MODEL useful in some situations is FAULT AND EVENT TREE ANALYSIS.

14   Monte Carlo simulation

Example: A building firm that makes many bids for contracts might start Monte Carlo simulation by taking existing spreadsheets used for bids. Views about uncertain inputs would be captured using software and then their combined implications for important summary variables like the overall job cost, overall profit, and overall chance of winning the work would be calculated at the click of a button. Over time these estimates could improve as past actual results are used to improve judgements.

MONTE CARLO SIMULATION is a way to increase the power of CAUSAL MODELS and FAULT TREE ANALYSIS AND EVENT TREE ANALYSIS by calculating the combined impact of multiple uncertainties.

Uncertainties combine in complicated ways, but calculating the combined impact is surprisingly simple and useful.

If MONTE CARLO SIMULATION sounds complicated, too hard, or too mathematical for you, don't stop reading. This is a technique where the hard stuff is done by a computer program. It takes pictures of your uncertainties about individual things and converts them into pictures showing what they imply for your uncertainties about overall results. They can also tell you how important each individual uncertainty is to the overall uncertainty. You can benefit from this even if you only have gut feeling to go on, though as with any technique more data will give better results. Many people start with existing spreadsheets and just add extra information about the uncertain inputs.

MONTE CARLO SIMULATION is well worth considering whenever the things you are interested in can be described with numbers, even if you don't know what the numbers should be. This includes models of money, time, quantities of goods, kilometres travelled, quality of products, and so on. It is easiest if you already have a spreadsheet model to start with.

Once you have the basic model with no uncertainty shown the next stage is to add information about how uncertain you are about input variables. Uncertainty can come in lots of shapes and the good tools show you lots of options then let you set up the ranges and details you want to enter.

For example, suppose the cost of a job is just the sum of five different, independent input costs, two of which are uncertain. The model is trivial: just add up the input costs. It might be that with one of the uncertain ones you think the highest it could be is 100 and the lowest is 50, but the most likely is about 85. There are various ways to set this up so that costs of around 85 are more likely than costs of 50 or 100, and costs are not outside this range. Do a similar input for the other uncertain variable and you are ready to simulate.

Most Monte Carlo simulation tools work in a similar way. To run the simulation you have to tell it which output variables you are interested in and say how many simulation iterations you want it to do. How many to do is a matter of how accurate you want to be. I usually start with a small number of simulations – say around 1,000 – and then increase it if needed.

A moment later the tool will tell you it has finished and start showing the results. These usually include graphs and summary statistics for the variables you asked about and 'tornado diagrams' showing the uncertain inputs in descending order of their importance for the overall uncertainty, with bar graphs for the amount of uncertainty from each one. (Tornado diagrams can be calculated in different ways.)

These outputs are useful in the following ways:

- The main variables of interest (e.g. total profit) are given as a graph showing the relative chances of different results rather than just as a single best guess, which is what ordinary spreadsheets produce. This helps to convey uncertainty about the estimate and keep minds open.
- The Tornado diagram shows the importance of uncertainty around each of the inputs allowing you to focus efforts to gather better information, improve/ extend the model, and think of controls.

Monte Carlo simulation also makes numerical modelling overall more attractive. One reason that numerical models are not used more often than they are is that people know a lot of guesswork went into them and therefore do not trust the outputs. Monte Carlo simulation is a way to be open about how much uncertainty went into the model and how much came out.

In business, spreadsheets with Monte Carlo simulation are probably the most common example of mathematically inspired risk-thinking. The uncertainties of each variable in the spreadsheet are the 'risks' and the tornado diagram shows the relative importance of each risk for the overall results of interest (e.g. overall profit).

The most common software tools for Monte Carlo simulation are spreadsheet 'add-ins' that integrate with Microsoft's Excel, giving it extra features. However, this kind of simulation is built into many other tools too.

Monte Carlo simulation works by doing thousands of 'what if?' calculations and recording the results of each one. Each calculation is done by giving values to all the uncertain inputs at random, but according to the uncertainty distributions set. The resulting output values are calculated using the spreadsheet model. These results are stored and then it's time to move on to the next 'what if'.

This simple technique means that Monte Carlo simulation can be used with an amazing variety of models regardless of how complicated their logic and non-linear their relationships. Although it is very easy to get started there is scope for taking things to a high level of sophistication.

The main limitation is that if you are particularly interested in very unlikely combinations of events then, just as in real life, these don't happen often in the simulations so results for these extremes can be unreliable.

Lack of data is not a reason for ignoring simulation. Monte Carlo simulation can be applied to objectively verified frequency data (one interpretation of 'probability') but usually it is for combining subjective uncertainties.

If you are interested in understanding the difference then consider this example. Imagine you are forced to bet on the outcome of the toss of a coin that is clearly bent. If, by some miracle, you could take time out to toss the coin a million times and record the proportion of heads then you would have a good idea of the relative frequency of heads. Unfortunately, you don't have that luxury and so are uncertain about what the relative frequency of heads would be. Uncertainty about relative frequencies is almost always present in real life (unlike school mathematics) but doesn't stop us from betting and doesn't stop experts from betting better than non-experts.

You can express your views about heads versus tails either directly by saying, for example, that you are '60 per cent certain of heads' or indirectly by having a view about the relative likelihood of the coin having different long run frequencies of heads and then combining those two together to reach a number for certainty of heads.

Situations where all relative frequencies are known with such accuracy that the uncertainty can be ignored are very rare in real life so, generally, we must think of probabilities as being expressions of certainty.

In summary, MONTE CARLO SIMULATION is a simple yet powerful way to compute and visualize the combined effect of multiple uncertainties and usually easier but better than sensitivity analysis. Therefore:

Once you have a largely quantified model of some kind do Monte Carlo simulation.

There are no subsidiary control patterns to this one in this book.

15   Fault and event tree analysis

Example: Engineers designing the control systems of a new type of aeroplane
are usually concerned with whether the control system is operating
normally or is broken, and with whether its components are operating
normally or broken. It makes sense to think in terms of just broken or
not broken and go through the various ways that failure could arise.

FAULT AND EVENT TREE ANALYSES are simplified versions of CAUSAL MODELS that are
applicable only when performance can be thought of simply in terms of success
and failure with no significant loss of information.

Sometimes it is enough to think in terms of success and failure.

Sometimes risk analyses can be done entirely in terms of the binary outcomes:
success and failure. This is common in analysing the reliability or safety of machines,
for example. The simple, success/failure nature of events makes very elaborate
modelling and sophisticated computer analysis possible. Leading examples of this
are Fault Tree Analysis and Event Tree Analysis.

Fault Tree Analyses (FTA) look like logic circuit diagrams in a hierarchical tree
shape. FTA works top down from a defined failure event, such as an explosion
in an engine, fire in a building, or injury at the doors of a lift. The analyst has to
think what could cause the top event and in what way. Potential causes are placed
lower on the diagram and linked to the top event using a 'gate', which is a piece of
logic about how the events combine. (The terminology comes from the design of
electronic logic circuits.)

For example, the top-level event 'gas explosion' could be the result of 'gas leak'
AND 'naked flame'. The gate would be an AND gate. The causal events can themselves
have causes and so on. A big model may have thousands of events and gates in it.

Computer tools can analyse the model once it is created to find out how much
influence on eventual reliability each event has, if there are any events that, on
their own, can lead to overall failure, and which sets of events happening together
could cause the failure.

Probabilities can be added to the basic events (i.e. the ones not caused by
anything shown on the diagram) and the probability of other failures worked out.

Event Tree Analysis (ETA) looks more like a decision tree. ETA starts with a
single defined event, such as an explosion in an engine, fire in a building, etc.
The analyst then has to think about what could happen as a result, including how
safety systems like alarms might affect the impact. The possible combinations of
circumstances branch out from the starting event on the left hand side. Again, by
applying probabilities the likelihood of various different impacts can be estimated.

Many situations in organizations do *not* fit this kind of model. For example,
revenues are not intrinsically a success or a failure. The revenues are somewhere on
a scale. Although it is possible to see the actual revenues achieved as a success or a

failure by comparison with a target this is ignoring a lot of information and creates difficulties. Suppose total revenues depend on Product A revenues and Product B revenues. Then each of these needs a success/failure target. This is not uncommon – budgets do this all the time – but there is a problem. Any combination of revenues from Product A and Product B that adds up to the overall target is a success, but this is not captured in the target levels for Product A and Product B.

So, what simplifies analysis of reliability in machinery turns out to be a mess when applied to unsuitable systems such as business performance.

In summary, Fault Tree and Event Tree analysis are powerful tools for understanding success and failure in suitable systems and very powerful software tools are available to build such models. Therefore:

If performance can be modelled in simple success/failure terms then build a cause-effect model on that basis to take advantage of the analysis available.

There are no subsidiary control patterns to this one in this book.

16   Story-telling about the future

Example: Imagine you are due to speak at a conference and plan for it using scenario planning. You decide that the top two uncertainties for your speech are the size of the audience and the quality of the sound system and projector. Then you take the highest and lowest credible values for each uncertainty and generate the four permutations for the speech, with inspirational names:

- Audience = hundreds, AV = clear and big: 'Professional'.
- Audience = hundreds, AV = not working: 'Out of earshot'.
- Audience = 3, AV = clear and big: 'Booming'.
- Audience = 3, AV = not working: 'Cosy chat'.

These need to be thought about to eliminate mutually incompatible combinations, and then to generate stories about how these scenarios might come to pass. For 'Out of earshot' the story will probably involve a series of last minute calamities, or perhaps abysmal organization at the venue.

This is particularly useful for opening minds to more future possibilities when planning, for example in conjunction with EVOLVING UNCERTAINTY LISTS.

*Thinking through how things **could** happen makes it seem more likely that they **will** happen.*

One way to combat the tendency to see the future too narrowly is to take outcomes that seem very unlikely, or even impossible, and try to work out stories that tell how they might come about. This is sometimes used routinely in procedures for eliciting subjective probabilities from experts. The facilitator might say, 'I know that it seems very unlikely that X will happen, but let's just assume for a moment that it has happened. What could be the explanation?' Once we've thought of a way for something to happen we tend to see it as more likely.

This is also a useful way to get people thinking about how events might unfold over time.

The disadvantage is that it doesn't necessarily mean that perceptions of probability are any more accurate. We've just countered a bias with another bias.

A well-known management technique which uses this principle is scenario planning. If the scenarios cover all possible outcomes then this extra analysis can help clarify the likelihood of each scenario. However, if the scenarios do not cover all possible outcomes the apparent likelihood of different outcomes is distorted by the story-telling. Yet scenario planning is still a great way to open minds to possibilities that otherwise would have been missed, and to prepare those minds to react more quickly to events as they unfold.

A typical approach is to establish a scope and then spend time analysing the way the business and its environment work, and what is going on. This leads to a clearer model. Next, the analysis tries to separate what is certain about the future ('trends') from what is not ('uncertainties').

The two most important uncertainties are then chosen and used to generate four scenarios.

After that the problem is to generate strategies that work well across a wide range of scenarios, and more specialized options that are, nevertheless, worthwhile. A number of methods are possible.

The main benefits of this kind of work are thought to be in expanding management's view of the future, leading to plans that deal with uncertainty better, and preparing them to recognize and respond to scenarios, or parts of them, if they actually occur. Consequently, the benefit is mainly with the individuals who participate in the story-telling.

Most examples of scenario planning show it being used to look far into the future at big questions, like the future of whole industries and even the human race itself. However, it is just as applicable to the everyday planning problems we face. Perhaps more so.

One of the method's big contributions is in preparing our minds to recognize and react quickly to future events as they unfold. Isn't it ironic that so many applications of the technique concentrate on events that will play out over years or even decades. Surely we'll have plenty of time to think! By contrast, everyday challenges that are over in a few minutes, hours, or days, give us very little time to think so mental preparation is more important.

In summary, STORY-TELLING ABOUT THE FUTURE has a powerful and helpful psychological effect, opening minds to future possibilities. Therefore:

Incorporate story-telling about possible futures into planning activities large and small. Consider the main drivers, imagine extremes, then consider the permutations and plan accordingly.

There are no subsidiary control patterns to this one in this book.

17 Generic control design library

Example: A company that wants to get better at managing risk on projects might start with a generic scheme of controls for projects of all types that is used with a guide to how to flex it to fit specific projects. After a year or so the generic scheme will have been used in a variety of projects and some of the more successful ones will provide the basis for developing generic schemes for more specific types of project. For example, alongside the general scheme they might be able to add a scheme for construction projects, another for IT infrastructure projects, another for marketing projects, and another for business change projects. All of these have a guide to flexing as well, but the more specific ones need less flexing and are more helpful.

A GENERIC CONTROL DESIGN LIBRARY helps people to think of controls and is useful with TOP-DOWN DESIGN WITH SCHEMES, FACTOR-DRIVEN DESIGN, RISK REGISTERS, EVOLVING UNCERTAINTY LISTS, and CAUSAL MODELS. They are an alternative to CONTROL PATTERNS.

It is helpful to have ready-made ideas for controls but they have to be adapted and good ideas aren't always available immediately.

This control pattern combines three ideas. The first idea is to create generic control schemes (i.e. designs, but not necessarily fully detailed) and make them available as a source of ideas or as a default design.

The second idea is to combine this with a guide to how to tailor and detail the generic scheme to fit specific circumstances. This covers what to consider and some guidelines on how to respond to different situations.

The third idea is to build, incrementally, a library of such schemes (with their tailoring guides) by making use of experience with earlier schemes. The initial schemes can be few in number (even just one) but rely heavily on sensible tailoring. Once this scheme has been used on a few occasions the designs they created can be turned into more specific schemes to suit more specific situations. When these new schemes are used there is less need for tailoring.

The initial schemes can also be improved in light of experience.

In summary, a GENERIC CONTROL DESIGN LIBRARY can be developed incrementally and helps people think of good controls. Schemes can strongly anchor design work to good designs. Therefore:

Start with generic but complete schemes and adopt more specific variants when a good starting point is generated through actual use. Always provide some guidance on tailoring.

A GENERIC CONTROL DESIGN LIBRARY can be organized using frameworks such as a PROCESS CONTROL FRAMEWORK or a PROJECT CONTROL FRAMEWORK.

18 Control patterns

Example: Suppose a small company wants to increase its ability to design efficient, effective controls and so gathers a collection of good control ideas and organizes them into the form of a pattern language i.e. a collection of linked problems and their solutions, structured into layers or groups.

CONTROL PATTERNS are a powerful way of organizing design knowledge and are helpful when used with FACTOR-DRIVEN DESIGN and TOP-DOWN DESIGN WITH SCHEMES.

Expert controls design requires a large body of knowledge about good solutions to common requirements/problems.

Expert designers rely on a lot of knowledge. Exactly what this knowledge is and how it is represented is not clear and probably varies between designers. However, psychologists and design theorists have established that there are at least two important components of this knowledge.

First, there is a small but crucial component about design processes – what questions to ask, how to make inferences about solutions, how to use existing knowledge, etc.

Second, there is a vast and equally crucial component that is something like a database of good solutions to common problems. It is quite possible that great designers are great precisely because they are keen and able to build this kind of storehouse of ready-made answers.

Although the exact structure of this 'solutions database' is not known an inspiring example of what it might or perhaps should be like has emerged in architecture from Christopher Alexander and colleagues. The idea is called a 'pattern language'. The control ideas in this book have been presented as patterns.

In summary, CONTROL PATTERNS if well done can provide a natural input to controls design that increases the design abilities of people who use them. Therefore:

> *Build a pattern language of control solutions and make it available to anyone who might need to design controls.*

CONTROL PATTERNS can be organized using frameworks such as a PROCESS CONTROL FRAMEWORK or a PROJECT CONTROL FRAMEWORK.

19   Process control framework

> *Example*: A controls team in a medium-sized charity wishing to think of better controls for processes more quickly might adopt a framework of control mechanisms with sufficient detail to be a practical memory jogger. This would have layers made with different mechanisms, represented by headings and subheadings, and perhaps some logic linking the layers.

A PROCESS CONTROL FRAMEWORK is useful as the backbone of a GENERIC CONTROL DESIGN LIBRARY or in CONTROL PATTERNS where it helps people think of good controls in an organized way.

> *Controls need to cover risks, but that doesn't mean that thinking of risks first is the easiest way.*

Many years ago I was a trainee accountant studying to pass professional examinations. The audit paper had questions that asked for suitable internal controls to cover a given accounting process. The advice on how to think of controls was to run through the control objectives one by one (completeness, accuracy, validity) and try to think of at least one control to hit each objective.

This didn't work well for me but I soon discovered that if I ignored the control objectives and instead ran through a mental list of types of control mechanism I could generate more control ideas more quickly, and cover the objectives as well or better than using the tutor's method. I put the control mechanism types into a logical order with groups and subgroups so it was easy to remember. My list of control objectives grew to have a dozen or so headings on it and helped me give more layers of control and produce them in a logical order, usually starting with management monitoring and working down.

Later, when I started working on real projects designing real controls I found that this approach still worked a lot better than trying to use control objectives as memory prompts. I have also learned through experiments in seminars I have presented that other people usually prefer mechanism prompts too.

Risk coverage is ensured by:

1. generating a well-formed, multi-layered control system quickly using combinations of controls that typically provide good coverage; and
2. having immediate feedback on coverage from a risk control mapping tool.

The ideal control framework groups all possible controls into a set of layers, or lines of defence, on the basis of the nature of the control. By finding or designing controls under each category it should be possible to produce a complete system covering all relevant levels of management control. If it is difficult to design effective controls at one level it should be easy to see the other levels at which compensating strength can be designed.

As an example, here's the multi-layer model I like and recommend for controlling financial cycles, starting at the top:

- **Management monitoring**
  - Process monitoring
    - Monitor *past effectiveness of the controls* and take corrective action, for example by tracking error rates, transactions via exception streams, and lost revenue then changing the process to make it inherently more reliable, or adding checks.
    - Monitor *future events* and adapt the process and its controls in good time, for example through capacity planning, looking ahead for high risk changes and spreading them out, and checking for forthcoming contract changes that will be difficult and time consuming to implement.
    - Monitor the controls to ensure they *are operating*, for example through audit work, reviewing reports of control performance, and control self-assessment. Where reliance is placed on exception reporting no news is good news – or the controls have stopped operating. This is particularly important for controls that aim to cover risks that rarely occur.
  - Business monitoring
    - Report *trading performance* through information derived through the process itself. In a business unit there may be many business processes, each with monitoring as above, each providing information about trading performance. This is relevant to ensuring financial information is correct because scrutiny of trading performance can identify unexpected numbers that may then be incorrect.

- **Control activities**
  - *Protect* the process from interference, using physical and software security measures.
  - Make the process *recoverable*, for example through data backups, disaster recovery planning, and building resilience and recoverability into every interface.

— Make the process *inherently reliable*, for example, by assuring software quality, testing the usability of software which interacts with humans, and using reliable hardware.

— Put *checks on data and processing* in place, with associated corrective action, to detect process errors, interference with the process such as fraud, and attempts to pass fraud through the process.

— Put *audit trails* in place, so that auditors can gain assurance of correct functioning, and so that errors can be investigated and corrected easily.

Of course other control frameworks can be used, but whatever framework you use it is a good idea to use headings and subheadings at least to organize the list of controls in the control matrix.

Controls can be given a code so that if they get out of order they can be sorted back into the original order of the control framework.

This is particularly useful if you build a database of controls and control types. By selecting the controls that apply to a particular process you can sort them up into the control matrix area. For example, if you go for the WebTrust[2] seal of approval there is quite detailed guidance about the controls expected so these can be used as a starting point in any analysis under WebTrust.

Table 6.8 is an example illustrating control framework headings and sort codes within MATRIX MAPPING OF RISKS AND CONTROLS. Note that only some of the controls are shown, in order to keep the example short, and the new elements are outlined in grey.

Another refinement of matrix mapping is to add a summary worksheet that computes the coverage achieved from each type of control within the control framework. This could be useful if you have a high-level design for the controls that specifies certain levels of control from each type of control.

In summary, a framework for process controls helps organize thinking about process controls and generates ideas. Therefore:

> *Think of controls by using types of control mechanism as a memory prompt. Have a suitable framework or other source to work from.*

There are no subsidiary control patterns to this one in this book.

20   Project control framework

Example: An IT consultancy that carries out projects for its customers might decide to accelerate risk management on projects by creating and using a framework of project control mechanisms. The framework puts mechanisms into layers and links them. This would help people think of cohesive controls fluently.

Table 6.8   Control layers with a risk control matrix

	Sort	C	A	V	U	Step A	Step B	Step C	Step D	etc.
MONITORING	A									
BUSINESS MONITORING	AA									
Weekly margin analysis and meeting	AA1	1	1	1	1	1	1	1	1	1
PROCESS MONITORING	AB									
Downtime analysis and meeting	AB1	1	1	1	1		1	1		
Quality review statistics	AB2		1			1				
End-to-end reconciliation summary	AB3	1		1	1	1	1	1	1	1
CONTROL ACTIVITIES	C									
PROTECTION	CA									
Building security guards and alarms	CA1	1	1	1	1	1	1	1	1	1
Computer room security	CA2	1	1	1	1		1	1		
Operating system-level passwords	CA3	1	1	1	1		1	1		
RECOVERY CONTROLS	CB									
Nightly backups of main servers	CB1	1		1	1		1	1		
etc.										

A PROJECT CONTROL FRAMEWORK is useful as the backbone of a GENERIC CONTROL DESIGN LIBRARY or in CONTROL PATTERNS where it helps people think of good controls in an organized way.

Managing risk on projects can be harder than for processes because there is less time to think but there are more individual controls to think of.

The justification for using a PROJECT CONTROL FRAMEWORK is almost the same as the justification for using a PROCESS CONTROL FRAMEWORK. It is easier to think of controls if you have a memory prompt list based on control mechanisms.

The situation with projects is perhaps more challenging because so many unique controls have to be designed and so quickly.

Many different schemes could be a good basis but here's one I like that is broad and meets most of the criteria set out above. Responses are divided into six types and these form a system. Within each type there are various alternative techniques and another way you can tailor the scheme is by deciding where to place your emphasis, building up from no focus through broad decisions about emphasis, then adding more specific points of interest. To begin with, Figure 6.4 is a picture of the six elements of the system.

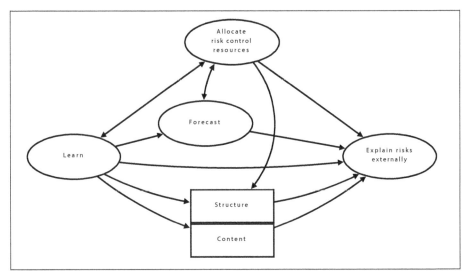

Figure 6.4   Elements of a project controls structure

At the top, directing resources and attention is 'allocate risk control resources.' It takes information from learning and other activities and decides where to put the risk control effort. That risk control effort goes into learning, into structuring the plans to control risks, into changing the content of plans to control risk, and into forecasting risk and communicating it externally to stakeholders. Obviously this is to be a continuous, or at least frequent, activity that should start as soon as possible.

There is no need to wait to start thinking about how to allocate risk control resources. Don't wait for an agreed scope or any of that paperwork. As soon as you have some scraps of rumours about the project that is enough to begin making deductions about how to cope.

Within each of the six activities emphasis can be placed in various ways. By default, your approach will be fairly general with few if any specific points of focus. However, more analysis will allow tighter focus of resources on more specific areas or even particular outcomes, layered on top of a safety net of general risk control procedures. Dimensions along which you might choose to focus resources include:

- *Phase of the project.* (For projects done using evolutionary deliveries this means concentrating on particular deliveries or groups of deliveries.)
- *Internal versus external to the project.* Some projects have to be done in a very hostile or opportunity rich external environment, while the success of others

is more dependent on competence, organization, and honesty in the project team. These demand an external and internal focus respectively.

*   *Upside versus downside.* In the past risk management has nearly always concentrated on downside risks i.e. things that could go wrong. This is changing as it is gradually recognized that a more balanced approach within one management system is more effective and efficient.
*   *Responses versus meta-responses.* A risk response might be to do some market research. A meta-response might be to get better at doing market research.
*   *Stakeholders.* Different stakeholders may have different needs for risk information.

Typical specific responses and techniques in each of the six groups are as follows:

*   **Allocate risk control resources**
    *   Factor-driven design
    *   Risk structuring through to response planning
        *   Analysis by examining each project step
        *   Analysis by stakeholder/value driver/objective
        *   Causal modelling, fault tree analysis/dependency analysis
        *   Analysis of risk factors
    *   Educating project team to be open about risk and uncertainty and manage it explicitly

*   **Learn**
    *   Acquiring expertise
        *   Training
        *   Recruitment
    *   Tracking of generic risk factor trends
    *   Ongoing monitoring of specific areas of uncertainty
        *   External horizon scanning, including
            *   Repeated discussions with stakeholders
            *   Monitoring other sources of news about the circumstances of stakeholders ...
            *   ... and other factors that affect the project
        *   Internal horizon scanning, including looking for signs of weakness and growing issues
    *   Clarifying requirements and objectives
    *   Research
    *   Prototyping

*   **Structure plans using inherently risk-smart patterns**
    *   Incremental delivery
        *   Evolutionary delivery i.e. ideally around 50 deliveries of real benefits to at least some stakeholders, with rethinking at each delivery. Massive risk reduction effect even with fewer such deliveries

- o Portfolio of activities i.e. in parallel and success of each is largely independent of the others, though it may be correlated. Similar to evolutionary, but in parallel. In general it helps to *reduce dependencies*
- — Redundancy – multiple chances to achieve something
- — Real options i.e. giving yourself more choices in future by keeping options open and creating new options. Could be as simple as having some contingency in the schedule or cost estimate
- — Critical chain buffering
  - o Put all 'padding' into an overall project buffer
  - o Put feed buffers in front of activities on the critical chain
- — Do project steps early that will give information that reduces uncertainty

- • **Content changes to manage risk**
  - — *Routing*
    - o Away from downside risks
      - ▪ Just don't do the thing with too much downside risk
      - ▪ Also do something else e.g. choose less innovative technology
    - o Towards upside risks
      - ▪ Just don't do the thing with not enough upside risk
      - ▪ Also do something else e.g. make more experiments
  - — *Modify causes*
    - o Reduce/enhance causes
      - ▪ Reduce or increase the level of a driver somewhere in the causal chain leading up to the outcome you are concerned with
      - ▪ Break or strengthen a link in the causal chain
    - o Add new causes
  - — *Modify impacts*
    - o Reduce/enhance impacts
      - ▪ Pick up impacts very quickly and limit their effect e.g. inspection of documents through all project stages as in Gilb's Defect Detection Process
      - ▪ Make a contingency plan, i.e. just think about what you would do
      - ▪ Have resources for the contingency, or otherwise create an option in advance
        - ~ Specific to identified risks
        - ~ Generally for unidentified risks
      - ▪ Exchange risk with contractors or joint venture partners or employees
        - ~ Contract with contractor
          - – Fixed price contract
          - – Risk-reward and risk-sharing contracts
          - – Target cost incentivization
          - – Specific risks (included or excluded)
          - – Liquidated damages
          - – Incentive/penalty payments

- ~ Contracts with joint venture partners
  - Reduce total involvement
  - Avoid downside risks
  - Retain upside risks
- ■ Add new impacts
  - ~ Insurance and similar
    - Insurance
    - Self-insurance
    - Captives (owned or rented)
    - Performance bonds, warranties, guarantees

- **Forecasting**
  - Subjective estimates by experts
  - Monte Carlo simulation – easier than it sounds
  - Model future decisions within your Monte Carlo simulation
  - Bayesian Model Averaging to deal with model uncertainty

- **Communicate risk externally**
  - Probability distribution(s) for future outcomes
  - Explanation of specific areas of residual uncertainty

A number of things in this suggested scheme need additional explanation.

The list of techniques may look long, but it is still far from complete. If possible a scheme more specifically tailored to the type of project an organization typically does should be used instead of a totally generic scheme. For example, if your organization does civil engineering projects then a scheme that lists the things often done on such projects will be more useful. Devising such schemes is part of embedding risk control.

The output of rapid risk control planning is a mixture of specific responses and decisions to do more risk management analysis. In practice it is often hard to draw a clear distinction, and not important to do so. What is important is to direct attention appropriately, and that can be done by gradually working down to more and more detail, but only where it is worthwhile.

Risks should usually be met by multiple controls, and controls should usually meet multiple risks. In other words, the control scheme should be multi-layered. For example, you may take actions to make some bad event less likely to occur, and also plan for the contingency should prevention fail.

In the suggested scheme above I have not made it clear which actions are alternatives and which should be used together. Typically you should build a multi-layered control system so the individual controls accumulate. How much depends on how much emphasis you need. However, some controls are incompatible and cannot be used together.

This breakdown uses the preventive versus contingency distinction rather than the probability versus impact distinction. (It's in the section on modifying content.) These distinctions are very similar in practice but I suggest thinking about cause and effect because it refers more directly to what you have to think to find risk responses.

A single possible event can have both positive and negative effects, even from the point of view of one person. Look for ways to make events that are unhelpful overall less likely. Look for ways to make events that are helpful overall more likely. This may not be obvious as it is the net impact *after* possible modifications of the impact that matters.

Certain activities tend to merge in practice. Learning and allocating risk control resources tend to be very close and often done in the same activity. Learning and forecasting are also very close. Communicating risk externally to stakeholders and hearing their news is often done in the same meeting.

The value of continuing with a project should be reviewed from time to time, but I have not included this under risk control activities. Some other approaches do.

In summary, a framework for project controls helps organize thinking about project controls and generates ideas. Therefore:

Create a breakdown of control mechanism types for use on projects and use it to help think of appropriate controls.

There are no subsidiary control patterns to this one in this book.

Notes

1 A good description of this appears in Stephen Ward's (2005) *Risk Management: Organization and Context* (London: Witherby's), in which he suggests putting obvious, important controls into the causal model quite early on so that their impact can be understood, including uncertainties arising from their use.
2 One of a number of assurance badges for websites. WebTrust has been developed and promoted by the American Institute of Certified Public Accountants. See www.webtrust.org.

7 *Audits, Reviews and Efficient Monitoring*

This is a second chapter of intelligent internal controls but, before the patterns begin, here is another reason for paying particular attention to intelligent controls: they are less likely to be in place already.

In the summer of 2004 I conducted a survey to find out more about the scope for adding value by recommending intelligent internal controls.

In this online Internet survey respondents were asked to consider eight hypothetical reviews of business activities and consider for each review a list of five potential recommendations for improvement. For each recommendation, respondents were asked:

- if, in their experience of organizations, the recommendation would probably already be in place;
- if the recommendation was probably a good one, assuming it wasn't already in place; and
- if they thought they were probably expected to make such recommendations. (If the respondent did not make recommendations in their job they were asked to consider if they would expect such recommendations to be made.)

This combination of questions revealed that recommendations of intelligent internal controls were as likely to be recognized as good recommendations as traditional favourites like sign-offs, documentation, segregation of duties, and reconciliations, but were much less likely to be in place already. They were also less likely to be 'expected' of the recommender.

Making these types of recommendation requires greater knowledge of risk and uncertainty but someone who has that knowledge would be able to use it often because the controls in question are rarely in place.

The survey showed no differences between the public and private sectors, except that public sector respondents thought a much wider range of recommendations was expected of them. This finding contradicts opinions expressed to me at the time by some, who speculated that the public sector was not interested in risk taking or risk management. In fact, the public sector respondents felt they were expected to make more wide-ranging and sophisticated recommendations than did the private sector respondents.

The results of this research strongly suggested that auditors, risk managers, and others who make recommendations for improving internal control and risk management can benefit from giving more attention to recommendations beyond the usual repertoire of sign-offs, documentation, segregation of duties, and reconciliations.

In summary, the reasons for focusing on intelligent controls are that:

- they are directly involved in the most important activities of the most important people in an organization;
- they are as likely to be seen as good recommendations as other, more traditional controls; and
- they are much less likely to be in place already.

The control patterns start here.

21   Controls supervision hierarchy

Example: Imagine Ann works in a small theatre taking telephone bookings and dealing with bookings by email. As part of her job Ann carries out a number of controls to make sure bookings are correct and credit card payments are processed. Each week her boss, Bob, asks her how things are going and she explains (among other things) the controls she has been able to do, what she found, and ideas she has as a result. Bob listens to what she tells him and also collects some statistics that are generated as a by-product of Ann's work and that they both look at. Each month he discusses this information (among other things) with his boss, Carmel, who adds her own observations and discusses what she thinks are the key points at a regular management meeting she attends. This process collects information about control performance and makes sure it is used and summarized. The top team know about controls performance throughout the theatre throughout the year.

A CONTROLS SUPERVISION HIERARCHY is a vital part of overall monitoring of an organization.

Supervision of control activities by a hierarchy of people is a traditional idea but usually waiting to be done well.

The idea is very simple. Each person who is involved in operating controls provides information to their boss about controls operation and performance within their area of responsibility regularly, in writing and/or conversation. Done properly this does not have to be a dreary formality, an inquisition, or an invitation to add extra layers of management.

It is best done with a combination of data and explanations.

Each person reports on the controls they personally have carried out (including supervisory conversations) and controls carried out by people beneath them in the organizational hierarchy.

This simple and traditional control can be carried out more thoroughly and with greater benefits than it usually is. It is an important means of taking the burden off costly audits and integrating control into business as usual. This is also the right thing to do for compliance with the Sarbanes-Oxley Act of 2002. Therefore:

Design control systems so that each person enjoys the benefits of effective and helpful supervision while information about control performance is moved efficiently upwards and used.

A CONTROLS SUPERVISION HIERARCHY is maintained by having HEALTHY CONVERSATIONS ABOUT CONTROL PERFORMANCE and works better in conjunction with PROCESS MANAGEMENT CONTROL.

22   Process management control

Example: A large UK telecommunications company is determined to keep its billing as near to complete and accurate as reasonably possible and has a committee representing all the organizational units involved in billing. This group gets regular reports on statistics of errors, losses, backlogs, IT support levels, and throughput. It meets to discuss them and to initiate and monitor actions to reduce problems. It also looks ahead at events that might threaten process performance to identify action needed in advance.

PROCESS MANAGEMENT CONTROL is useful for large-scale processes, particularly those that cut across organizational boundaries. It strengthens a CONTROLS SUPERVISION HIERARCHY and provides powerful evidence for ALL EVIDENCE AUDIT at virtually no extra cost.

Processes need to be refined and improved, which requires information and cooperation.

Process management control reaches its most developed form when applied to large-scale business processes. These processes usually cut across organizational boundaries and mistakes made in one department tend to generate problems and work for departments later in the process. The high volume and need for low cost mean it is vital to minimize the number of things that go wrong as this is much more efficient than detecting and correcting errors, however early you do it. The elements of this form of control are:

- **A management group with end-to-end responsibility:** It is important to get representatives together who, collectively, can take responsibility for the process, end-to-end because the process cuts across organizational boundaries and errors in one department often cause problems for others.

- **Process measures and summarized reporting:** To focus their conversations and reveal what is happening across the whole process it is important to collect data on process performance (including volumes, resources used, errors, and backlogs) and summarize them as time series and to give an end-to-end picture.
- **Work to improve inherent reliability:** The team needs to understand what types of error and delay are occurring and why, then initiate actions to remove their causes. These may include system bugs, ergonomic problems, and the skills of individuals.
- **Proactive management of risk factors and adaptation of controls:** Reacting to past problems is not enough. The team needs to look ahead for demands that may be beyond the current configuration of the process, and initiate actions to adapt the process in good time. It is also important to reduce future challenges if possible, for example by spreading change over time.

In summary, this is one of the most important controls for large-scale processes because it pulls together and uses so much management information about controls. It also makes more efficient audits possible. Therefore:

Manage process health by creating a team that collectively controls the process, providing them with suitable information, and requiring them to improve the process continually and proactively.

PROCESS MANAGEMENT CONTROL requires a regular PROCESS STATS PACK and can be used as the focus for a CONTROLS SUPERVISION HIERARCHY.

23   Process stats pack

Example: A telecoms company has process management control operating to control its complex, high-volume billing. It aims to minimize errors arising because this is efficient. To support the management committee it has a regular pack of statistics about the billing process covering volumes and revenues (of course) but also statistics on errors found of various types at various stages, backlogs, system down time, people working on billing, system bugs on hand, incidents, future changes, and progress of actions to improve errors.

A PROCESS STATS PACK is usually an important part of PROCESS MANAGEMENT CONTROL.

Most management reports about process performance have lots about how much work has been done but little about how many errors there were; but which tells you more about how to increase the work done?

Managing a large-scale process can be difficult because you can't see all the activities involved (many of which are within a computer) and some changes happen over long periods of time. There is often a lot to know about.

To manage the reliability and performance of a process in an organization you need to know what is going on. It is helpful to hear from people how they are coping, but it is vital to measure the health of your process by collecting statistics and presenting them in a regular report.

Companies sometimes feel that this kind of information gathering is not worth the effort, but when they find themselves under pressure to improve a poorly performing process they naturally begin to measure and report at increasing frequency!

The reports should show:

- workload e.g. how many invoices were raised, how many receipts were posted;
- discovered error rates (i.e. as uncovered by controls and usually corrected later) and write-offs/uncorrectable errors;
- numbers of items processed as exceptions e.g. special rush jobs;
- backlogs e.g. unmatched receipts, invoices on hold, orders with errors;
- system support e.g. availability, response time; and
- resources used e.g. head-counts, storage space.

Too many reports just show workload and resources, which is not so helpful.

The ideal report will also contain information about forthcoming changes and challenges, such as trends in workload and new software releases, so that the process owners can take action in advance to manage the risks involved. People who measure the health of their process learn that they must manage in advance to keep their numbers looking good.

This kind of monitoring is extremely useful in meeting the requirements of Section 302 of the Sarbanes-Oxley Act as it helps meet the requirement for notifying changes affecting controls and the stats themselves are powerful evidence of the effectiveness of internal controls, which also helps with Section 404 of that Act.

One of the most important objectives is to improve inherent reliability and so reduce original error rates. This is the only feasible, economic strategy for most really large-scale processes. To do this the report should also show breakdowns of errors into error types (classified by cause or potential fix if possible), showing them in descending order of their impact so that actions can be prioritized.

The report takes time to compile. To minimize that time follow these guidelines:

- Don't be idealistic. Design your report to use the data you can easily get.

- Don't assume you need a computer system to do it, but consider getting one once you have some experience of doing it by hand. Initially it is usually best to collect figures by hand and emails to colleagues and compile them on a spreadsheet. You can start immediately and the knowledge gained about what is available and useful, and what it means, is invaluable if later you decide to automate properly.
- Drop stats from the report once they tell you nothing new. If an issue arises then track stats about it until it is resolved, then drop the detailed analysis. Pareto analysis breakdowns of errors by type usually don't need to be repeated often.
- Don't skimp on presentation. Use graphs, calculate averages and ratios, and generally make sure you get full value from the data collected.

In summary, these packs provide essential information in a form that promotes action. Data does not have to be comprehensive or perfect to be very useful. Therefore:

> *Collect information about process performance (including errors found, throughput, delays, resources used, and control improvement actions in progress) and provide it in a clear, regular report.*

A PROCESS STATS PACK can usefully contain many types of information, including PERSONAL COMPARATIVES, results from STATISTICAL PROCESS CONTROL, and data for RISK-FACTOR MONITORING.

24   Personal comparatives

> *Example*: A commodity trading system records deals made and keeps records of who did what and exactly when, to the second. This immense amount of data can provide insight into working patterns, errors, and contacts.

A PERSONAL COMPARATIVES are just one of many useful inputs to PROCESS MANAGEMENT CONTROL and may be relatively efficient where the alternative control is segregation of duties.

> *Computer systems record information about who did what and when in great detail; this can be used for risk control by comparing individuals.*

PERSONAL COMPARATIVES is another control that's useful if you want to reduce segregation of duties. It is only possible if you have lots of people doing basically the same job with data arising from it automatically recorded.

The technique is simply to develop and use analytics that are calculated for each individual person and compared with others to reveal unusual patterns of behaviour, especially those believed to be linked to fraud or incompetence.

For example, these could relate to the number of transactions processed that are just below control escalation criteria, delays, and dealing with certain parties more than expected.

This kind of analysis can also be used to provide routine feedback to people to help them improve performance.

In summary, these comparisons can reduce the need for splitting up jobs to segregate duties, and can also provide people with greater insight into how they do their jobs and how it compares with others. Therefore:

Consider specific ways to use existing data to compare the work of individuals so that reliance on segregation of duties can be reduced.

There are no subsidiary control patterns to this one in this book.

25   Statistical process control

Example: Imagine that in a potato crisp factory there is a machine that drops crisps into bags and seals them. The amount to put in needs to be just right. Too much and profit is lost. Too little and a customer might complain leading to a scandal. The weight of crisps of a given bulk varies according to the number, size, and shape of the crisps, the potatoes used, the oil used, air temperature, and other factors not yet understood. A persistent step change in any of these variables could lead to bags being consistently over- or under-filled. The factory uses control charts to keep an eye out for problems. The weights of sample bags are plotted on a graph over time and rules are applied to detect when there might be a problem so that it can be investigated.

STATISTICAL PROCESS CONTROL is useful for repetitive processes that are required to produce the same output at all times. It may provide input to a PROCESS STATS PACK.

Where variations in the output of a process need to be limited but there are many inputs that can affect the output, it can sometimes be difficult to know when a problem has developed.

Statistical Process Control (SPC) is another set of ideas and tools for dealing with uncertainty from the field of quality management. The usual set-up is a process that is producing some output whose characteristics are measurable and can be compared with customers' expectations. The element of uncertainty comes in because, in practice, processes do not produce exactly the same output every time. If the output strays too far from the ideal it won't be acceptable.

The usual roles of SPC tools are:

1. to help reduce the variation; and
2. to identify when the factors driving the variation in output have changed significantly.

The usual assumption is that drivers of variation that have recently changed significantly are more interesting and deserving of management than drivers that have not changed.

Some SPC tools are concerned with pinpointing the most influential causes of variation so that they can be controlled. This may take experiments to see what effect deliberate variations seem to have.

Other techniques, such as the famous control charts, are designed to pinpoint when something important has changed. For example, a failure of the thermostat in an oven could produce a significant change to the average temperature and the variation of temperature. Control charts are designed to pick that up as quickly as possible without raising too many false alarms in respect of variation that is not due to some special cause.

The usual design of control charts is that each measurement is plotted on a graph, moving left to right. There are also two horizontal lines called the Upper and Lower Control Limits. Various rules can be applied to decide when there has probably been a significant change to the drivers of variation. These rules relate to things like the number of consecutive measurements outside the control limits, the number of consecutive measurements that move in one direction, and the moving average of the absolute difference between successive measurements. By varying parameters of these rules it is possible to adjust the probability of missing a genuine change on conditions, and of having false alarms.

In summary, STATISTICAL PROCESS CONTROL offers a well-developed range of techniques for understanding and controlling processes quantitatively. Therefore:

> *Measure relevant aspects of outputs and chart them, with control limits and trend detection, to point out when a problem may have developed. Consider the wider range of SPC tools.*

There are no subsidiary control patterns to this one in this book.

26   Risk-factor monitoring

> *Example*: A government department with major projects going on might track risk factors against each project and use these as a basis for challenging risk analyses and overall progress summaries and predictions made by project

managers. Typical risk factors would include the benefits as seen by each stakeholder, the time pressure, extent of novelty, extent of business change, size of increments, and track record of actual delivery of benefits to stakeholders.

RISK-FACTOR MONITORING is useful as a top layer over risk analyses that allows senior levels of management to challenge opinions on risk given by lower levels. It can be presented within a PROCESS STATS PACK.

Facts or opinions; which should you trust? Both together.

A risk factor is something that is a fact or expected with reasonable certainty to be a fact in future and that drives risk levels. For example, reliance on pioneering technology is a classic project risk factor. The more the reliance the greater the risks involved. In contrast, a typical risk register item like 'failure to secure adequate resources in stage B' is a risk and not a risk factor.

The basic procedure of RISK-FACTOR MONITORING is to identify important risk factors for whatever is to be monitored (e.g. a project, service improvement over a year, process performance) and then track those factors over time, using them as comparators to judge risk ratings and statements of confidence given by project managers.

For example, suppose several service managers in a local authority are asked how confident they are that they can achieve improved efficiency targets. Their responses will be, at least in part, rather subjective and may reflect their personalities as much as the facts. Risk factors can be used to challenge their views. For example, if someone's target is for an increase twice that of any other service and the service has never achieved improvements in any of the previous four years then, on the basis of those two risk factors, a highly confident prognosis needs to be challenged.

This technique compensates for the occasional weakness of risk analyses. Risk analyses may be undermined by anything from deliberate spin-doctoring to simple neglect, but most often they omit politically difficult topics and give risk ratings without empirical support. Risk analyses that start out well enough often get out of date.

Which factors to track depends on the situation. Ideally, factors should be:

- easy to track;
- based on facts not opinions;
- sourced independently of the project manager; and
- important and strongly related to the actual risks (which might be known from statistical analysis of similar situations, for example).

Not every analysis that claims to be of risk factors is what it appears to be. Most risk factor questionnaires rely on risk opinions in disguise rather than simply asking for facts. For example, the respondent might be asked to rate 'reliance on new technology' on a scale of 0 to 10. In addition to this being a quantitatively vague question (How new is new? How reliant is a score of 5?), the rating of 'reliance' is a risk judgement in disguise. It allows people with a hidden agenda to assign ratings to give the impression they want to give.

Questionnaires answered by project participants that give summary scores are a reasonable way to do RISK-FACTOR MONITORING but it is vital to stick to factual questions.

Here are two examples from part of a collective intelligence tool developed by Asuret.[1] Its questions are by far the most objective of their type that I have seen and a great model.

RELATIVE SIZE

- In terms of implementation cost and duration, the project is smaller than average for us.
- The project is above average in cost and duration, but not by more than 50 per cent.
- The project is one of the largest implementations we've ever undertaken.
- The project is more than three times larger than our largest implementation in the last five years.

MATURITY

- The application is a widely adopted, well-tested version in a mature product category.
- The version we're installing is a major upgrade of a well-established product.
- We're installing a version 1.0 release of new a product in a mature category.
- The product is an early release in a new category.

In summary, monitoring risk factors complements other methods of thinking about risk. It is relatively easy and quick yet provides most of what you want to know and is resistant to distortion. Therefore:

Identify important risk factors that are bias resistant, track them objectively, and use them to prompt questions about risk opinions.

RISK-FACTOR MONITORING can be more effective if the data are well presented, as in GRAPHICAL BUSINESS ANALYTICS. Risk factors can be included in HEALTHY CONVERSATIONS ABOUT CONTROL PERFORMANCE.

27 Healthy conversations about control performance

Example: Suppose Peter works for Linda in a government department that makes grants. Peter is one of the people who receives applications for grants, carries out various checks on them, then passes them on for a decision on whether a grant will be made. Each week, as part of her routine supervision of Peter, Linda asks him about the control aspects of his job. Peter tells her about the controls he has performed and what he found by doing them. He confirms that he was able to carry out the standard checks on all but a few of the applications and explains the problems with the others. Linda and Peter can see there is a problem with the process and agree that Linda will pass the information on. Peter also talks about the errors he found in application forms and what might have caused them. He suggests a change that could prevent one type of error.

Within a hierarchy of assurance from routine monitoring HEALTHY CONVERSATIONS ABOUT CONTROL PERFORMANCE complement purely statistical reporting.

Conversations about control performance should lead to honest answers that are hard to fake, and to rapid learning.

There are several reasons why people need to have good conversations about controls performance and why it should be an integral part of supervisory management. In most cases some kind of conversation is unavoidable because problems with uncertainty and with controls are the most complex and mentally demanding part of many jobs. Control problems create work and headaches.

With effective conversations about control performance we should expect to:

- encourage people to carry out the controls they are supposed to carry out;
- stimulate interest in controls and how they are performing;
- encourage a culture of continuous improvement that involves people at as many organizational levels as possible;
- get ideas and actions that will improve processes, systems, controls, and skills;
- gather information about the performance of the process and its controls; and
- obtain assurance as to the functioning of the control system.

The last of these reasons is increasingly seen as important to complying efficiently with Section 404 of the Sarbanes-Oxley Act. Since 2005 the Securities Exchange Commission (SEC) and Public Companies Accounting Oversight Board (PCAOB) have been encouraging companies to get more assurance from routine monitoring so they need to spend less on special testing and audits. What that means in practice is still being worked out, but already it is clear that this is more than just another certification pyramid.

Although certification (i.e. people signing documents stating that the controls they are responsible for have operated effectively and passing them up the line) has become very popular over the last two decades or so there are problems with it in its purest, crudest form.

There are three problems with simply asking someone to answer and sign off a series of questions about whether they have done their job correctly:

- It's a loaded question. Everyone knows what the expected answer is and there is great pressure to give it. Having done so the less obvious danger is that people come to believe what they have signed for.
- The certification provides little information, even when it is reliable. Exactly how well did the controls perform? What have we learned about risk levels? Are there ideas for improvement? None of these is provided.
- The experience can generate resentment. Certification conveys three unwelcome messages to employees. First, it says they are not trusted; not trusted to do their jobs and not trusted to give a straight answer in conversation. Second, it says they are to blame if something should go wrong. The certification exercise looks and feels like a systematic exercise in delegating blame in advance. Third, it says the boss is not interested in anything more they may have to say on this topic, even if there are problems outside their control.

Better questions to ask include the following.

- To what extent did you carry out the controls that were prescribed or needed?
- What were the problems in carrying out the controls?
- Do you have any ideas to improve the efficiency and effectiveness of the controls you are responsible for?
- How well do you think the controls you are responsible for have performed?
- What did you find using your controls (e.g. errors, backlogs, missing information, delays)?
- What do those findings suggest and what could we do better (including problems generated in other organizational units)?
- How well do you think processes and controls have operated in other areas based on the problems you have found using your control checks?

These questions can be asked of the individuals who actually perform controls, and of their supervisors, and of their supervisors, and so on. Information will flow up the hierarchy alongside the statistical information it helps to explain.

In summary, the right questions can generate more learning and tighter control while building relationships and skills. Therefore:

Ask questions about controls operation and performance that show trust in people and encourage them to contribute.

These conversations can also incorporate ideas from CONTROL INTERVIEW QUESTIONS.

28   Control interview questions

Example: Imagine Jill is a manager with seven direct reports, each working on different things. From time to time Jill has meetings with each one individually to discuss how things are going. Keen to improve the way risk and uncertainty are managed, Jill begins to focus more and more on risk control in these conversations, following a pattern of questioning that helps people think through their approach. She begins with questions about what is happening that involves risk and uncertainty, then moves on to what is being done about them, and then probes for evidence on whether the approach is working.

CONTROL INTERVIEW QUESTIONS are useful in interviews within ADAPTIVE AUDITS and ALL EVIDENCE AUDITS, and during HEALTHY CONVERSATIONS ABOUT CONTROL PERFORMANCE.

Getting the key information about risk and control, quickly and easily, depends on asking the right questions.

The questions that work well in risk control interviews encourage the interviewee to go through a process of thinking. General interviewing advice, such as distinguishing between open and closed questions, or following a pattern of progressive narrowing down, is not as helpful as questions specific to the risk control interview.

Use the right types of question in the right order and the interview will flow naturally and productively as one thought leads to another.

For each type of question there are a number of recommended wordings. Although it is very effective to use these tried-and-tested phrases, anything that achieves the same basic message will do. One of my favourite questions is 'What are the changes and challenges you face this year?' but not everyone feels comfortable asking this. If you think this sounds cheesy use other words or practice in front of a mirror until you can do it with a straight face and a look of genuine interest in the answer. Trust me. This question works like magic because it asks people to talk about the things they are thinking about most at work.

If you ask your questions correctly an interviewee who knows the answers will sometimes answer your next question before you can ask it. Ask the right type of question at the right time. The general flow of questions is shown in Table 7.1.

Normally the questions to ensure complete coverage would be asked first for a topic, followed by inherent risk questions, control questions, control result questions, validation questions, and then a final completeness question. Questions to get specific/validate, stay relevant, or check understanding are often needed throughout.

It may be that the interview as a whole moves in this way, or that sections of it do, or that, with some backtracking and jumping around, the sections of the interview that relate to controls follow this pattern.

Table 7.1   Risk control question types

Scope out the area with . . .   questions to ensure that everything relevant has been identified.
Then find what the risks might be with . . .   questions to help people think of inherent risk facts   (including how things work).
And move on to what people are doing about those risks using . . .   questions to help people think of control facts.
Followed by evidence on whether those actions are working using . . .   questions to help people think of control results   (i.e. whether they work).
Then grind down as far as necessary to get comfortable with . . .   questions to get down to specifics and to verify.
As you go you will often need to ask . . .   questions to check understanding.
And occasionally use . . .   questions or statements to stay relevant.

Here are some details on each question type, including suggested wordings.

QUESTIONS TO ENSURE THAT EVERYTHING RELEVANT HAS BEEN IDENTIFIED

Most auditors have had the experience of discovering something quite important that should really have been discovered in a previous conversation, and line managers are not immune to this mistake either. It is stressful to find something out late. On an unknown number of occasions we miss something big completely and it is others who will find our mistakes.

When an interviewee is chatting happily about his or her job it is easy to go with the flow and not realize that you have missed something huge and important. Avoid that mistake using questions that scope out the area thoroughly.

Recommended wordings include:

- Could you give me a brief overview of the organization structure for [the area of interest]? / What's your role/job? / What goes on in your team/department/ division?
- Could you give us a brief overview of the products/services/platforms/ applications?
- What are all these other files/computers/people/etc. for? / Is there anyone else who does that?
- What's changed since we last met/this year? / What are the plans for the future?
- Is there anything we've missed? / Is there anything I should have asked you about but didn't?

Asking about organization structure is probably the most useful opener in most situations (except where you should already know!). Asking if there is anything else you should have asked about makes you look a fool if your previous questions have been weak, but is quite easy to ask if you have been going well.

QUESTIONS TO HELP PEOPLE THINK OF INHERENT RISK FACTS (INCLUDING HOW THINGS WORK)

Some people are happy to be asked directly what risks they face, but others feel they cannot answer that question. They can, but they just need the right encouragement and help.

Recommended wordings include:

- Tell me about the changes and challenges you see this year/at the moment?
- How do the systems work? / Then what? / How does ...? / Can you talk me through the process please?
- What's changed? / What changes are happening?
- How often does that happen? / How many times? / What financial value? / How long has this been happening?
- What makes your job hard? / How complex is that? Show me please. / Manual or automated?

Asking about change is probably the most important and useful line of questioning in most situations. If it is not clear what a person is supposed to be achieving it is helpful to ask for an explanation at this point. Some styles of risk analysis make objectives the main source of risk, but this tends to lead to rather theoretical risks. Many people have jobs where they chase vague and continually moving objectives. It is more productive for you to ask about projects and changes in circumstances.

Once the risks begin to surface people naturally start to think about what they are doing about them.

QUESTIONS TO HELP PEOPLE THINK OF CONTROL FACTS

Asking directly what controls someone is using sometimes works but more often people are not sure what a control is or have a very narrow concept of controls and so do not give themselves credit for good things they are doing. It is best to start questions of this type with open, non-leading questions but if the interviewee is struggling move into making more suggestions to help them remember relevant facts. The better your skill at anticipating what should be in place the easier it is to do this.

Recommended wordings include:

- How do you know you can rely on that information/system? / How do you know that's worked? / How do you know you've entered everything? / How do you know you haven't entered something twice? / etc
- Do you have/do [a control you expect]?

QUESTIONS TO HELP PEOPLE THINK OF CONTROL RESULTS (I.E. WHETHER THEY WORK)

Audit theory books tend to suggest that the only way to see if controls are working is to decide if they are well designed and test if they are operating. Fortunately, this is not true.

There is usually plenty of direct evidence of success in the form of error statistics, backlogs, delays, and the time people spend firefighting. Always probe for it.

Recommended wordings include:

- What issues are you working on? / What issues are there? / What outstanding system bugs are there?
- Do you track those backlogs/errors/complaints? / Can I see the figures please? / What's the situation now?

QUESTIONS TO GET DOWN TO SPECIFICS AND TO VERIFY

Probing for specifics is often necessary because people tend to talk in generalizations and abstractions. Statements like 'We've taken a root and branch approach to our internal control framework process' and 'We've had some minor issues with run time compatibility and user reactions' are so vague they are barely worth noting down. Since you want to know the truth they cannot be allowed to pass and asking for specifics is a powerful way to get to the truth.

Verification means seeking additional evidence. It may not be possible to do it in the interview so decide quickly what verification you want and go ahead if there is time, or make a date to follow up later.

Recommended wordings include:

- When you say [vague term used by interviewee], what do you mean? / Can you give me some examples? / Would you mind talking me through an example?
- Can you show me? / What does that look like? / Why don't we do this at your desk then you can easily show me?
- Can we look at some examples at random? / How could I see that? / How could I confirm or corroborate that?
- How often does this happen? / When was the last time? / How many times has that happened so far this year?
- Then what? / What do you do if X?

QUESTIONS TO CHECK UNDERSTANDING

Clarity is important. The most intricate parts of processes are often the controls, not the underlying work.

Getting people to start making some sense requires persistence in many cases. It is easy to feel that you ought to have understood what they just said and to shy away from asking for clarification. Occasionally people do react angrily to patient questioning that checks understanding often, but this is rare and a small risk compared to misunderstanding.

Most people find it difficult to give a good explanation of something to someone whose knowledge is not the same as theirs. When someone's explanation does not allow for your lack of knowledge the best approach is to take firm control of the conversation and direct them to give you the information you need to make sense of what they are saying. If you do not take control then an interviewee who is keen to make you understand will often repeat themselves at ever greater length, often with complicated examples explained in excruciating detail you cannot begin to follow.

Recommended wordings include:

- I don't understand. / Can you just say that last sentence again please? / I'm not sure I got that. Can you please say that again – just the same words.
- So, let me see if I've understood. [Summarize] / In summary, then, X: correct?
- You're saying that X. So, presumably Y [inference]? / Does that mean that X? / So X, but earlier I thought you said Y [contradictory]?

QUESTIONS OR STATEMENTS TO STAY RELEVANT

Sometimes people have to be politely redirected. Recommended wordings include:

- Thank you, that's fine/enough. I wonder if we could move on to X. / We've only got another 20 minutes, so I wonder if we could move on to X.
- What I am trying to establish is X.

If you want to go on and fix control problems then you need to explore solutions and begin gathering support for them. Two further types of question become important as well:

QUESTIONS TO GET THE INTERVIEWEE TO THINK ABOUT CAUSES AND EFFECTS

If you think it may be possible to control a risk better it is important to get people considering the importance of reducing the weakness. Asking them about implications is a powerful way to do this. You may find that in fact the weakness is not important, but more often you will find it is.

Recommended wordings include:

- What are the implications of that problem/risk/issue? / What other implications might there be? / Can we try to list/quantify the effects to see just how serious that might be? / What would that lead to?
- Why does that happen? / What are the main causes of this problem? / What is creating/driving this risk?

QUESTIONS TO PREPARE THE WAY FOR PROPOSING A SOLUTION

Without actually proposing a specific solution it is useful to test points for intervention. Recommended wordings include:

- If we could improve X/stop X happening/reduce X/increase X/etc. [a particular point in the cause-effect network built through the previous type of question], would that provide at least a partial solution? / Suppose there was a way to X. Wouldn't that help?
- Can you think of any other effects of improving X?

These two types of question are useful for bringing interviewees along with you. Once you've found out some facts and identified a problem, the 'cause and effect' questions can be used to assess the importance of the problem, and get the interviewee to understand it too. The more they understand the impact of a problem the more they want to solve it, if that is justified.

When the interviewee is sufficiently concerned about a problem to want to solve it, they will begin to consider the options seriously. The temptation is to produce a solution at this point (if you have one) but even that is often too early. Hence, questions are needed to confirm that the interviewee agrees an intervention at a particular point (or set of points) could be effective. This requires an 'If we could improve ...' type of question.

Once there is agreement in principle that an intervention at particular points could be effective, finally, you can present your solutions and demonstrate as far as possible that they would work.

In summary, the right interview questions used in the right way can dramatically improve audit performance and how it is perceived. The conversation flows naturally and omissions are reduced. Therefore:

> *Use patterns of questioning that establish what needs to be talked about, what is going on that generates risk, what people are doing about it, whether that is working, and how the interviewer can check it.*

There are no subsidiary control patterns to this one in this book.

29   Reporting with uncertainty

Example: A factory that makes glass could have a policy that all management information must provide at least some indication of its measurement uncertainty (i.e. reliability). For example, recorded stock levels are rarely exactly correct due to errors, theft, and breakage. Stock values are less reliable because of valuation uncertainties. Costs depend on the policies applied and can move unpredictably when accounting errors and unexpected costs arrive. Quality measures are often based on samples, introducing sampling errors, while the quality tests themselves do not pick up all quality problems.

REPORTING WITH UNCERTAINTY is applicable to virtually all internally reported information. It improves a CONTROLS SUPERVISION HIERARCHY and is relevant within a PROCESS STATS PACK and when using GRAPHICAL BUSINESS ANALYTICS.

Much internally reported management information is unreliable, even when it appears to be factual.

How much of the information passed around in organizations as management information is totally accurate and reliable? Not much. Even externally reported and independently audited information like financial statements has its limitations. The reported numbers are just one set from a range that the auditors would have accepted. Accounting estimates and judgements can make a considerable difference to reported results. Small errors happen all the time.

Many numbers are based on samples. Others are generated by quality checks that themselves are unreliable. One company tracked errors in processing insurance claims, noting with satisfaction the small but steady improvements. The errors were detected by a quality reviewer who looked at processed claims and identified the errors made. One day someone from internal audit re-performed some quality reviews and found twice as many errors as had been reported by the quality reviewer.

Other reports are based on data in computer systems which sometimes have not been checked adequately and whose meanings are unclear. The data may have been extracted incorrectly. The data may not be what they seem to be. For example, it may be an estimate instead of a faithful record.

This is uncertainty that is rarely given enough attention so get people to give information about the uncertainty inherent in management information they provide. Do this with as much information as you can. Even audited financial statements are not above such caveats (internally at least!) because it can be helpful to understand how much the results rested on accounting judgements and estimates.

Do this and suddenly the illusion of certainty is shattered and the value of learning more is clearer. There may also be useful but unreliable information that has not previously been used because a satisfactory way to show the uncertainty was not thought about.

Here are some specific techniques that can be useful:

- **State the source of information:** Even if the source is 'John Smith's gut feeling' that is a source so state it.
- **State assumptions:** This is not an ideal approach because lists of assumptions tend to convey the impression that the conclusions are worthless, but it is better than nothing.
- **Quantify the empirical support:** For example, if the information is based on a survey, how big was the survey?

- **Show confidence limits:** For example, what is the upper level such that you are 90 per cent sure the result is less, and the lower level such that you are 90 per cent sure it is more?
- **Show the whole probability distribution:** The previous idea can be taken further by showing a full probability distribution for the number in question.
- **List sources of uncertainty:** This is another simple technique that can be applied to any type of management information.
- **Analyse out components that have higher uncertainty:** If some parts of a number are subject to more uncertainty than others then analyse them out. For example, a company's profits for a period may be influenced by a number of accounting estimates and judgements. Show how much those are worth.

In summary, REPORTING WITH UNCERTAINTY is one of the most pervasive ways to remind people to be open about uncertainty and a strong indicator of embedded risk control. It can help avert poor decisions. Therefore:

Almost all internally reported information is uncertain to some extent and this should be disclosed informatively as near to the information as reasonably possible.

There are no subsidiary control patterns to this one in this book.

30   Explanation first analytics

Example: A bank with multiple branches might have an understanding of how conditions and events affect branch performance and use this to predict results. It can then use information about the major events and changes in conditions during a period to form expectations about results and compare these with actual reported results.

EXPLANATION FIRST ANALYTICS are an important part of overall business monitoring and especially useful if analytics are used heavily, which they should be.

Hindsight is dangerous; it undermines analytical reviews of performance.

Years ago when I was a trainee accountant I went to audit an expensive private school for girls. The standard audit procedure I was learning to follow included an 'analytical review' of the profit and loss figures that aimed to find possible misstatements. This was done by calculating, for each figure in the detailed profit and loss breakdown, the percentage change from the previous year, then asking the bursar (the school's accountant) to explain all the larger changes.

During my conversation with the bursar I looked down at my schedule and asked him why a particular type of expense was *lower* than in the previous year. He gave me two or three convincing reasons for this and I wrote them down. When I looked at my schedule to ask the next question I realized I had made a mistake. In fact the expense he had just explained was *higher*, not lower. I apologized and asked the correct question. He laughed at me and gave convincing reasons why the expenses had been higher.

The problem was that when we know what we are trying to explain we can easily remember potential explanations, even if they are not the whole story or even important. My review procedure involved making a crude comparison between actual results and expectations based on last year's numbers (though it could have been a budget) without any knowledge of more recent events.

A stronger procedure is to:

1. ask for the main trends, events, and other changes that would have affected results in the period compared to the previous period;
2. estimate their impact, for example by adjusting last year's figures or some earlier forecast;
3. calculate variances from these new expectations; and
4. enquire as to possible reasons for the remaining variances.

In summary, this approach increases the power of business analytics and provides another reason for using predictive models of performance. Therefore:

> *Build a numerical model of performance during a period, ask for information about conditions and events that should have affected performance during that period, build them into the model by some kind of adjustment, and then ask for explanations of the remaining differences between predicted and actual performance.*

EXPLANATION FIRST ANALYTICS can be more effective when enhanced with GRAPHICAL BUSINESS ANALYTICS.

31   Graphical business analytics

Example: A training business wishing to understand and control its revenues and costs better supplemented its existing budget variance analysis and year-to-date management accounts pack with graphs showing numbers month by month, with coloured breakdowns, moving annual totals, and even scatter plots to reveal possible causal links, or the lack of them.

GRAPHICAL BUSINESS ANALYTICS give a better understanding of what has been happening and, also, often reveal incorrect management information. They can increase the power of EXPLANATION FIRST ANALYTICS.

Business leaders usually want to know more about what is going on but prefer to be given fewer papers.

One of the ironies of management accounting and performance measurement is that users of this information usually want more and more analyses and yet often complain of being given too much information.

Very occasionally it is possible to meet this requirement by finding a small set of indicators that are so far reaching and yet so sensitive that anything important that is going on will be visible in the key indicators and will prompt users to look at more detailed information to fully understand what is happening.

Unfortunately, this is rare. More often any small set of indicators that is wide in scope is also rather insensitive. They are so summarized that really major things have to be happening to show up. It is also hard to be sure if a supposed key indicator (e.g. customer satisfaction scores on a survey) really is linked reliably to performance in the way that one imagines. Statistical analysis can provide some evidence that an indicator truly is important but few bother with the analysis.

A technique that nearly always helps to make it easier for users of reports to process the data they are given is to give them in appropriate graphs. This does not mean just adding traffic-light colours to variances compared with targets or budgets!

The best displays are usually based on time series. In other words don't just show the total profit in the year to date. Instead, show the profit month by month for the year to date and the year before that so that cycles and trends can be seen. Moving annual totals are helpful too. Also, if two numbers, such as monthly expenditure and monthly revenue should correlate try putting them on a scatter plot to confirm that they do and see how they vary.

A very important part of making this work is to give graphs that are clean and clear. Every technique for improving the quality should be used and there is no better source of ideas for this than Edward Tufte's books.[2]

Graphs, however well designed, usually do not replace tables of figures entirely, but they can certainly make them more digestible.

In summary, good information graphics are an easy way to gain dramatic new insights and stimulate more productive management conversations. Therefore:

Show key numerical information using clean, clear information graphics, especially using time series. Maximize their data density and data-ink ratios.

The reports are improved by REPORTING WITH UNCERTAINTY.

32   Random fraud audits

Example: Tax collection agencies in some countries use random audits to deter tax evasion. The reviews have to be thorough to be effective so it is not practical to audit everyone and auditing only in situations where there is already evidence of evasion would invite tax dodgers to think they are safe if they are careful. Citizens complain, but the alternative is worse.

RANDOM FRAUD AUDITS are applicable to most forms of fraud.

Fraud is much harder to detect and to control than error.

The controls, including audits, which guard against error are not enough to prevent fraud.

People commit fraud deliberately and take care to conceal what they have done. They often know what checks are in place and even know what auditors usually do. Whether they are perpetrating their fraud using a control weakness they found by accident or by deliberate searching, they have carefully studied that weakness and how to exploit it with minimum risk to themselves. They may set up false evidence and may collude with others to conceal the fraud.

Audits which effectively search for fraud have to be rigorous, detailed, time consuming, and inconvenient. They can easily leave innocent people feeling unfairly persecuted and distrusted.

In view of the cost, inconvenience, and emotional impact of effective fraud audits most audit departments have a choice between:

1. doing no specific fraud reviews and hoping to pick up obvious, badly concealed fraud almost by luck; and
2. doing a very few fraud audits in special circumstances.

RANDOM FRAUD AUDITS are a way to create a wide-acting deterrent while only doing limited fraud audits. The alternative is to do fraud audits only when there is a specific reason to think fraud is going on. That is rather narrow and invites fraudsters to learn what signs to avoid giving.

The emotional impact can be improved using the following approach:

•   Make it quite clear that inclusion in random audits is random, though it may be weighted by value, role, extent of normal supervision – that is, anything that is not personal. Therefore we can say 'It's nothing personal. You/your team/these transactions were picked at random on the basis of factors that are to do with your role, not you. Nobody is accusing you of anything or distrusts you personally.'

- Invite people caught up in a fraud audit to help make the audit a success and so maintain a deterrent without which much more costly and inconvenient controls would be needed.
- Compensate people inconvenienced by a fraud audit or otherwise mitigate the effects for them. For example, their boss can be told what has happened and the time taken.
- Encourage auditors to be polite and respectful, treating people as innocent, even though they must follow rigorous procedures without concessions for special pleading or seniority.
- Specify the rigour of the procedures in written rules that do not involve significant judgement. This allows the auditor to reassure people that they are not distrusted but nevertheless the procedures have to be followed to the letter or the credibility of the audits and their deterrent is undermined.

In the interests of efficiency it makes sense to weight the random selection towards higher-risk items and roles. Fraud can be targeted more effectively by including personal factors such as a reputation for sharp practice, driving an expensive car, taking no holidays, and spending time in the office when nobody else is around. However, these are dangerously personal factors and may be seen as unfair by very hard-working people from wealthy families.

If fraud audits can be made effective they can reduce the need for segregation of duties, which is sometimes an inconvenient or wasteful type of control that increases error risk because of the hand-offs involved.

In short, fraud audits carried out on a (partly) random basis are a way to spread fraud audit resources more efficiently and create a deterrent. Therefore:

Trust but verify. Apply some audit resource to intensive audits for fraud, choosing targets on a random basis that is fair and an acceptable alternative to other, less appealing controls.

There are no subsidiary control patterns to this one in this book.

33   Adaptive audit

Example: The internal audit team of a listed electronics company might approach reviews with a focus on risk that drives down into every detail of their reviews. They would begin each review with interviews of relevant senior or central people and analysis of process health statistics then work down to lower levels in the organization and more detailed information. At each stage they would ask about the changes and challenges people face and how they have tried to maintain control. This highlights inherent risk factors, issues, and controls, many of which can be tested immediately. The next step in their audit is always decided in response to findings so far.

ADAPTIVE AUDIT is relevant for audits, Sarbanes-Oxley reviews, and when a line manager wants to go into something in more depth.

A problem with audits is that you don't know how much audit work is needed until after you've done it.

It's an inconvenient fact of life that the amount of work an auditor should do depends on what the auditor finds. There are three major reasons for this.

• Issues, if found, generate a lot of work often by senior people. Issues have to be discussed and investigated further.
• The amount of work needed depends on how near actual control performance is to required performance. If controls are much, much better or worse than needed it is usually easy to show it without a lot of work. If controls are very near to the required level it may be theoretically impossible to decide and in practice it will at least involve more work.
• Some controls are much easier to test than others.

Even if you know what controls to expect in advance the amount of work needed and how to focus it are still uncertain. Genuine responsiveness to risk is not compatible with a pre-determined audit programme.

The idea of adaptive auditing is to make the audit approach up as you go along, responding to what you find and focusing on the highest areas of risk and most cost-effective controls.

If this sounds crazy or impractical you may be reassured to learn that it was the global standard audit approach of PricewaterhouseCoopers (the world's largest audit firm) just before Sarbanes-Oxley came along and put things back ten years. Done well it works and does not cause resource problems. In fact saving audit costs was one of the reasons PricewaterhouseCoopers started doing it in the first place.

Adaptive audits are efficient for two reasons:

• The audit is highly risk focused.
• The audit does not include precautionary work.

The second point is not obvious. Remember that the amount of work needed depends on what is found. If you had to choose a pre-determined audit programme to be sure of getting enough evidence then you would need to plan for the worst. Most of the time that will mean doing work you will discover you don't need.

Adaptive audits are sometimes more expensive than non-adaptive audits of the same area, but on average they are cheaper.

Adaptive auditing requires skill and the right approach. Some points to bear in mind are as follows.

• Start with interviews of people near the top of the hierarchy and work down.

- Auditors need to be able to make good decisions about what to do, and make them quickly, often during interviews.
- Teamwork is important. The team needs to share its discoveries and the evolving plan.
- Asking the right questions in interviews is crucial.
- If the review is big enough to need resource management, it is a bad idea to manage mindlessly against a fixed budget. Have an expectation in mind, but repeatedly forecast the work needed to complete the review based on the latest information and use this as an input to decisions about what work to do. On average these reviews are more efficient.

In summary, this approach reduces the average cost of audits and promotes highly risk focused reviews. Therefore:

> *Conduct audits and reviews of controls so that as information is gained it is quickly used to plan the further work.*

ADAPTIVE AUDIT is much more effective when appropriate CONTROL INTERVIEW QUESTIONS are used. It can also benefit from AGILE DOCUMENTATION REVIEWS.

34   Audit against controls designed

> *Example*: A company with a large number of similar UNIX servers in different buildings might go through a controls design exercise to decide exactly what security parameters should be set on UNIX. An element of audit work on computer security might then be to compare the actual parameter settings on some or all of the servers against the design. This might be made much more efficient using a software tool that makes the comparisons automatically.

AUDIT AGAINST CONTROLS DESIGNED is possible where controls have been designed and documentation of controls was produced as a by-product.

> *If controls have been designed and the design has been documented then a different kind of audit is possible.*

In a traditional audit review of controls the procedure goes like this. The auditors ask questions to find out what controls are supposed to be in place and consider if the controls seem to be adequate given their perception of the risks and the design of the controls. Next the auditors test the individual controls to see if they are operating as they perceive they should. If everything meets their expectations then they give a clean report, otherwise they point to weaknesses and usually make recommendations for remediation of controls. The controls tested are the auditors' choice and usually management never finds out which controls were tested. Because the reporting is on an exception basis not much information is reported.

However, if the controls have been deliberately designed and documented, and if management wants detailed information on the implementation and operation of controls, then a very efficient and informative audit is possible. The idea is simply to audit the controls in the design only and report full details of results.

At the planning stage the scope needs to be agreed in detail:

- Is the auditor to evaluate and test the level of inherent risk?
- Is the auditor to evaluate and report on the design of controls?
- Which controls is the auditor to test and to what extent?
- If the results are very poor should the auditor move on to other procedures to try to find the extent of the resulting issues or uncover mitigating controls outside the intended design?
- Is the auditor to evaluate and report on direct evidence of controls performance such as error statistics?

When the testing of individual controls is executed the task is simply to test the agreed controls and record the results. There is no filtering to be done.

The results of the review are reported in detail. This allows management to track implementation and operation of designs in detail.

The efficiency advantage of this kind of testing is greatest if the same tests need to be performed in many places or at different times. Audits of computer security and parameterization of ERP software can be automated to a degree.

In summary, this kind of review provides a lot of information to management for reduced work and judgement by the auditor. Therefore:

Audit against the controls that have been designed and are supposed to be in place and provide detailed reporting of results.

There are no subsidiary control patterns to this one in this book.

35   All evidence audit

Example: A large banking group, determined to comply with Section 404 of the Sarbanes-Oxley Act more efficiently, expanded its search for evidence beyond the usual design and operation tests on individual controls to include evidence of actual inherent risk levels and performance of control systems as measured by error statistics. Having looked more widely it could be more selective in the evidence it used from each source.

ALL EVIDENCE AUDIT is part of monitoring controls performance through audit and works with ADAPTIVE AUDIT.

The total pool of evidence of controls effectiveness is broader than most people think and nuggets of high-value, low-cost evidence lie all around.

In a typical area of potential audit evidence the items of evidence vary in how much evidence value they provide for the effort of getting them. Some evidence is easy to acquire and highly informative. At the other extreme some evidence is a long grind to obtain but adds little. Obviously an auditor, or anyone trying to assess the performance of some controls, should focus on the evidence that is easy to get and highly informative.

The wider the search for evidence the more selective you can be in your choice of which evidence items to go for. For example, if you have previously ignored computer controls then adding them should allow for an audit approach that is, overall, more cost-effective. Extending to include evidence from entity-level business analytics, if not considered before, will also make a more efficient review possible.

These are well-known examples, but there are much more powerful and less well-known opportunities to extend the search for evidence.

Conventional controls audit theory focuses exclusively on two types of evidence:

1. the apparent design of the controls and control system; and
2. the operation of individual controls.

The idea is that if the controls look like they should make an effective system and individual controls are being operated diligently then all should be well.

Conventional controls audit theory is missing some other evidence that virtually everyone recognizes as relevant and useful. In 2004 I carried out an online survey to find out what volunteers thought was relevant evidence when assessing the effectiveness of a control system.

In addition to design and operation of controls, respondents (including external auditors, internal auditors, and non-auditors) were virtually unanimous in agreeing that statistics on errors found (for example, customer complaints about billing) and evidence of inherent risk levels (for example, actual extent of change to software during a period) were relevant. In fact statistics on errors found were the most strongly supported evidence type of all, and considered much more relevant than tests of the control environment (for example, existence of policies about control).

Only one respondent remembered his textbook learning and disregarded everything except design and operation evidence.

If an organization systematically gathers, reports, and monitors evidence of controls performance – in particular error and delay statistics – then this is extremely informative evidence the reviewer can obtain with almost no effort.

Audit procedures, papers, and other tools should be designed to encourage people to consider and use the best from all types of evidence. A wider variety of testing techniques is required to cover a wider variety of evidence types.

Since most audit materials are designed to focus only on the two textbook types this is another massive opportunity for greater efficiency.

In summary, selecting from all relevant forms of evidence allows a more efficient and effective audit to be done and is particularly powerful in an organization that has well-designed controls. Therefore:

Conduct audits and reviews so that all sources and types of evidence are drawn from appropriately, including direct information on controls performance.

These audits can make heavy use of data generated by PROCESS MANAGEMENT CONTROL and will also benefit from AGILE DOCUMENTATION REVIEWS.

36 Agile documentation reviews

Example: A team of risk control specialists re-engineering controls in a business process, and generating documentation showing what is happening and what could happen instead, will need to do reviews of their own documentation to ensure it is of adequate quality. It could do this efficiently by reviewing samples of documentation very slowly and thoroughly against predefined quality rules, starting from an early stage.

AGILE DOCUMENTATION REVIEWS are useful during monitoring by audit and in controls design work, and should be considered in any situation where large-scale quality reviews of documentation are needed.

The economics of working paper quality reviews are astonishing.

It is a long-established tradition in auditing that all working papers are reviewed by someone else, almost always someone at a higher organizational level than the author. This helps to improve quality and promotes learning by authors, and it is a good practice that should always be followed.

Although there have been dozens of studies of the reliability of these reviews there seems to be little if anything on their economics. In contrast, inspection of documentation has been less consistently applied in the world of software development but it has been done on a large scale and its economics have been studied in a scientific way. It is from this research that some astonishing facts have emerged with major practical implications.

Suppose someone reviews some papers and marks all the defects they can see. Does that mean we have a list of all the defects present? Far from it. If another person does a similar review they will find some of the same defects plus others. If a third person does a review then yet more new defects will be found. And so on.

Most astonishing is the effect of review speed. Experiment has shown that if you review at the usual audit manager's pace of perhaps 10 to 50 pages an hour you will do no more than scrape the surface of the defects present. The slower the review speed the greater the number of defects found and if speed goes down to one page every 30 to 60 minutes the number of defects found is several times higher than at one page every five minutes.

Reviews of typical documentation at this speed will often find *hundreds* of defects per page, even if you ignore trivia that does not undermine the value of the documentation produced.

I have reproduced these findings in seminars and found that almost everyone is able to find many defects in controls documentation of typical quality.

What can be done about this? Obviously, if all controls documentation was reviewed at a rate of one page every 30 minutes it would be astonishingly time consuming to do and would generate a mountain of corrections to be made by authors. It would be a disaster.

Fortunately, it is not necessary to review every page of every document this way. It can be done on a sample basis. This makes sense because the main benefit of inspection is not the clean up that occurs but the increase in the *skill* of authors that is caused.

When someone has their work inspected rigorously for the first time the number of defects is the usual frightening number. However, their second attempt will have half as many errors in it, their third will have half as many errors again, and so on. Progress is rapid and does not require every page to be inspected.

This approach also implies that the best time to begin to review a person's work is as soon as there is a large enough sample to look at, that is, once about half a page of work exists.

In practice most early writing is not clear enough to tell if it makes sense. Early reviews often have to focus on clarity until the document is ready to be reviewed seriously for its suitability.

In summary, intensive reviews of samples of documentation, used as a coaching tool, are a good use of time and most review time should be used this way. Therefore:

Review controls and audit documentation as early as possible, very slowly against rules, feed the results back fairly, and demand low defect rates for work to be accepted.

There are no subsidiary control patterns to this one in this book.

Notes

1   Asuret Inc., at Asuret.com
2   A good starting point is Tufte, E.R. (1983) *The Visual Display of Quantitative Information*. Cheshire, CT: Graphics Press.

8 *Learning and Adapting*

Managing uncertainty through agility, adaptiveness, learning, and anticipation is often more efficient and effective than trying to do it through standardization, tightness, fixedness, barriers, and restrictions. It's more popular too.

People in organizations often see risk control as being negative. The risk manager is the 'No' man. Internal controls are limits, checks, barriers, hurdles, shields. Risk control makes things harder than they should be. Often people are right to see risk control in that way because in their organization it really is negative.

Companies sometimes try to cut expenditures by increasing the bureaucratic barriers in the way of spending money. They set hurdle rates for investments. They institute filters to weed out bids that are too risky. They limit authority, limit budgets, and put limits on risk.

These 'negative' controls are not inherently a bad idea but they can create a costly bureaucratic strait-jacket. They even carry a subtle insult to employees, saying 'You're not trusted'.

Ideally, we would like to be able to cope with uncertainty without putting on heavy armour. Controls need to be light and intelligent.

This chapter is about control mechanisms based on this idea but, before the control patterns are presented, here's an overview with some more detail on what positive qualities are and what evidence shows that they can be effective.

An overview of learning and adapting

This is a huge area, but is all based on the simple idea that one way to tackle uncertainty is to learn faster and be more flexible. That can involve getting set up to learn faster, doing things to generate learning, getting more feedback faster, making use of learning more often, and creating flexibility to respond to what you learn. Although this is common sense it is surprising how often organizations do none of this, instead carrying on as if they know everything from the outset and do not need to learn or adapt.

- **Getting set to learn:** If you promise your boss something will happen in a certain way and then you start revising your priorities and methods as you go along that looks out of control. In contrast, if you say at the start that you will be monitoring events and progress frequently and adjusting to take advantage of new information then that looks like good, responsible management! More seriously:

- Documents like approved plans and agreed contracts need to be written in a way that gives room for learning and adjustment or, better still, requires them.
- Plans need to allocate time and resources to learning and adjusting.
- People need to understand that this is expected of them.
- Often, the whole structure of a plan needs to be designed to create a situation in which you can learn quickly and have the flexibility to adapt instead of being stuck with the consequences of old decisions.
- Finally, it helps to allocate responsibilities to people in a way that allows flexibility. For example, if you have a set of five products to manage, then allocating a manager to each product creates a defender for each product who may well block attempts to manage the products as a portfolio. You may want the product management team to pull support for products that are failing and give it to the successes, but the managers will resist. In contrast, if managers are responsible for the *portfolio* they will be more willing to change things.

- **Doing things to learn more, faster:** Although much can be achieved by retrospectively trying to make sense of what has been happening it is hard to learn how the world works and what you can do to influence it by monitoring trends. You have to *experiment.* In other words, try different things and see what happens. Making lots of small, quick experiments is a common management strategy that you can see, for example, guiding the development of websites and the selection of new products. Our ability to spot potential winners is so poor that trial and error turns out to be a good strategy, provided you can do it quickly and cheaply. There's a fascinating literature on 'design of experiments' which is all about designing efficient experiments. One interesting technique is Evolutionary Operation (EVOP), which involves making small changes to input parameters of a live process to see what effect it has on the output. Provided those changes are small enough the customer receiving the output won't mind, but the tiny changes can be enough to guide continuous optimization.
  - Other fact-finding and research techniques can be useful, and even just thinking more is an important option.
  - Sometimes in a project you have a choice about when you do tasks whose outcome is very uncertain but important to the overall outcome of the project. Unless there are special circumstances do them as early as you can.

- **Get more feedback, faster:** Include performance measures that give fast feedback. For example, if you are trying to improve educational standards in a school then exam results are an important measure but cannot be used alone because they are only available once a year, which is far too infrequent. We really need to know *next week* if something seems to be working.

- **Adapt often and in a quick but controlled way:** We're used to discussions about objectives, priorities, resources, and plans being tough and often political. They are something we would perhaps prefer to do no more than annually. There's no room for that kind of discussion if you are reviewing everything monthly. If the monthly reviews lead to violent fluctuations in approach as warring factions struggle for the upper hand then adaptation will not work. Fortunately, if reviews are more frequent they are naturally easier and quicker. People get used to the routine. (You rarely get used to an annual review process, particularly as they are often reinvented.) People know the issues. They've discussed many of the alternative actions before. The more frequent the reviews the easier they are and the smaller the adjustments.

- **Build flexibility:** Learning and thinking about what you have learned give no advantage if there is nothing you can do differently as a result. These options might be devised after the learning takes place but it is helpful to have given yourself flexibility beforehand. Here are some types of flexibility to aim for:
  - Flexibility as to *extent*:
    - o   Scalability: Look for ways to make it possible to increase or decrease the investment, to any extent required, and at low cost.
    - o   Incremental delivery: Look for ways to deliver in small increments, with the opportunity to assess the situation after each. (See EVOLUTIONARY PROJECT MANAGEMENT.)
    - o   Flexible timing: Look for flexibility on when you do things, including when you make decisions.
    - o   Easy termination: Look for ways to get out quickly and easily if necessary.

  - Flexibility as to *purpose*:
    - o   Commonality and multifunctionality: Do things that will be useful in all or many anticipated futures. This may be because the action has several helpful effects.
    - o   Reconfigurability: If the investment or product cannot be made multifunctional, can it be made configurable? This might take the form of last minute customization.
    - o   Reusable components: If the investment or product cannot be made multifunctional or reconfigurable, can it be made so that it is possible to reuse parts of it? Make it modular, re-manufacturable, or recyclable.

Gaining information and flexibility often involve extra costs. There's a fine line between intelligent flexibility and being weighed down by dabbling in fringe activities, and that line tends to move with expectations of the economy. In good times people are happy to expand and try ideas, encouraged by optimistic expectations of the future. In bad times the new management cuts away what is now described as 'non-core activities'.

As mentioned earlier, the usual human tendency is to see the future too narrowly. In good times, when our expectations are high, we are too confident that our investments will be successful and tend to make too many of them. In bad times, when our expectations are low, we are too confident that investments will fail and tend to make too few of them. In both cases, we tend to make too little effort to maximize the learning and flexibility in our plans.

Most of the time the right balance is best struck by judgement, with the hard thinking going into finding efficient ways to build flexibility and learning into our plans. Occasionally a big decision has to be made that justifies quantitative methods.

Qualities of adaptive control systems

Imagine you've set out to design a management system from scratch. You might start by writing down some rough ideas about how you would like it to be: effective, fast, responsive, proactive, adaptive, stable, low cost, simple. Perhaps you want to do something more than annual target setting and monthly reviews of plans against targets.

In recent years the Beyond Budgeting Round Table (BBRT) has claimed that organizations can be more adaptive if they abandon budgetary control, and other management systems involving fixed absolute targets, and adopt different practices. The BBRT has reported many fascinating case studies[1] of companies that have stopped using fixed targets. (The Beyond Budgeting model is a collection of generalizations about the case studies expressed as principles, but these cover a wide range of practices.)

Successful large companies without budgetary control systems include IKEA, Svenska Handelsbanken, Borealis, UBS Global Wealth & Business Banking, and Rhodia, to name just a few.

The BBRT case studies show that there are many alternatives to annually fixed targets that work even with very large organizations. They also strongly suggest that *accelerating* management is an important part of the way forward.

Acceleration is the theme on which the following framework is based. Imagine an organization. It has people, structures, processes, knowledge, and so on. There are things that might happen in the future that will affect the organization and for each it might be that some kind of management action might be advantageous for the organization.

Here is a way to analyse the performance characteristics of a management system in terms of five dimensions.

DIMENSION 1: FORWARD VIEW

The earlier management considers action in relation to a future event the greater the choice of alternative actions. (They have all the options that will be available later, plus those available only to the early bird.) It may be that the time it takes to implement certain potential actions means they are only available if an early decision to act is taken. Also, some chains of events are more easily influenced early on, before they have built up momentum.

Forward view is improved by (a) looking further ahead, (b) considering more of the set of possible futures, and (c) being better able to identify the most likely futures and focus attention on them. Most of the time we are not as good at predicting and controlling the future as we think. Our view is too narrow and should be wider. This is the main way of improving the forward view.

DIMENSION 2: SCOPE

The greater the extent of reconsideration the greater the potential advantage. (Management has all the options that are available from limited changes, plus those available only to those who dig deeper.)

Scope is usually improved by moving along some continuum of deeper consideration. For example, one might increase scope by reconsidering goals up to a higher level in a hierarchy of goals, or by reviewing things you have previously considered more and more certain. Another possibility when looking at learning from performance indicators and experience is to progress up the following scale:

- *Numbers we report*: What do we have to say to our shareholders, employees, the regulator etc.? (And, how will they react and how should we explain it?)
- *Reality*: What is the situation, really, and what is going on?
- *Understanding*: Why is this happening? This is the first level at which modelling, perhaps informally, becomes important.
- *Prediction*: What could happen in the future?
- *Action*: What can we do that works, and how well does it work?

DIMENSION 3: INPUT

The greater the amount of relevant information used the better the potential outcome of the deliberations.

DIMENSION 4: FREQUENCY

The more frequently management considers action the earlier actions can be considered, on average, and the higher the value of options. (Management can time their exercise of options more precisely, leaving decisions closer to the last possible moment.)

DIMENSION 5: SPEED

The faster the deliberations the less the delay between information being obtained and action resulting, and so the lower the risk of obsolete action.

The greater the Forward View, the more proactive the system is. The greater its Scope, Input, Frequency, and Speed the greater its responsiveness and adaptiveness. The other features of management systems can be understood as ways to increase these five.

In judging a management system against this framework we must recognize that there may be more than one cycle, and each cycle will have its own Frequency, Forward View, and so on. Some of the most important cycles (usually because of their good Forward View and Frequency) will be informal, making it hard to judge them.

Obviously, there's a problem. You could easily sacrifice quality of decision-making for speed. Progress in Forward View, Scope, Input, Frequency, and Speed are only beneficial if they are not offset by a drop in decision quality.

Getting information, thinking about it, and communicating new plans all takes time to do effectively. The speed with which these can be done limits the Forward View, Scope, Input, Frequency, and Speed of a management system.

Beyond Budgeting cases

The main characteristics of 'Beyond Budgeting' case studies can be understood in terms of their effect on information processing and the five dimensions:

- **Removal of fixed absolute targets:** In a typical late-twentieth-century management control system, targets and resource allocations are set annually and rarely adjusted. In between target setting other things can change, but not the targets or resource allocations. If targets and resource allocations are allowed to change more frequently then the Scope of the monthly or quarterly deliberations is increased.

- **Relative and aspirational targets:** Organizations that have done away with budgets often use targets expressed in relative terms compared with competitors, or aspirational targets (i.e. way above any realistic expectation for achievement). The effect of these is to split the concept of an 'objective' into two parts. One part shows that a particular performance characteristic is important and indicates the direction that is desirable e.g. more profit, less pollution, longer life expectancy. The other part is the specific value that is currently used for planning e.g. profit of £34 mn this year, pollution down to 100 tonnes this year, life expectancy up to 82 years by five years from now. Typically, companies have changed the first part very infrequently (not more than once a year) but the second part much more frequently (monthly or quarterly). This separation enables the specific planned objective levels to be changed more easily and often.

- **Increased Frequency:** Along with this increased Frequency goes a reduction in the duration of deliberations. Each review takes less time because the issues are fresh in everyone's minds and changes tend to be fewer and less dramatic.

- **Not negotiating targets:** Targets, if used, tend to be aspirational i.e. higher than any reasonable outcome. Also, reward is often on the basis of performance taking into consideration the conditions experienced rather than by comparison with originally agreed targets. There is little or no negotiation of targets between levels of management and this dramatically speeds up the whole planning process.

- **Rolling forecasts:** These improve the Forward View. The crucial difference between a rolling forecast and a budget in a budgetary control system is that the rolling forecast is a view of what may actually happen in the future, whereas the budget is a desire. The most useful rolling forecasts look at a range of outcomes and at the events that may cause them.

- **Faster accounting:** In several examples companies have moved closer to real time accounting, which increases Speed.
- **Decentralization:** A few of the case studies include decentralization. In the right circumstances it is possible to increase the total amount of management brain power available by distributing decision-making. Also, if the alternative would be for decisions to be passed up the line for consideration then decentralized decision-making can be faster.

Other methods of increasing management thinking include:

- ergonomics/information design, for example replacing a sea of figures with graphs that directly support the required thinking;
- accelerated forms of risk and uncertainty management;
- multi-level teams to integrate strategic and tactical reviews;
- assembly of solutions from existing components, which is possible when planning is frequent and managers have developed a repertoire of potential action plan ideas;
- legal terms that promote rethinking more frequently; and
- open-ended architectures so that change can be made frequently as a regular part of business rather than by irregular upheaval.

Control patterns for management under uncertainty

The following patterns provide a range of mechanisms for learning and adapting in an agile, proactive, accelerated way.

37   Flexible requirements

Example: An oil refining company employs traders to buy crude oil of various kinds on the open market. Based on their stocks, markets for different oil products, prices for different types of crude, and various other factors the refinery planners calculate what, ideally, they would like to have bought each week. However, it is rarely possible for traders to buy exactly what is in the plan because of moment to moment variations in pricing and availability of crude, so traders are given flexible requirements with guidance that helps them decide, on behalf of the refinery and at high speed, what they will buy.

FLEXIBLE REQUIREMENTS are useful in the many delegation/hand-off situations where what the other party will be able to provide in response to a request is not predictable and so flexibility is required. This is especially true if the parties cannot confer after the request is made or don't think it worth the effort.

Simple, specific, fixed requests stating what we want are natural in everyday life but often give disappointing results when applied in large organizations or indeed any situation where what the other party is able to provide is not predictable.

'Please pass me the butter', 'Could I have two kilos of potatoes?', 'Throw me the big one will you?' These are the sort of simple requests we make all the time in our daily lives. Rarely is there any doubt that the other person is able to provide exactly what we have asked for and if there is a problem they can tell us immediately and we can try again.

Unfortunately, requests on a larger scale at work do not meet these conditions. For example, consider 'Please win four new customers this month', 'Get this ready for the launch date', and 'Buy the barrels listed on this schedule for the prices given'. There is a very real chance that the other person will not win exactly four new customers this month, that being ready by the launch date is not feasible, and market prices will not match those on the schedule.

Thanks to delegation, agency, and partnerships people in organizations frequently make requests (or give orders) where there is considerable uncertainty about what will actually be provided in response. Furthermore, thanks to complexity, overwork, and lack of time the people trying to meet those requests often cannot reply to ask about alternatives.

One response to this problem is to make flexible requests that provide more guidance to the other person. Here are some specific mechanisms for doing that:

- **Vague requests:** Often we tackle this problem by just being vague; for example, 'Don't spend too much'. It works because people have some idea of what these vague phrases mean.
- **Contingent requests:** Last week my wife sent me to the shops and expressed her requirements using a contingency: 'Get two of the blue ones, but if they've only got one blue one then get a blue one and a red one because they're on a two-for-one offer at the moment.'
- **Policies:** If the potential contingencies are complex it may be possible to express a request as a set of policies.
- **Qualities and priorities:** If the contingencies are too complex or too little known we can fall back on expressing our values in some way and trusting the other person to do their best to give us the best value available. One way to do that is to state the qualities we are looking for (e.g. 'soft, strong, not too expensive') and then express priorities (e.g. first, it mustn't be too expensive, and after that I'm more concerned with softness than strength).
- **Value functions:** The qualities and priorities approach often doesn't work very well. For example, if we are looking for 'speed' in a car it may be that this is because a very slow car would be unbearable but as long as the car can go above a certain speed there isn't much to be gained by it being even faster. A more sophisticated way to capture these nuances is to create a 'value function'. This is a mathematical formula (or table) that gives a value in some suitable units for any reasonable combination of performance levels on the qualities of interest. For example, a value function might be something like 'Zero points

if the car can't manage at least 120 km per hour, then a point for each 10 km per hour above that level that it can do up to a maximum of 10 points.' There are many different ways to set up value functions and simple software to help express your views by answering questions about what you want.

In summary, FLEXIBLE REQUIREMENTS give others more information about what we will value so that they can act for us in situations where what they can give us is not entirely predictable and there is limited scope for them to refer back to us for more information. This makes delegation work better in uncertain situations. Therefore:

Write requirements with appropriate flexibility deliberately built in.

A specific aspect of FLEXIBLE REQUIREMENTS involves expressing a value for risk using RISK WEIGHTING. Requirements can be expressed as FLEXIBLE AGREEMENTS and achieving them usually requires FLEXIBLE PLANS.

38   Risk weighting

Example: Large banks are now calculating the cost of operational risk in terms of expected losses and the cost of economic capital required to cover extreme losses from operational risk events. This means that if they can project the implications of action plans for operational risk then they can put a cost on that risk and include the cost along with other money amounts when making decisions.

RISK WEIGHTING is a way of expressing FLEXIBLE REQUIREMENTS about risk and can be used to guide people in any decision, including decisions about controls.

When decision-making under uncertainty is delegated it should be controlled.

In large organizations there is a need to delegate decision-making, including decision-making under risk and uncertainty. This doesn't always bring happy results. For example, when people are worried that their performance is poor (perhaps compared to targets they have been given) they tend to be more willing to take poor risks in the hope of getting lucky and seeing a sharp improvement in results. Usually this makes things worse.

This can be more dangerous if the system for deciding rewards and promotions does not recognize differences in the circumstances under which people work and severely punishes poor performance relative to others even though it is partly caused by those circumstances. For example, the performance of bank branch managers is not directly comparable because some branches have more favourable locations than others. Sales people are given territories or types of customer or product, which again can be inherently different. Indeed it is difficult to think of situations where conditions are not different in some way.

This means that managers working under less favourable conditions are faced with a stark choice: find a way to raise performance despite the circumstances or get the sack. This makes poor risk-taking rational from a manager's point of view because if the manager doesn't take the risk it's the sack anyway. This is thought to have been one of the risk factors at work in Enron.

Clearly, risk is an important factor in decisions and it helps to give it explicit consideration within sensible guidelines.

The control mechanism in RISK WEIGHTING, in its most sophisticated form, is to prescribe (at least partially) the way risk is to be calculated and the way that risk is to be weighted in decision-making. Other forms do not involve explicit consideration of risk but instead focus on limits for risk factors, including behaviour. This can be used in different ways:

- By asking individuals and teams to follow the prescribed approach.
- By applying the prescribed approach when giving approval for actions.
- By measuring performance using the prescribed approach.

Situations where this is relevant include ongoing business activities whose risks and results fluctuate with changing conditions, activities that involve frequent but relatively small investment decisions (e.g. trading in securities), and investments in relatively larger projects where it is possible to give deeper consideration to each investment. It is commonly applied to decision-making about what controls are worthwhile.

There are many examples of weighting risks and they illustrate different approaches:

- 'Risk appetite statements' often include many total bans on specific activities. In effect this is saying that a huge negative weight is attached to the risk arising from those activities.
- 'Risk appetite statements' also contain statements saying that activities or, alternatively, the risk arising from them must not go beyond certain levels. In effect, these say that any extent below the limit is fine, but any extent above the limit has a massive negative weight. Sometimes the implied weighting below the limit is equal for all levels and sometimes it varies with extent of activity/risk.
- Project business cases sometimes include a financial projection using discounted cash flow methods. The discount rate used can depend on risk, or the rate of return required of a project can be adjusted depending on the level of risk.
- Some project business case methods use a risk scorecard of some kind and a crude system of points to reach a risk score, which then feeds into the decision-making in some way.
- A very simple approach is to ask people how much they would be willing to pay for complete mitigation of a (downside) risk. This provides very useful guidance to controls design and Willing To Pay (WTP) protocols have a huge

scientific literature which provides guidance on how to ask the questions and where people usually give good answers.

- In financial services a very widely used approach at a high level is to calculate risk adjusted performance measures, usually Risk Adjusted Return on Capital (RAROC) and sometimes Economic Value Added (EVA).[2]
- Another approach is to charge for capital at a rate that varies with the amount of capital according to a simple formula. The greater the amount of money at risk, the higher the charge rate, reflecting the impact on the risk position of the organization as a whole.
- If alternative courses of action (e.g. investments or sets of investments) are evaluated to give each an estimated return and an estimated risk level then these can be plotted on a scatter graph and most alternatives can usually be eliminated from consideration by very simple logic. A course of action can be taken out of consideration if there is another that offers the same rewards for lower risk, greater rewards for the same risk, or of course greater rewards for less risk. The alternatives that remain after doing this trace out the risk-efficient frontier. Some further judgements are needed to decide between actions on the risk-efficient frontier but this can be done by direct comparisons or by plotting risk-indifference lines i.e. lines that connect points on the scatter graph where combinations of risk and return are equally desirable.

Risk-weighting methods that link risk to weights smoothly are usually better than crude limits. People do not act within a limit just because it is set. They need to feel that more downside risk is worse, even before a very dangerous level is reached. This discourages them from playing the game of spending their risk budget up to the limit on poor risks in the hope of rescuing poor performance. They also need to feel that even for risk levels beyond those their organization will approve, the further they go the worse it is. This again discourages the 'What the heck, I'm in trouble anyway' attitude.

In summary, RISK WEIGHTING gives guidance and/or instruction to people about how to weigh risk in decisions, encouraging effective delegation. If a smooth weighting function is used this encourages sensible decision-making. Therefore:

Devise, agree, and communicate appropriate policies on measuring and weighting risk in decision-making.

There are no subsidiary control patterns to this one in this book.

39   Flexible agreements

Example: Imagine that officers in a local government organization have
developed a plan for improving services to disabled people within their area
that includes 28 initiatives. The council approves this plan for implementation,
but specifies the exact meaning of its approval. Rather than being an
agreement that the plan shall be carried out exactly as written, the approval
is given with the explicit understanding that many of the initiatives are
innovative and their costs and results are uncertain. The plan is approved on
the basis that it will be continually revised in the light of the latest information
about costs and results and changes will be handled in a specified way.

FLEXIBLE AGREEMENTS are often useful in carrying through FLEXIBLE PLANS.

*Sometimes we make an agreement with another party to do something in a certain
way and then someone realizes that there is a way that would be better for both
parties.*

Most likely nobody knows how many agreements are made only for a better idea to
appear later. However, we can be confident it is not as many as would be the case if
people remained open to improvements and carried on looking for them after an
agreement is made, rather than sticking doggedly to the agreement.

Often an agreement is a reason for not exploiting new information and new
ideas that would be beneficial to all parties.

Fortunately there are ways to word agreements so that the flexibility is built in
and defined. Usually this means agreeing a procedure for agreeing future changes
that requires mutual agreement. This means that the gains from a better idea have to
be shared between the parties in some way so that both have an incentive to agree.

This is relevant to internal agreements, such as approvals to do things and inter-
departmental service-level agreements, and to external, contractual agreements.

In summary, FLEXIBLE AGREEMENTS allow better ideas to be exploited and
encourage people to look for those ideas. Therefore:

*Make agreements flexible in specified ways, recognizing that future ideas are likely
to be better ideas.*

There are no subsidiary control patterns to this one in this book.

40   Flexible plans

Example: The risk manager of an international group of companies who wants to implement a new risk database system may well have to make a flexible plan. This will recognize possible differences in willingness and ability to use the system in different countries, potential technical problems with the system itself, and the potential need to make changes to improve the system's usability.

FLEXIBLE PLANS are useful in the many planning situations where the future is not predictable and so flexibility is required. This includes where action is guided by FLEXIBLE REQUIREMENTS.

Fixed, specific plans can seem easier to write and more reassuring, but they rarely last long.

Delays are so common in real life that we tend to assume an implicit flexibility in dates of actions, but this is not as good as explicitly planning with flexibility. Flexibility in all aspects of plans, not just dates, is usually necessary and there are various ways to achieve it. Each of these is an intelligent control mechanism that we can decide to deploy.

- **Leaving things unstated in the plan:** You could leave unstated any combination of details (who, what, when, etc.). Real-life plans do not go down to complete detail on how things are to be done so this form of flexibility is expected; the only question is how much of it is best in a given situation.
- **Stating a plan with alternative paths:** 'If this happens then do that, otherwise do this ...' In the extreme such a plan could look like a computer program in a parallel programming language, with communication between parallel processes, and within each process any combination of sequence, selection, and iteration of actions. In practice we might just suggest some alternative actions and decisions rules in plans to increase their flexibility, or insert some contingency actions.
- **Using policies:** Sometimes it helps to give up on the programming style and construct an approach that is a collection of policies rather than a recipe. Some have suggested that an organization's policies are its DNA and that experience can be used to select the DNA/policies that work.
- **Planning to do more planning:** This is simple and effective. How many plans should have planning activities within them but don't?

In summary, FLEXIBLE PLANS make flexibility more explicit, clarify when flexibility is not allowed, and encourage sensible management in the face of uncertainty. Therefore:

Write plans with appropriate flexibility deliberately built in.

FLEXIBLE PLANS can be realized in a number of ways including EVOLUTIONARY PROJECT MANAGEMENT and THE CRITICAL CHAIN METHOD, which specifically focuses on schedule uncertainty.

41   The critical chain method

Example: A project to build a bridge is naturally high risk because it is rarely possible to deliver useful increments of the bridge and activities follow on in sequence. A builder might estimate the durations for various stages of work but recognize the uncertainty in these estimates. Consequently, the builder could plan flexibly so that a step like road surfacing, for example, can be started later *or earlier* than the schedule depending on the durations of previous steps.

THE CRITICAL CHAIN METHOD is applicable to managing schedule uncertainty for any project where EVOLUTIONARY PROJECT MANAGEMENT either is not applicable at all or does not provide sufficient risk control. It is useful for managing FLEXIBLE PLANS.

Even unbiased task duration estimates can be too high or too low, but without flexibility in executing project activities these estimation errors do not balance out.

This is a good example of a risk analysis based on a model. The model is the project plan. The risks are the uncertain durations of each task on the plan, and the uncertain completion dates of tasks and the project as a whole. How can these uncertainties be managed?

One approach is to pretend you know how long things should or will take and try to keep to that schedule by making adjustments of some kind when things go awry. This has a number of drawbacks and doesn't work very well. It encourages blinkered thinking about the future and the schedule becomes a target rather than a reliable projection. People try to catch up when they fall behind (with only partial success), but ease up if they happen to get ahead of schedule. The result is that it is very rare to finish ahead of schedule.

(A better approach is to represent the uncertainty in plans explicitly, for example by showing the duration range such that you are, say, 80 per cent confident that the task will be finished in the time (neither earlier nor later). Simulation can show the implications for the overall schedule of these uncertainties, summarizing them as the distribution of finish dates for the project as a whole.)

The critical chain approach to this has these elements:

- **Careful analysis of dependencies, considering resource constraints:** The starting point is to draw up the project with tasks and dependencies shown. The critical chain method emphasizes the importance of searching for dependencies created by scarce resources as well as those that arise when an activity cannot be started until another is finished.
- **Durations estimated as a range:** Durations are estimated as a range and to get a 50 per cent confidence duration i.e. the duration such that you are 50 per cent confident of finishing within that time.
- **Plans based on 50 per cent estimates:** Plans are drawn initially with times set at the 50 per cent confidence level, but with the understanding that dates are uncertain.
- **Buffers at the end of the project and before tasks that feed into the critical chain:** Some tasks will be done in less time than expected, and some will take more time. A time buffer is inserted after the final task in the project plan to show the overall buffer. Where tasks feed into the critical chain and, if delayed sufficiently, could delay the overall project, a time buffer is inserted between the tributary and the critical chain. The intention is to cut the risk of delaying the overall project.
- **Starting tasks as early as possible, not simply when the schedule says they should start:** Tasks start as soon as possible. If tasks only start on schedule or later (due to delays) then the overall project is almost certain to be delayed. If it is hard to get flexibility in timing then more analysis may be needed to identify when having the flexibility to start earlier if possible is most useful and worth pushing for.

In summary, this is a well-thought out method for managing schedule uncertainty in projects with significant dependencies. Therefore:

Estimate each task duration as a range but use the 50 per cent confidence-level durations for the central project plan. Organize to be ready to start tasks earlier than scheduled as well as later and manage the time buffers.

There are no subsidiary control patterns to this one in this book.

42   Evolutionary project management

Example: A Norwegian company providing online research services improved the usability and other qualities of its reporting software by a series of fortnightly increments, each time measuring their progress. They dramatically improved the usability, lowered training requirements, and delighted their customers.

EVOLUTIONARY PROJECT MANAGEMENT is applicable to virtually any project or continuous improvement process.

The bigger a project the bigger its risk of failure.

Big projects fail more often, but if you can efficiently restructure a big project into lots of smaller projects the overall downside risk is dramatically reduced and the upside risk is boosted.

Almost anything that can be thought of as a form of project (or process improvement) is an opportunity to apply Evolutionary Project Management (Evo for short), and the more difficult and risky the project the greater the benefit of doing so.

Although we're used to the idea that a project is a big, dramatic change the problem is that investing resources for months or even years without having anything useful delivered until the end is taking a big chance. What if our initial idea for what we needed turns out to be wrong?

It is much better to rethink our project as a series of smaller deliveries, and rethink the rest of our project each time we deliver something and see how it performs.

The idea that a project is a long build-up to a single delivery comes from the roots of project management itself in construction and space projects. It's hard to see how you can incrementally deliver a bridge or a man on the moon. Until you have a bridge that you can use or a man on the moon you have nothing but a lot of expenditure.

However, computer projects are usually different. It's quite possible to deliver a system in stages, or to roll it out gradually. Indeed, this happens to just about all systems because at some point in their lives they move from 'development' to 'maintenance'. 'Maintenance' means that the pace of changes and enhancements has slowed down and become business as usual.

Not surprisingly it is in the world of IT projects that the philosophy of incremental delivery has blossomed over the last few decades. For example, the Dynamic Systems Development Method (DSDM) is based on the simple idea that delivering what was required is *not* the objective of the project. The true objective is to deliver what is required at the time of delivery, which of course may be rather different from the original requirements.

Evo, devised by Tom Gilb, is the form of incremental delivery that has gone furthest in spreading from the IT world to be applied to any project. Three key ideas in Evo are these:

- **Incremental delivery:** The project is divided up into (ideally) 50 deliveries of value to at least one stakeholder, which are delivered in sequence so that the delay between each delivery is kept small (a matter of several weeks at most). Delivering something to the next stage of a project (e.g. a technical specification) does not count as a delivery of value. There is usually a need for some 'back room' work to set up an open ended architecture that makes incremental delivery efficient.

- **Evolving requirements and plans:** One of the major advantages of delivering something is that you can learn from people using it. Another is that you learn quickly what it takes to make a delivery in the project. To capitalize on this learning it is important to review and revise the remaining project plan after each delivery.
- **Performance characteristics:** The improvements we want as a result of the project are defined in terms of measurable scales called 'performance characteristics'. The idea is that these are scales of degree, not simple success/fail criteria. This mental shift makes it possible to think of just about any project in terms of incremental improvements. For example, the objective 'Put a man on the moon' is not helpful to incremental delivery because until a man gets on the moon (a tough thing to do) we've delivered nothing. In contrast improving on 'Knowledge of space travel' and 'Knowledge of the moon' is easy to think of in incremental terms, and while we're about it why not aim for more 'Useful applications of space travel' as well. This kind of objective is perhaps not so good for election year speeches but it is good for the space programme.

    Tom Gilb's Impact Estimation tables help to judge the impact of potential deliveries on the performance characteristics and resources.

EVOLUTIONARY PROJECT MANAGEMENT does not mean plunging in and making it up as you go along. It is a highly disciplined method of incremental delivery that drastically improves the risk profile of most projects.

Evo or variations on it is used by a number of top companies and is the preferred approach to acquisition projects for the United States Department of Defense.

In summary, Evo has a dramatic positive impact on the risk profile of nearly all projects and is probably the most important control pattern that exists for managing projects. Therefore:

Manage projects and process improvement using evolutionary project management. Identify a large number of incremental deliveries of value to stakeholders and measure their impact as they are delivered in rapid succession. Review the remaining plan of increments in each cycle based on the latest information and ideas.

EVOLUTIONARY PROJECT MANAGEMENT requires frequent revisions of expectations, which can be done using REFORECASTING TO COMPLETION.

43   Portfolio management

Example: A manufacturer of chocolate bars might view its products as a portfolio, monitoring the returns from each product, introducing new products, and removing failing products. It might also view launches of new products as another exercise in portfolio management. It expects each product to be a failure, because most are, but it continues investing in new launches because some of them are, against the odds, successful. The performance of the portfolio is what matters, not individual products alone.

PORTFOLIO MANAGEMENT is useful when you have a collection of investments whose performance is at least partly unpredictable and uncontrollable.

In percentage terms, individual success is less predictable than collective results.

Techniques and theory developed to help investors make money from shares and other securities have wider applications.

The portfolio management perspective is applicable in far more situations than most people realize and helps to tame our worries about individual failures. It is especially helpful in situations where individual investments typically have a low chance of success.

For example, a local authority given the task of improving education in its schools might have scores of ideas for improvements but will usually lack hard information about which will work and to what extent. Even costs may be difficult to estimate accurately. If it views each idea as part of a portfolio it can see them as a set of experiments from which the successful ideas will be identified for further exploitation while others will be dropped.

There are two statistical effects at work in portfolio management.

Diversification is simply not putting all your eggs in one basket. If you invest your money in a mix of different securities the variance of returns from those investments will be lower than if you had invested the same money in just one security, provided the returns of the securities in the diversified portfolio are not perfectly positively correlated.

In the language of finance, the mix of 'risk' (i.e. variance of returns) and returns is better if you diversify.

Curiously enough, if you could divide your money between two securities that were perfectly *negatively* correlated the variance of returns from your portfolio would be zero. Rises in one share would always be tracked by falls in the other. In practice, this is not achievable in real stock markets so investors usually hold between 15 and 20 securities and cannot diversify away the variance resulting from overall economic cycles.

The diversification principles apply to other situations, such as portfolios of projects or the performance of sales people. (1) The variation of performance of the whole portfolio is less than the variation in individual items, *in percentage terms*. (2) Combinations that tend to be affected in opposite ways by the same factors have results that are more predictable overall, though not necessarily higher on average.

Rebalancing is the inevitable consequence of trying to maintain a portfolio with the same balance of different types of security. From time to time, securities whose price has risen are sold and securities whose price has fallen are bought, so that the total value of securities of each type returns to the original ratios. This tends to increase returns through buying low and selling high, even though it may involve buying more of securities that are falling for good reasons and will fall further.

In other portfolio situations, like projects, rebalancing is still necessary but your policy will be different. Whereas in securities markets it is not known which direction the price will go next, in real projects you know that a failing project is not something you want to invest more into, so your rebalancing policy should be different. Typically, although you need to be experimenting with new items in your portfolio, ones that are going well should get more investment while ones that are not should get less.

In summary, portfolio management is a powerful way to exploit statistical effects and applicable to many situations outside stock markets. Therefore:

Identify populations of similar investments and manage them as portfolios, rebalancing according to appropriate policies.

There are no subsidiary control patterns to this one in this book.

44   Negative feedback control loops

Example: A charity, wishing to balance its expenditure with its income, will usually try to keep the difference between the two within a narrow range year by year and can do this by setting a target 'surplus' then monitoring its results month by month and making adjustments to its plans over time to keep the surplus steering towards the target.

NEGATIVE FEEDBACK CONTROL LOOPS are useful at many levels of an organization in situations that are relatively stable and where actions are available that will keep moving results towards a target.

Some things are hard to anticipate but easy to adjust for when they happen.

A thermostat is a negative feedback control loop. You simply set the temperature you want and the device compares the actual temperature with the target to decide on an action to reduce the difference. ('Negative' just means that the feedback reduces the difference.) The same idea is often relied on in organizations and some management textbooks even go so far as to state that management control is no more or less than setting clear targets, holding them fixed for a year or so, and motivating subordinates to reduce the difference between actual and target values.

Negative feedback control loops have often been seen as a way of managing uncertainty about the future in organizations, and they are, but they are far less widely effective than generally thought and in most business situations other techniques are preferable. Problems with negative feedback as a control mechanism in organizations include the following:

- **Assumption that an effective action exists:** The logic of negative feedback control seems persuasive until you realize that it rests on the assumption that there is some action that will get you 'back on track' when something unexpected happens. In practice this is rarely the case in business situations. Typically we are constrained on quality, deadline, and resources so if we get into trouble we can usually do no better than limit the damage by trading off our priorities.

  Example from auditing: During my training as an auditor all audit work was to a predetermined budget, usually derived by taking the agreed overall fee/cost and dividing it between tasks in what seemed, at the outset, to be a reasonable way. If progress seemed slower than expected so a budget over-run had occurred or was feared on a part of the audit then the team leader would scold the offending person for getting 'bogged down' and warn everyone else not to get 'bogged down' before saying we would have to 'find some efficiencies'.

  Audit work is fully constrained and usually if things start to go badly it is because the work that needs to be done is messier and more complex than originally thought. If you fall behind the chances are that you will fall further behind as the work progresses unless you are prepared to accept less evidence or blow the budget. Since team leaders do not want to overspend the true meaning of 'find efficiencies' is 'convince ourselves we don't need so much evidence'.

- **Purely reactive:** One reason there is rarely a way to get back on track is that negative feedback loops are purely reactive. We have to wait for a difference between desired and actual results before anything different happens. By that stage it is often too late. Other methods for coping with future uncertainty that involve looking ahead at potential future events are better in this respect than negative feedback loops.
- **Failure to adjust targets:** One characteristic of negative feedback control is that the target is held constant. This is an artificial constraint and people usually find it easier to adjust targets as well as action plans as new information is obtained. There has to be a compelling reason for trying to hold to a target to compensate for the disadvantages.
- **Effect on behaviour:** When people are motivated to achieve some agreed and fixed target, rather than to act in the best interests of the organization, they close their minds to uncertainties and focus on their personal interests. People play games to meet targets. They begin to confuse targets with what will actually happen. They stop questioning whether the target is still appropriate.

The more variable and unpredictable actual results are the harder it is to make NEGATIVE FEEDBACK CONTROL LOOPS work. Stable, predictable results are more common with very large organizations, by the law of large numbers, so this is where budgetary control systems, for example, are most often found. Small organizations and small teams within larger organizations tend to rely on different controls.

In short, negative feedback loops are fine in situations where the task they perform is simple and unchallenging and the loop itself has very little intelligence. A thermostat is an ideal example, but a division of a company is not.

Responsiveness can be improved by resetting targets more frequently. Therefore:

Provided actions exist that will bring things back 'on track' and the anticipatory control is not worth the effort, set clear targets, monitor actual results against targets, and take actions to reduce variances.

NEGATIVE FEEDBACK CONTROL LOOPS can be made more responsive by using ACCELERATED TARGETS.

45   Accelerated targets

Example: Suppose that targets are used to direct and motivate the sales force of an office supplies company. There are targets for individuals and also for different customer segments and product types reflecting the company's views on where sales people should concentrate their efforts. After relying on annual targets for some time the company gets fed up with the game playing involved and the continual complaints that the targets are obsolete almost as soon as they have been agreed. They move from annual targets to quarterly targets and cut down the negotiation process to something less time consuming. They then move to monthly target revisions, finding that each revision is easy and less contentious when less rides on it.

ACCELERATED TARGETS make NEGATIVE FEEDBACK CONTROL LOOPS more adaptive.

Adjusting targets more often could lead to more time being spent on debating and communicating targets and to more manipulation and evasion of targets, but it doesn't.

It is obvious that targets (with the possible exception of some relative targets) get obsolete eventually and need to be revised. When targets are out of date resources are wasted trying to do things that are no longer a good aim. Perhaps people ease off because conditions have improved but the target has not been raised. Perhaps they take unnecessary risks trying to hit a target that is no longer feasible.

There are two things that can be done to accelerate targets.

- Shorten the period of time to which each target applies. For example, a target for annual sales might be changed to 12 targets for monthly sales.

- Quicken the frequency of revisions to targets. For example, an annual target might go from being revised annually to being revised quarterly.

It is hard to judge how often targets should be revised and what period of time they should apply to. However, most organizations could benefit from acceleration.

Partly this is because we tend to have a blinkered view of the future and so undervalue flexibility and responsiveness. We think the targets will be relevant longer than is actually the case.

It may also be because we think the target revisions will be time consuming and unpleasant. Some annual target setting processes take months to complete and involve emotionally charged and drawn out negotiations. This is hardly surprising as it is often pay and promotions that are at stake. It is not unheard of for budget discussions to begin months before the year for which the budget will apply, to conclude after the year has already begun, and for the budget to be obsolete from the moment it comes into force. The thought of going through this process more than once a year is unattractive.

However, if targets are revised more often the effort and pain of each revision are reduced. To take an extreme case, suppose annual target sets were revised weekly. What would happen? There would be much less riding on each round of target setting. Instead of negotiating the year's bonus in one go people would be negotiating a tiny fraction of it. Instead of having to make guesses about things that might happen in a year's time people would usually be looking forward less time than that. Instead of following a complex procedure they haven't seen for almost a year they would be following a simpler procedure that they last followed a week ago. Targets would usually be changed by only small amounts if at all.

What about manipulation? Would frequent opportunities to revise targets allow people to erode the challenge in targets, gradually grinding ambition away? It's possible, if allowed to happen, but unlikely. Gaming is encouraged by lack of information. If everything is subjective guesswork negotiating power takes over. However, if there is more information to go on and less guessing to do, as with frequent revisions over shorter time periods, it is easier to base target setting on facts and harder to manipulate it.

In summary, ACCELERATED TARGETS is a way for organizations to become more adaptive gradually and can be taken further than most people imagine. Therefore:

Find ways to set targets for shorter periods of time and revise them more often.
Simplify and refine the process of revising targets.

There are no subsidiary control patterns to this one in this book.

46   Reforecasting to completion

Example: A marketing research company that does multi-stage research for its customers might find that large research projects involve significant uncertainties and, while customers usually have budgets that limit their expenditure, there is some flexibility in what is done in response to findings from initial research. To discuss research plans with customers it could track expenses and results during projects and periodically revise plans to estimate the cost to complete the work currently envisaged. It would discuss this information with its customers and show them the implications of alternative plans to completion.

REFORECASTING TO COMPLETION is relevant on projects where there is some flexibility but still an interest in managing overall costs and results. It is especially useful where expectations are frequently revised, such as when using EVOLUTIONARY PROJECT MANAGEMENT.

Often we need to have conversations about how to complete a project because of new information or ideas.

These conversations are usually far more productive if everyone involved can see immediately the implications for costs and results of doing things in different ways. Decades ago this kind of calculation would have been too slow to do during a conversation but today's computer spreadsheets make it easy.

Ideally the forecasts will give estimates as ranges rather than best guesses, and wider ranges will reflect lack of clear ideas for action, among other things. It is dangerous to allow people to work with best guesses on the grounds that they are sure they will think of something to make those numbers happen. People are usually overconfident of their estimates and believe they have more control than they really do.

The steps involved are as follows:

- Track actual costs and other results of interest at least as frequently as you need to re-plan and reforecast (which will be more often than most people think).
- Create a spreadsheet model of the project's costs and other results of interest in such a way that these are computed automatically from a representation of the project plan and this can be changed quickly and easily. For example, the work might be broken into lots of small activities, each with an estimated cost against it. These can be added or deleted from the model quickly giving revised total costs immediately.
- Periodically combine actual costs and results to date with a projection for the remaining project done using the model and the latest plan to give overall costs and results.
- Discuss the plan with others who are interested and use the model to explore alternative courses of action before deciding what to do.
- Communicate the revised plans and forecasts.

In summary, this control pattern makes forecasts useful and encourages sensible conversations about actions rather than mere negotiations about targets. Therefore:

> *Track actual costs and results to date and estimate future costs and other results of interest to completion under the latest plan. Discuss alternative plans and use a computer model to estimate their implications for costs and results. Repeat periodically.*

The work of reforecasting can sometimes be reduced by FORECASTING WITH STATISTICAL EXTRAPOLATION.

47   Forecasting with statistical extrapolation

> *Example*: A company that hires audio visual equipment for use at conferences and in companies found that asking sales managers and other managers for forecast financial numbers was time consuming and rarely accurate, but statistical extrapolation from past results was more reliable and less subject to manipulation and bias. They were then in a position to move to an approach that combined statistical extrapolation with judgements and plans input by managers.

FORECASTING WITH STATISTICAL EXTRAPOLATION is useful for forecasting and as a comparator that allows managers to review critically and challenge forecasts submitted by other managers. This control is only applicable where the results are sufficiently regular. It can be used in REFORECASTING TO COMPLETION.

> *If you have a history of past results and a computer then reforecasting by statistical extrapolation is quick and easy.*

A forecast made by statistical extrapolation is a forecast that uses mathematics to guess what the future will be like assuming it is similar to the past. Similarity to the past can be quite sophisticated, picking up cycles, trends, and variability. There are many different formulae that could be used, though happily studies of accuracy in practical use tend to show that it is the simplest methods (e.g. exponentially smoothed moving averages) that tend to work best.

If you break a number down and forecast each component then a slightly better forecast may result, with some types of extrapolation, but usually the advantage is slight so it makes sense to work with numbers that are already summarized enough to fit on a spreadsheet.

Calculating statistical extrapolations is very easy and quick compared to asking lots of managers to give their best estimate of their contribution to an overall result.

Also, formulae do not try to manipulate expectations or suffer from secret biases. In addition, statistical extrapolations should reflect an overview of all relevant data from which regular patterns can be seen, whereas individual managers tend to see only part of the picture so things look less regular to them. On the other hand, formulae do not understand about unrepresentative events in the past or future changes or plans.

Experience shows that statistical extrapolations are more accurate and reliable than we like to admit, and often more reliable and accurate than human estimates even though the human estimator has access to more information.

The performance of a statistical extrapolation formula can be tested by seeing what it would have predicted for numbers you now know. If you have, say, two years of past numbers and need six months of data for the rule to make an extrapolation then that gives 18 months where extrapolations can be compared with actuals.

This analysis can also be used to calculate prediction intervals. A prediction interval is a range around a predicted number that indicates how likely it is that the actual value, when known, will be near to the predicted number. For example, looking back at past forecasts and actuals may show that 90 per cent of the time the forecast has been right to within plus or minus 5 per cent. Plus or minus 5 per cent would then be a good choice of prediction interval.

Prediction intervals should always be given. They remind readers that the forecast is only a forecast, not a fact, and they quantify the uncertainty involved.

Statistical extrapolations can be used to review and challenge estimates submitted. If an estimate seems very much out of line with the extrapolation then that means the person who made the estimate thinks things are going to be very different in future. Why? They need to be able to give some good reasons for that, especially if they have an obvious motive for trying to manipulate expectations.

A statistical extrapolation that is giving results comparable with adding up human estimates can usefully replace those estimates because it will be easier and quicker to do and its weaknesses can be understood.

However, there is one more problem to solve that is at the heart of making forecasting valuable. A forecasting model should allow users to try alternative action plans and see what the implications for results might be. A statistical extrapolation on its own does not allow that.

Fortunately, there is a simple way to add this functionality to a statistical extrapolation and so combine the ease of these forecasts with the engagement and what-if capability of other forecasting methods.

The technique is to create lists of 'variations' i.e. events or actions that are either unrepresentative blips in the past history or are actions planned or events anticipated in the future that will be different from normal past practice. Against each of these the impact for results (e.g. costs) needs to be estimated period by period. Software then:

1. runs through the variations erasing blips from past history;
2. re-extrapolates; and then
3. adds future variations to the new extrapolation to produce the final forecast.

Past history, the raw extrapolation, and the projection incorporating variations can be shown using time series line graphs. This makes reviews and conversations easier because everyone can see how the forward numbers compare to the past and what impact doing things differently is expected to have.

With this technique discussions of what-if forecasts can focus on what actions will be different and what their implications will be. It is only necessary to consider variations for important items.

This means that the statistical extrapolation still takes away a lot of the drudgery of forecasting but gives freedom to adjust though in a way that is easy to review and challenge.

The usual alternative that most managers will be familiar with is one person adjusting aspirational numbers in a bunch of budget spreadsheets and then another person hunting through trying to find out what they have done. All of this happens without ever having to discuss how actions will be different.

In summary, this control cuts the cost of forecasting and helps reduce gaming by forecasters. Therefore:

Test the possibility of using statistical extrapolation for forecasting and if the data support it then use this in combination with human input.

There are no subsidiary control patterns to this one in this book.

Notes

1   A small selection of these cases is reported in their book: Hope, J., and Fraser, R. (2003) *Beyond Budgeting*. Cambridge, MA: Harvard Business School Press.

2   According to recent surveys risk-adjusted performance measures are about as common in financial services as risk appetite statements (laying down a list of limits). Deloitte's fifth Global Risk Management survey found that 66 per cent of their sample of large institutions around the world had a formal statement of overall risk appetite, while PRMIA's global survey, 'Risk Adjusted Performance Measurement', found that 44 per cent of organizations were already using risk adjusted performance measures and a further 45 per cent were in various stages of planning to. Both surveys were conducted in the latter part of 2006 and published in 2007.

9 *Protection and Inherent Reliability*

Many traditional internal controls are checks on data or processing, but it is usually cheaper and better to stop things going wrong than to detect and correct problems later.

The two main ways to do this are to improve protection and inherent reliability.

- *Protection* aims to minimize possible contact between hazardous things (e.g. people) and the process or asset to be protected.
- *Inherent reliability* aims to create a process or system that does not go wrong often, at least when protected.

Controls that do these things are not quite the same as 'preventive controls'. Traditionally, 'preventive controls' refers to controls done to prevent errors getting into a computer system and may include checks on data just before they are entered on the system.

Protection involves using barriers and other techniques to keep hazards away from precious assets, including information.

Inherent reliability involves removing reasons for errors by techniques like removing or preventing software bugs, by simplification, ergonomic improvements, and automation. Ideally the impact of all these efforts is measured and the process continues relentlessly towards extremely low error rates.

This chapter is relatively short, but not because protection and inherent reliability are unimportant. Usually they are the best type of control to focus on, long term, and everything else is just something done to survive until they are in place or to manage progress towards high inherent reliability and protection.

The control patterns start here.

48   Multi-layered access restriction

Example: A typical building used by a large company has a special room for the most important computer systems, with powerful air conditioning and other protective features, and a locked door. Only a few people have access to that room and to certain computer consoles with very special access. Beyond the computer room lie offices for employees of the company and getting into these offices means passing a security barrier. Elsewhere is an area of meeting rooms that has more visitors from outside. Getting into the building at all involves passing from the public part of the reception area to the private part via another security barrier. These physical barriers are complemented by barriers in accessing computer systems, even when this is done remotely via networks.

MULTI-LAYERED ACCESS RESTRICTION should always be attempted in some form and in large organizations should be carried through rigorously and in detail.

Access must be restricted but some people need access in their work.

Restricting access to data and assets requires a multi-layered approach in two senses:

1. the journey from the outside world to a precious asset involves moving past several natural barriers; and
2. multiple control mechanisms are usually used at each of these barriers.

The idea of multiple barriers is familiar. If we imagine moving from outside an organization to some precious data inside it the objective of protection by access restriction is to minimize the number of people who have access beyond each barrier without undue inconvenience to people with a legitimate need for access. The number of people with access will usually get smaller as we pass through the following stages:

- Access to the organization's computer network(s) from outside computer/ telecommunications networks.
- Access to buildings.
- Access to sections of buildings and to specific rooms. (Computer operations rooms usually have very limited access.)
- Sitting at a terminal or personal computer.
- Getting the terminal or personal computer switched on.
- Logging onto the terminal or personal computer.
- Access to the corporate network from an internal computer.
- Access to sections of the corporate network.
- Access to particular servers on the network.
- Access to particular software applications.
- Access to particular data files on a server.
- Access to particular data records and functionality within a software application.

In the interests of efficiency a controls designer may choose to impose no additional access restriction at some of these stages, but the implications of doing so should be understood.

Computer security is an interesting but complex area with a lot of abstract jargon. To understand the idea of multiple control techniques at each barrier I think it helps to approach it from a more familiar and tangible point of view. Imagine you have a collection of valuable gold coins with historical value – treasure in fact – and keep them in your home. How could you secure the coins?

- Make it hard to steal the coins.
  - Hide the fact that the coins exist and are in your home.
  - Hide your home or, more sensibly, hide the coins.
  - Keep the coins in a locked strong box, in a built-in safe, in a locked room, and keep the doors and windows of the house locked whenever possible. Have strong locks and strong doors, windows, and walls.
  - Have as few copies of keys as possible.
  - Entrust keys to as few people as possible and choose those people carefully.
  - Have an alarm system installed that is sensitive to movement, body heat, and opening doors and windows.
  - Supervise legitimate visitors at all times.

- Make it hard to get away with it.
  - Use recorded CCTV at all times so that it is harder for someone to break in and get away without being identified. Put an exploding paint bomb in the strongbox so that anyone opening the box will be marked.
  - Hide among the coins a radio device that will allow the collection to be tracked if stolen.
  - Mark every coin with invisible identification chemicals.
  - Have a record of every coin in the collection and store it, hidden, separately from the coins themselves. Be ready to make this list available to the police immediately a theft occurs.

- Make it hard to profit from theft.
  - Separate the collection into two or three parts and store each separately, dividing the coins in such a way that *sets* of coins that are more valuable together are stored separately.
  - Have the coins etched with a tiny mark that identifies them as your property.

All these physical techniques have computer equivalents. An effective control system needs to use at least a handful of them at each level of access to be effective.

For example, a lot of emphasis is placed on passwords (rightly) but there are disappointing limits to their effectiveness. The more you encourage people to use passwords that are hard to guess and change them frequently the more often people will write them down, making them easier to discover.

One way to think about password strength is to calculate the maximum rate of password guessing that would be possible for a cracker who knew the rules. For example, suppose that a password barrier is set up so that users are locked out for

24 hours if they enter an incorrect password three consecutive times in a 60-minute period and there are 25 user profiles that are set up but no longer used. The system allows a person to log on only once and will report attempts to log on twice.

In this situation a cracker's best approach is to guess twice an hour on each of the 25 safe user profiles. The maximum guessing rate is 50 guesses per hour – during working hours at least.

On this basis most ordinary business security arrangements that I have seen allow guessing at surprisingly high rates. If you do an audit test by running a suitable cracker's dictionary file against a password file you can find out how many guesses it takes to crack a password in the file and so estimate how long it would take to break in.

Another common weakness is to focus on passwords but not monitor for attempted and successful break-ins. In effect, this is focusing on making theft hard but forgetting to make it hard for the thief to get away with it.

In summary, MULTI-LAYERED ACCESS RESTRICTION is a way to structure protection controls and stimulates thinking widely about possible combinations of controls. Therefore:

Design protection to have multiple barriers and use multiple controls at each barrier to get a good balance between security and convenience.

One of the most complex parts of this pattern is to manage the access rights of many individuals and this can be done using SEGREGATION RULES ON ROLES.

49   Segregation rules on roles

Example: Implementing a new ERP system involves deciding who has access to what functionality and data. This can be done in terms of roles and general rules about their access, from which specific access profiles can be derived.

SEGREGATION RULES ON ROLES is useful when deciding roles as part of MULTI-LAYERED ACCESS RESTRICTION and where the goal is to segregate duties appropriately.

Segregation of duties is a traditional protection control against fraud, but it has its problems.

Segregation of duties is a traditional internal control that combats fraud by preventing individuals from being able to do all the things that a fraud requires. For example, a person who can set up accounts for suppliers would usually be prevented from approving supplier invoices for payment. If a person could do both it would be harder to prevent them setting up a fake supplier, sending in fake invoices, then approving payment to their fake supplier i.e. themselves.

However, segregation of duties can create some big problems.

- If a job has to be split between several people then several people need to be employed to do the job. Perhaps there is not enough work to keep them all efficiently busy.
- If a job has to be split between several people then this creates more hand-offs and these can lead to communication delays, errors, and overall loss of time and efficiency. A common pattern in business process reengineering is to create case workers who do every part of a job, eliminating hand-offs. Segregation of duties can be inconvenient and frustrating, especially in small organizations.
- Managing segregation of duties for large numbers of people in modern software systems can be complex, skilled work. In the leading ERP packages (i.e. packages that do just about everything like SAP and Oracle Applications) it is possible to set up fantastically detailed and complicated profiles, though this takes a long time and is difficult to maintain. Sometimes software does not offer good programs for managing segregation of duties.

Although segregation of duties to some extent is unavoidable in an effective control system it can be reduced by relying more on other controls instead. For example, sometimes it is possible to compare individuals who all do the same job using analytics (PERSONAL COMPARATIVES) that reveal suspicious behaviour. Also, RANDOM FRAUD AUDITS create a deterrent at controllable cost.

SEGREGATION RULES ON ROLES is a technique for specifying segregation of duties rules in a way that makes them easier to understand and design.

It is obvious that segregation rules should be written that refer to jobs rather than to named individuals, because segregation requirements are related to the nature of jobs, not to the individuals who happen to occupy them.

What is less obvious is that recognizing a small set of generic roles in jobs helps to understand and specify segregation rules.

There are a number of bases for segregation and some can be used in combination. These are the most common, written in a notation suited to high-level design work:

- custodian of asset DOES NOT keep records of the asset
- record keeper DOES NOT check the records
- checker of the records DOES NOT review the checks
- approver DOES NOT enter data
- person who enters reference data DOES NOT enter transaction data
- contract maker DOES NOT raise/receive invoices
- raiser/receiver of invoices DOES NOT handle receipts/payments.

It is rarely appropriate to apply all the bases at the same time. Choose the most appropriate and vary the tightness depending on the risks and scope for alternative controls. When designing controls in detail, interpret the rules according to the job roles that exist or are being considered.

In summary, SEGREGATION RULES ON ROLES makes it easier to derive specific access profiles from a much smaller set of design decisions and provides a way of writing succinct policies. Therefore:

Define roles and the bases for segregation that are applicable in different situations, and from these derive specific access profiles.

There are no subsidiary control patterns to this one in this book.

50   Cognitive ergonomics

Example: The design of road signs in most developed countries is carefully standardized and internally consistent. New designs are often tested to make sure their meaning is either obvious without explanation or, in the worst case, easy to learn. Imagine the carnage if this effort was not made.

COGNITIVE ERGONOMICS should always be an important area of a control scheme.

Ultimately nearly everything that goes wrong in a system is directly or indirectly due to human error, so design it out.

Ergonomics is the most overlooked yet most important subject in internal controls design.

Almost all errors arise, directly or indirectly, because of human error. Mis-coded transactions, bugs in software, a wrong VAT code entered – all human error. Even a computer hardware failure comes from the mistakes of the engineers who designed the robot that built the component. Training helps, but ergonomic improvements are more effective and far more cost-effective.

Some human errors are outside your control because they happened too long ago, are outside the company, or are caused by something you cannot change. However, there are many errors you can reduce by paying attention to ergonomics. It is also vital to consider ergonomics when designing the details of internal controls.

The main tool in ergonomics is redesign driven by usability testing.

The following information comes from Thomas K. Landauer's book[1] and is derived from a series of studies of usability testing in practice:

- User-centred design typically cuts errors in user-system interactions from 5 per cent down to 1 per cent, and reduces training time by 25 per cent.

- The average interface has around 40 usability defects in need of repair. (Typically, about 50 per cent of flaws found get fixed successfully.)
- Two usability evaluations or user tests usually will find half the flaws; six will find almost 90 per cent. This work will only take a day or two.
- After six tests, one can estimate accurately the number of remaining flaws and the rate at which they are being found.
- Usability assessment has very large benefits relative to cost. The work efficiency effect of a software system can be expected to improve by around 25 per cent as a result of a single day of usability testing. Intensive user-centred design efforts have typically improved efficiency effects by about 50 per cent. (However, fundamentally flawed system specifications can lead to minimal gains from user-centred design.)
- While specialists are better at usability design and at finding flaws, both systematic inspections and user tests can be done effectively by people with modest training.

These results, and experience as well, indicate that usability testing can reduce the difficulty and time for development while contributing dramatically to quality.

Jakob Nielsen[2] surveyed a wide range of usability testing techniques. These do *not* include releasing a beta test version and going ahead if nobody complains bitterly enough! The most important techniques include:

- Thinking aloud – a representative user is asked to perform representative asks using the software and says aloud what they are thinking as they do so. This can give insights into confusions that did not lead to an error for that person but would lead some people to make errors at least some of the time.
- Retrospective testing – after the user has finished a task the experimenter asks them to go back over the experience and report the problems and confusions they experienced.
- Coaching approach – the user performs the tasks as usual, but can ask for explanations or instructions if they get into difficulty. This helps to identify the information that would improve the user interface.
- Heuristic evaluation – this is different in that there is no user and no task. Reviewers inspect the interface in detail using a checklist of common usability faults as a guide.

Most work on usability is concerned with the design of new software. However, this is only one area where usability improvements are an important control. Here are some others:

- paper forms e.g. order forms
- computer reports from a report generator
- Perl and other scripts used by IT support people to make things happen behind the scenes
- spreadsheets
- scripted conversations e.g. in a call centre

- reference data wording e.g. the descriptions of items in a product catalogue
- workstation comfort and lighting
- readability of written instructions and crib sheets e.g. the product code sheets commonly seen at tills in shops, safety regulations, emails from the accounts department about how to claim your expenses.

If monitoring stats show errors arising then the most important action is usually to find out exactly where and why the errors occur. Typically, confusing design of something is the culprit and the cure is to improve the design so it helps people get things right instead of tricking them into getting it wrong.

Individual controls need to be designed with human factors in mind. For example, imagine a control that calls for someone to read computer reports looking for items that look suspicious and check them. If the report is long and suspicious items are very rare then even the most motivated and highly trained person will glaze over after a while and miss items they should have noticed. The control is ergonomically infeasible. It could be improved by designing a report that searches for suspicious items, or sorts items in a particular way that makes the search easier.

A very common mistake is to rely on people to spot errors in situations where they don't have enough time or information at hand to do it reliably.

In summary, there is overwhelming evidence that many errors are driven by human error and that usability techniques can reduce this cost-effectively. Therefore:

Invest in cognitive ergonomics wherever possible. Design, test, repeat, and repeat again to minimize the mental difficulty of doing jobs correctly.

There are no subsidiary control patterns to this one in this book.

Notes

1   Landauer, T.K. (1996) *The Trouble with Computers*. Cambridge, MA: MIT Press.
2   Neilsen, J. (1993) *Usability Engineering*. San Francisco, CA: Morgan Kaufmann Publishers.

10 *Checking and Correcting*

We have now worked our way down from intelligent controls that generate other controls, through management monitoring and other controls for managing under uncertainty, through protection and inherent reliability, to reach the lowest and most traditional form of controls: checks on data and processes.

Yet, even here, there is immense scope for improved value, typically through automation.

The control patterns start now.

51   Spreadsheet tightening or replacement

> *Example*: An organization trading in commodities found it relied heavily on a large number of spreadsheets that had been developed over a period of years and supported decisions involving vast sums of money. It created a team to replace those spreadsheets where appropriate and improve the others to make them clearer, easier to change, and better at flagging errors.

SPREADSHEET TIGHTENING OR REPLACEMENT is applicable to virtually any computerized spreadsheet, but especially to ones that are important.

We need computer spreadsheets but make errors creating and using them.

It is often said that computer spreadsheets are a control problem. It is true that there are some serious problems to deal with but spreadsheets also have some tremendous advantages from a broader risk control perspective. Spreadsheets are flexible and accessible. They allow people to use control techniques that would not be available economically any other way. Spreadsheets are great.

Unfortunately, a lot of spreadsheets contain errors,[1] and some are large and important. Spreadsheets get developed in informal ways by people with no training in software design and development. Some spreadsheets implement mathematical techniques incorrectly and, for example, incorrect net present value discounting is common. Spreadsheets often lack documentation for users or maintenance purposes. They may be inadequately backed up, insufficiently confidential, and spreadsheets that grow large can become agonizingly slow to run.

These problems have become increasingly well known over the last decade or so and now many spreadsheet audit tools are available to help find errors.

The idea of SPREADSHEET TIGHTENING OR REPLACEMENT is to find important spreadsheets in an organization and reduce the downside risk associated with them by either:

1. replacing them with another computer application developed in a more rigorous way, or
2. making changes to the spreadsheet to reduce the risk of error in its use and future development.

Design changes that tighten a spreadsheet include:

- Clarity improvements
  - An overall design that separates the spreadsheet into blocks with clear roles.
  - Separate areas for user data entry and entering instructions; not mixed with formulae.
  - Written instructions to users, including comments, especially where spreadsheets are to be used by many people or are not to be used frequently.
  - Comments within macro code to explain it and the data structures used.
  - Intuitive layouts and clear labels in plain English, or the nearest possible.

- Built-in checking
  - Formulae that cross-check totals and show prominent error messages when there is a problem. Often it is possible to carry control totals through a spreadsheet or even a chain of spreadsheets.
  - Improved data value validation e.g. using drop-down lists, lookups, and conditional formatting that colours errors.
  - Graphs that make errors stand out.
  - Comparatives, e.g. from a previous period, with big differences highlighted.
  - Calculation of ratios that can be scrutinized for suspicious variations.
  - Macros that just do a list of checks and report their findings.

- Simplifying future changes
  - Macros to perform error prone changes, such as shifting old data to receive a new period's data.
  - Taking numbers out of formulae and putting them in a field, visible and easier to edit without risk to the formulae.

- Audits of existing spreadsheets to remove current errors e.g. to find errors in NPV calculations.

The easiest spreadsheets to tighten in this way tend to be ones where control totals can be used extensively. For example, if an overall set of data is cut up into slices then the subtotals of all the slices should add up to the grand total of the original set.

In contrast, spreadsheets that work out things that are difficult to estimate and where control totals are not possible present special difficulties. Unfortunately, spreadsheets used for large financial decisions and incorporating net present value calculations are in this category.

Therefore:

Look for important spreadsheets and either replace them with something more rigorous or 'tighten' them by improving clarity, built-in checking, automation, and simply removing current errors.

SPREADSHEET TIGHTENING OR REPLACEMENT sometimes involves inserting EXTENDED EDIT CHECKS into spreadsheets.

52 Computer supported authorizations

Example: Decisions by a lending company on whether to lend to a potential customer are often computer supported – even to the point where many decisions are entirely automated. The system can summarize and present relevant facts, calculate risk scores, make recommendations, and collect and store decisions.

COMPUTER SUPPORTED AUTHORIZATIONS should be considered in any situation where data on a computer is to be checked or authorized by a person.

Some checks on data need too much real-world knowledge, flexibility, and judgement to be left to a computer, but computers can still help and often their help is essential.

Whether before or after some event, reviews to check data and give approvals to proceed are fundamental controls. Some can be fully automated because rules governing the decision can be identified, are fairly simple, and do not change over time.

Many cannot be entirely automated so human input is required. A problem is that we often have little understanding of how effective a human reviewer will be. Human approvers struggle in situations like these:

- Under time pressure, especially where effective review requires pulling together related documents and computer records.
- Where there are many items to look at and a very low rate of defects. People just glaze over and after a while do not see the problems.
- Where effective review requires accurate, detailed memory for events, people, products, and so on, that in fact people do not possess.

- Where there simply isn't much to go on.

To help out, computer power can be used to do a number of things:

- Identify subsets of items where a fully automated approval decision is possible, deal with those items, and present the remaining items for human input.
- Identify groups of items that are sufficiently similar that the human approver can give approval for whole sets of similar items in one action.
- Calculate statistics and search for anomalies in populations of items, highlighting certain items as suspicious. For example, numbers with unusual distributions, outliers, fields with more formats than would be expected, dates out of order, and correlations that normally hold but are broken.
- Highlight higher risk items or sort items into risk order for human consideration.
- Display items using information graphics (e.g. scatter plots) that help identify potential problems.
- Call up related computer records so that they can be seen easily.
- Capture and store evidence of the human approval given.

Therefore:

> *Look for ways to use computer power to make human authorizations easier and more effective.*

COMPUTER SUPPORTED AUTHORIZATIONS can make use of DISCREPANCY SEARCHING, ANOMALY SEARCHING, and EXTENDED EDIT CHECKS. There may be more opportunities for COMPUTER SUPPORTED AUTHORIZATIONS where there is a SHIFT FROM PRE TO POST.

53   Extended edit checks

Example: The R statistical programming environment stops running programs if it encounters an error, as you would expect. However, it also gives WARNING! Messages when it sees something that might be valid, but is still likely to be an error.

EXTENDED EDIT CHECKS are relevant wherever data are captured into a computer system, especially where human input is involved. They may enable COMPUTER SUPPORTED AUTHORIZATIONS.

In computer speak 'valid' is much narrower than 'correct'.

Computer people talk about 'validation'. The system will perform 'validation' on user input or when loading data from an external file. Since the system has 'validated' the data they are 'valid' right?

It depends what you mean by valid.

'Valid' in computer-speak just means the data conform to some basic requirements that allow the software to process them. For example, fields that should contain numbers are checked to make sure they have numbers. Text fields that should not be longer than a certain length are validated for length and to remove unprintable characters and trailing spaces. Field values that should match those of another record are matched. Validation often gets more subtle than this, for example to check that invoice detail lines add up to the invoice total, or that a person's date of birth is before their date of death, and so on.

'Valid' in computer-speak does not mean the data are the correct values or that they are genuine. You could enter your name as 'Mickey Mouse' and expect it to be accepted as valid. You could claim to have been born in 1853 and most systems would be happy.

'Validation' does help filter out data entry errors, but be aware of the limitations and examine the exact rules being applied before you decide what control the software is giving you.

The idea of EXTENDED VALIDATION CHECKS is to go beyond the bare minimum of validation and think of things software can check that will identify user input that must be wrong or even flag up user input that is likely to be wrong, giving the user a chance to check and confirm or correct the data.

In summary, the value of these extended checks is in detecting more errors at the data capture stage. Therefore:

When designing edit checks, look to go beyond the bare minimum of validation.

There are no subsidiary control patterns to this one in this book.

54   Shift from pre to post

Example: Organizations that empower their people to make more decisions for themselves often remove requirements for authorization of actions before they take place but can compensate to some extent by reviewing actions afterwards, effectively authorizing them post hoc.

SHIFT FROM PRE TO POST-authorization is relevant to any situation where authorizations are required, even when completely eliminating pre-event authorization is not possible.

Sometimes authorization is just as effective, and much more convenient, after the event.

A very traditional internal control in organizations is for actions (e.g. purchases, bids, sales contracts) to be authorized by someone *before* another person carries them out. This is a control mechanism that is often needed and can be very useful.

However, it does have some drawbacks and there are refinements that should always be considered when authorization is being designed.

The drawbacks relate to speed and rigour. Many years ago when I was a trainee auditor I performed an audit at a glass factory in the north of England which had the least efficient internal controls I have ever seen. Two of its worst designed controls illustrate, in extreme, the problems of pre-authorizations.

Delays are illustrated by the case of credit notes. From time to time customers would dispute an invoice and usually refused to pay until correction was made. The glass factory had a clear procedure for issuing credit notes to correct bills and this required signatures from some senior people in the company in a specific order, sometimes more than once. Unfortunately, these people worked at different premises in the same city. A draft credit note would collect a signature, be driven to another office, collect another signature, go back to the first office for a third signature and so on. I estimated that credit notes travelled more than 300 miles before they could be sent to a customer.

In addition, because senior people were involved, they often took some days each to get round to giving their signatures. All this time the much larger bill the customer should have paid was unpaid. Very often the credit note amounts were tiny, though the procedure applied to *all* credit notes regardless of value.

Clearly this was a stupid procedure but even in less extreme cases pre-authorization tends to introduce delays and when speed is important even small delays may be crucial.

The second example illustrates the potential problem of incompleteness. The glass factory had an elaborate purchasing procedure with many forms and stages that involved the usual, ultra-cautious pre-authorization signatures.

In fact the procedure was so slow that people began to bypass it. They made a purchase and then, usually, put the paperwork through the system to obtain permission to do something that in fact they had already done. Nobody reviewed purchases that came through to see if there were items that had not been pre-authorized.

To illustrate a third potential problem with pre-authorization here is an example from an entirely different business. The problem is lack of rigour and the example comes from an insurance broking firm in London. The finance director of the broker was determined to overcome internal control problems with accounting that had led to long delays in finalizing the annual accounts in previous years. One of his ideas was to insist that all journal vouchers were presented to him, with supporting documentation, for his authorization before the journal was posted.

It is true that journals are important. They include adjustments and corrections, occasionally of high value, as well as many routine inputs of data to the accounting system.

The problem was that *scores* of journals were created every day and he did not have time to study each one rigorously without causing delays.

This control idea, like others he had introduced, did not solve their accounting problems and the board of directors, fed up with his slowness, sacked him.

So, although pre-authorization has the advantage of preventing some badly chosen actions from being taken it usually introduces delays and on its own is not a complete or rigorous control mechanism.

One way to address these weaknesses is to shift the emphasis from pre-authorization to post-hoc authorization.

In the general case there is a stream of decisions to be taken each of which has some kind of value or size. There is a person who can take those decisions provided the value is not above their personal authorization limit. If it is, then the decision has to be passed on to someone else more senior within the hierarchy of the organization, or at least independent of the first person. That second person either takes the decision or confirms the decision made by the first person.

Shifting the emphasis towards post-hoc control involves:

- raising the authorization limit of the first person so that they are empowered to make decisions alone more often;
- providing them with the option of raising a decision to a higher level even if it is within their maximum authorization limit (e.g. because the decision is a difficult one or might link to other decisions);
- adding a rigorous post-hoc review that examines every decision once it has been taken and acted on; and
- making it clear that the post-hoc review is important and mistaken or dishonest decisions will be taken very seriously.

In this approach the first person cannot simply fill in forms and mindlessly pass them on for someone else to worry about. The person has to use his or her own intelligence and learn the job properly.

For the deterrent effect to be fully effective it is important that computer systems and/or paper records reliably record who did what.

In summary, this shift of focus reduces costs and delays, and helps people learn to make decisions competently themselves. Therefore:

> *Look for ways to shift the emphasis from authorizations before events take place to authorizations afterwards.*

The authorizations might be easier with COMPUTER SUPPORTED AUTHORIZATIONS, perhaps using DISCREPANCY SEARCHING and/or ANOMALY SEARCHING to highlight potential problems.

55   Recovery/cleansing project

Example: A large organization that uses office space it does not own might find that it is charged on the basis of floor space and that the floor space charged for is not the same as the floor space actually available. Measuring the space might give a basis for getting a lower rent and a refund of past over-charged amounts.

RECOVERY/CLEANSING PROJECTS are relevant to most large-scale processes, where even small percentage errors can have high value, and to processes at any scale that are known to be unreliable.

Even tiny flaws in the control system of a large scale information process can be costly. Something powerful needs to be done and often pays off handsomely.

Recovery/cleansing projects are projects that involve checking large quantities of data, typically using software 'power tools', to find what may be faults, then checking through them, leading to identification and correction of specific errors and other problems. This in turn leads to higher data quality and greater efficiency in future, ideas for improvements to controls, systems, and processes to prevent reoccurrence of the errors, and recovery of money from other parties e.g. customers, suppliers.

Recovery projects are often justified purely in terms of the financial recovery benefits, but these are not the only or even the main benefits to be gained. People who find themselves affected by recovery projects usually feel that improvements to prevent further problems are important and they want reassurance and evidence that these are part of the project.

One way to prevent a recovery project from starting is to demand proof in advance that it will be worthwhile. Usually nobody knows exactly what will be found or how much work will be required until the project is done.

It is better to consider all processes guilty until proven innocent and go ahead with a project that gives good information early on and keeps risks low. For example, if you involve external experts in the work they will often be used to working for a percentage of the money saved or recovered. If they find nothing then their client pays nothing – other than the minor inconvenience of supplying data downloads and answering questions.

This problem of not knowing if, or where, the problems lie is fundamental in recovery projects and solving it is at the heart of this control pattern.

A first step is to ask people in a position to know to help make a list of error types either known to exist or suspected. Usually there will be quite a list of things that are already being worked on in some way or are currently concerns. Each of these should be subjectively rated to capture their importance and the uncertainty around them at the outset. This should be done by, in effect, estimating a probability distribution over extent of loss. For example, you could ask for the chance that the annual loss is greater than £10,000, that it is greater than £100,000, and greater than £1,000,000.

Do *not* ask for an estimate of the annual losses from each issue because people do not know the amounts, usually, and this question will kill the project. It pushes people to pretend they know more than they do and it removes from consideration loss levels other than the best guesses provided.

It is quite possible to rate the losses in every individual possible location as being, at a best guess, too low to bother with even though there are some worthwhile losses to go for. Some loss levels will actually be lower than the best guess while others will be higher. Work in the areas of higher losses may be very worthwhile. The trick is to find those special areas as quickly and economically as possible.

Asking about known issues is an important step but should not be the only basis of initial plans. There will probably be other issues not yet known about. Look at *risk factors* in order to guide the hunt for those other issues.

Tabulate possible loss areas and consider each one. Rate each area on relevant risk factors. The choice of risk factors is judgemental because I'm not aware of published research on what is typically most useful. I suggest considering the following:

- **Overall value:** It helps to think in terms of the overall value affected by the process/data and the percentage rate of errors. Then multiply them.
- **Extent of automation:** Steps with a lot of human input tend to give high levels of errors, varied errors, and concessions to other parties made to preserve good relationships. Steps that are fully automated tend to be correct except when they are systematically and invisibly wrong. Automated steps are often easier to sort out but there is less certainty of finding at least some errors.
- **Extent of previous recovery projects and other investigations and reviews:** The prospects may be lower with processes that have already been studied in detail and improved.
- **Evidence from previous projects and reviews:** On the other hand, previous reviews may give evidence of remaining problems.
- **History of management and ownership:** Business units and systems that have been low priority for a long period, or have changed ownership once, twice, or more times in the last decade or so tend to have more problems.
- **Complexity of task:** If the process/system has to do something that is inherently complicated, under time pressure, and perhaps also despite poor cooperation by other parties, then there are likely to be more issues.
- **Age:** Very young and very old processes/systems are more likely to have issues. Very young processes/systems that have been created by a project that was out of control are particularly hot prospects for recovery work.
- **Extent of known issues:** Usually if more issues are known about that suggests there are yet more to discover, but not always.

These ratings need to be summarized and combined in some suitable way. Awarding points and adding them together is often as good as any other way and tends to be more consistent than unaided judgement as well as taking into account all the factors every time.

A more sophisticated alternative if you are confident with mathematics is to represent the probability density of different levels of percentage error using a beta distribution[2] and update its parameters in light of evidence as it is obtained.

An advantage of this is that it is easy to draw graphs that show the relative chances of different levels of loss. This keeps people aware of the possibility (even when slim) of high levels of loss being present.

Having analysed the total area to be covered by the recovery project and made an initial assessment of the extent of issues that might be found in each sub-area the next phase is to begin work checking data in such a way that more is learned about the true level of problems in each sub-area, as well as perhaps identifying some errors.

The three main techniques for this are as follows:

- **Searches for anomalies and discrepancies:** Identifying what *appear* to be incorrect data is not the same as finding all the errors. There will be errors that are not anomalous and do not create discrepancies. There will also be many items that appear to be incorrect but have legitimate but unexpected explanations and in fact are correct. Typically fewer than half of the items that at first appear wrong actually are, and often it is much less than half. If searches are hard to do they can be on a sample only. This work allows the probability distributions of loss to be revised judgementally but does not allow a point estimate because of the uncertainty over how much that is suspicious will turn out to be wrong.

- **Testing samples:** A more reliable guide to the actual error rate is to select a sample of items, run queries to find apparent errors, and follow them up fully to find the explanation and identify any true errors and their financial and other consequences. The extra follow-up work is time consuming but helpful, and can even be extended to trying to recover money from other parties (if appropriate). This technique also allows the probability distributions of loss (and possible recovery) to be revised but also does not allow a point estimate because of the sampling uncertainty. If beta distributions are used they can be updated very easily from sample information. Estimates of the work needed to process suspect items can be made but of course, over time, efficiency will improve so do not be put off by work that seems very slow initially.

- **Attempting reconciliations in total:** Sometimes it is possible to work out the total loss by comparing the value of data at one point with the value at some earlier, more reliable point. For example, you might know the goods sold and how much they should have been billed for and compare that with the total of bills actually raised. Sometimes this is the easiest and hardest hitting estimate of all. However, it is easy to misunderstand and to make a mistake in such reconciliations so again the probability distributions of loss should be revised but not reduced to a point estimate.

Exactly which errors are searched for and where may be guided by known issues and by knowledge of where the process is complex, manual, and poorly controlled.

The remainder of the project consists of increments of work after which estimates of losses, potential recoveries, and work to achieve them are revised and decisions taken.

Gradually the initially wide scope will narrow to a few areas of highest net reward.

Throughout it is important to estimate open-mindedly and to report progress without suppressing uncertainty. Always remember that apparent errors usually are not errors at all, and that a genuine error that should give rise to recovering money often will not. For example, some 'customers' who have been receiving services without being charged may defect when asked to pay and may then dodge outstanding bills.

In summary, a good project can claw back money, prevent future losses, and lead to better systems and controls. Many previous projects have paid for themselves many times over and in some areas specialist consultants offer services that are priced as a percentage of recoveries. Therefore:

Unless a process is known to be close to perfect consider a project to search hard with computer tools for errors whose correction might lead to benefits. Develop an improving capability for this kind of project.

These projects rely heavily on DISCREPANCY SEARCHING, ANOMALY SEARCHING, MASS CORRECTION TOOL use, and ERROR FILE REDUCTION BY CLUSTER. They may also use information from END-TO-END RECONCILIATION.

56 Discrepancy searching

Example: When a customer orders a new telephone service the telephone company records the order on an order processing system but many of the data are then copied on to billing systems and network management systems. Discrepancy searching is often used to compare data in these various systems, looking for differences that should not be there.

DISCREPANCY SEARCHING is useful in COMPUTER SUPPORTED AUTHORIZATIONS and other checks on data. It is also one of the primary tools of a RECOVERY/CLEANSING PROJECT.

If an organization has data that can be inconsistent then, probably, some are.

DISCREPANCY SEARCHING has a lot in common with ANOMALY SEARCHING. It can be routine or part of a project. It produces a set of items suspected of being wrong, invalid, or missing that usually need to be looked at more carefully.

The difference is that DISCREPANCY SEARCHING involves comparisons between two different sources of data that are supposed to be comparable, such as records of the same events taken from different stages of a business process.

Because this matching is needed there is a new complication because one needs to know how to relate data from one source to data in another. At the very least some of the data fields will have been given different names. Sometimes a calculation or some other logic is needed to make data from one place comparable with data from another.

The first step is simply to develop the tools to match up records that should be comparable and report records present in one source but missing in the other. This alone is a valuable step forward and the tool should be used on live data as soon as possible.

The next step is to add the comparisons that are well understood without much research and find out what they reveal in live data.

Finally, implement the more complex comparisons that seem to be worthwhile.

In summary, searching for discrepancies using computer power is an efficient way to find even rare errors in large volumes of data. Therefore:

Identify opportunities to compare data between data stores using software.

DISCREPANCY SEARCHING has similar uses to ANOMALY SEARCHING and they are often used together.

57   Anomaly searching

Example: Download a sample of several thousand deals from a commodity trading system and sort them into date order using the deal date as entered by the trader. You may find that some of those deals appear to have been made around hundred years ago. The date has been entered incorrectly and the anomaly is obvious.

ANOMALY SEARCHING is useful in COMPUTER SUPPORTED AUTHORIZATIONS and generally as a computerized check on data. It is also a primary weapon in a RECOVERY/CLEANSING PROJECT.

Ideally errors would not arise but they do so throw computer power at the data to find them.

Imagine that a process creates data records and these are stored in a computer system and also copied over to another computer system for further processing. By searching for *anomalies* I mean looking in just one of these computer systems for records that look odd for some reason. By searching for *discrepancies* I mean comparing the data records between the two computer systems for differences that indicate something has gone wrong.

Of course we prefer to avoid having incorrect data arise at all, and prefer to prevent incorrect data ever getting into computer systems, but these things happen so the next line of defence is to look for anomalies.

This may be particularly relevant if edit checks at the front end are weak, out of date, or were weak when the data was entered, perhaps years ago.

Searching for anomalies can be done routinely or as part of a special project. It is normally done using computer queries followed by more in-depth investigation by humans. Over time, anomaly search that is part of a project can become a routine control through greater automation.

Searching for anomalies in large populations of data records makes it possible to use techniques not available in edit checking because they rely on seeing a large sample of data records, against which anomalies can stand out.

Typical anomalies found in practice include:

- Empty fields.
- Numbers out of the reasonable range e.g. zero, much too large, negative, total does not exactly agree to the sum of details.
- Numbers vastly too large or too small, suggesting that the wrong units have been used e.g. user is supposed to enter a money figure in thousands of dollars but mistakenly enters it in dollars.
- Values that are not one of the valid list of values for that field.
- More field formats than should appear e.g. if the standard format for a customer code is three letters followed by five digits then other formats, if found, are anomalous.
- Dates that are obviously wrong e.g. from the wrong century.
- Dates out of order e.g. an item sold before it was bought.
- Wrong list of fields on a data record – possible with some kinds of database on very old systems.
- Flag values (i.e. fields which have simple codes) that are inconsistent with other field values or are in inconsistent combinations e.g. 'number of children=2' but 'parent(Y/N)=N'.
- Subsidiary record missing e.g. billing records for a telecom service that should always include a record to bill for the line, but where that record is sometimes missing.
- Subsidiary record present that should not be.
- Distribution of digits in a large population is different from Benford's law.[3]
- Combinations of field values that are statistically unusual.
- Field values that are statistically unlikely given the values of other fields on the record e.g. typically old items might have lower values so that an old item with a high value is unlikely. These can be shown on scatter plots.

Anomaly search can be done using implicit or explicit rules, and where explicit rules are used these can be identified by a person or created by software automatically.

Before thinking about explicit rules it is quite easy and productive simply to look at the data. Sort it on each numeric or date field and look at the top and bottom items, look at the number of formats used in each field, and generally get familiar with the records and fields in a file.

Information about what data should look like is often surprisingly hard to get, having been known only to the original programmers of a system, perhaps years ago, with no effective handover to the people who now support it.

As more knowledge is acquired it becomes possible to start formulating rules to check the data against, and putting these into software queries or just using them in spreadsheets.

If there are many data (hundreds of records at the very least) and you have the necessary skill it may be worthwhile trying data mining methods. Methods that 20 years ago would have seemed impossibly academic and difficult are now available in software that runs fast and costs little (or, in the case of R,[4] costs nothing).

One approach is to use some form of cluster analysis to break the population down into subpopulations on the basis of 'similarity'. Different algorithms have different capabilities. Some work only on number fields, some only on text fields, and a few can cope with both together. Clusters with few records in them are potentially anomalous.

Another approach is to use some variables on each record to predict the value of another variable and then search for records where the predicted and actual values are different or different by more than a certain amount. This could be done with neural network software, SVM software, or classification tree software to name just three well-known types. Again some techniques work only with text fields, some with numbers, and a few with both.

If anomaly searches are to become routine controls operating automatically then it may help to use techniques that automatically update the search rules. A decision needs to be made about how often the rules will be revised.

In summary, searching for anomalies using software is an efficient way to search for even small percentages of error in large data sets and finds more than most people expect. Therefore:

Search for anomalies in data using software tools and human expertise, progressing from simple reviews of sorted data to searches using explicit rules.

ANOMALY SEARCHING has similar uses to DISCREPANCY SEARCHING and they are often used together.

58   End-to-end reconciliation

Example: A telecommunications company with a data warehouse about telephone calls made on its network implemented an end-to-end reconciliation to check that the number of call records in files of call records gathered from mediation systems daily could be reconciled to the number of calls shown as being made daily on reports from the data warehouse.

END-TO-END RECONCILIATION is often a low-cost way to detect losses and distortions of assets and data in multi-stage processes, and can provide useful information to a RECOVERY/CLEANSING PROJECT.

Most high volume, multi-stage processes lose or distort items they are processing at various stages along the way, but when, where, and how much?

Many people imagine that if something has been done by a computer then it must be right. If a computer churns out a report showing that all data have been dealt with and there are no losses or errors they believe it. I have never believed this because my first proper job was as a computer programmer and I learned quickly that virtually all software has at least some bugs in it and even adding up numbers is a dodgy area.

However, I did once sign up to another popular myth which is that very large, successful companies do not make mistakes. Their work is reliable and their systems are solid.

Of course, once I started auditing the processes and systems of very large and impressive companies I realized the truth, which is that they go wrong in very large and impressive ways.

Computerization does improve reliability but it can also make some kinds of problem harder to see. The more complicated the technology the less likely it is to be working properly. Interfaces are often unreliable. Systems sometimes reject data when they fail validation routines, but the rejection is not reported or, if it is, nobody knows where or bothers to look.

Sometimes losses of data are the same as losses of money, such as when the data are records of purchases for which a customer can be billed.

Whether there is a direct cost or not we would like a quick and economical way to find out what losses are occurring, where, and to what extent. That's what END-TO-END RECONCILIATION is for.

It is applicable to multi-stage processes and processes that split off into two or more parallel data flows.

Before getting into the details of end-to-end reconciliation, here are the basics of reconciliations generally.

Reconciling two numbers means explaining the difference between them by showing a calculation that gets from one to the other using other numbers independently sourced. It is similar to agreeing or comparing numbers but different.

Agreeing numbers means matching them exactly with no differences to explain. *Comparing* numbers means looking at the difference between them, if any, but does not imply finding an explanation or insisting on exact matching. Making a comparison is the first step towards a reconciliation.

Sometimes what looks like a reconciliation is really just an incomplete reconciliation because one of the numbers in the calculation is a 'balancing figure' i.e. the number needed to make the reconciliation work. Badly worded or deliberately deceptive reconciliations may obscure the fact that the reconciliation is incomplete.

Comparisons/reconciliations can be done in total or in detail. For example, suppose there are two files representing data records before and after going through some processing. If the reconciliation is between the total number or total value of records before and after processing then it is at the total level. If the reconciliation matches individual data records and looks for individual differences then it is at the detail level.

An end-to-end reconciliation is actually a chain of reconciliations between numbers representing data or assets at different stages in a business or accounting process, and individual reconciliations do not necessarily use the same variable or basis of comparison.

With a little research it should be possible to design all, or nearly all, the steps quite early on but implementation is likely to take longer and should be incremental if it cannot be done immediately. Do what you can as soon as possible.

End-to-end reconciliations gradually improve in the following four ways:

- *Coverage of more links in the total chain.* For example, a process may have a series of steps of data transfer and processing and at first the reconciliations do not cover all those steps. Gradually more and more steps have at least one reconciliation across them.
- *More attributes in each link.* The most basic reconciliation is just to count items, but it is usually possible to create additional reconciliations using numeric data that are present from the start to finish of a step. For example, if the items in question all have a weight then the total weight at the start and finish of the step can be compared as well as the item count.
- *Progression from comparison to reconciliation at each link.* At first the comparisons may show differences between one stage and the next that are not understood, even if they are not the result of error or fraud. The most common reasons for reconciliations not working properly are timing differences and error data stores which are not accounted for. An example of a timing difference is where telephone call records are allocated to hours of the day on one system according to the time each call starts and on another system according to the time each call finishes. An example of an error data store is where one system sends data across an interface to another, which validates the data and rejects some of them into an error file for later reprocessing. The movements of data in and out of the error data store have to be accounted for to reach an exact reconciliation over the interface.

When designing a reconciliation it is usually best to start with readily available data, even if this does not give exact reconciliations, and then move towards accurate reconciliations by implementing software changes that will provide the data needed.

Comparisons are still useful because you can spot problems from statistical irregularities, and timing differences can be overcome by tracking cumulative differences (which should stay within a small and narrow band, not grow over time).

- *Moving from total-level to detail-level reconciliation.* Typically, the links in an end-to-end chain begin as reconciliations or comparisons in total and move on to the detail level. This is because reconciliations in total detect errors but do not give enough information for corrections. For that the individual errors need to be identified and that requires detail-level comparisons.

  If comparisons/reconciliations in total suggest significant problems then detailed comparison usually follows.

Another important design decision for each reconciliation is the level at which any counts or totals are calculated. Is it daily, hourly, for each file, for each customer each day, and so on? This is usually influenced by what is readily available.

In summary, reconciliations can quickly provide useful quantification of errors, including losses, with relatively little work and can be developed incrementally into very powerful controls. Therefore:

Design and implement, incrementally, a set of reconciliations that becomes progressively more comprehensive and more detailed as it is developed.

There are no subsidiary control patterns to this one in this book.

59   Mass correction tool

Example: A national telecommunications company will often process data on more than 100 million calls per day and at this rate even a small glitch somewhere can lead to thousands of faulty records piling up within minutes. A tool to examine and correct large sets of records damaged by much smaller numbers of faults is extremely useful.

A MASS CORRECTION TOOL is useful in any situation where high volumes of data need to be examined and corrected, which includes large-volume processes and RECOVERY/CLEANSING PROJECTS.

Sometimes errors are so numerous it helps to have software support for dealing with them.

In some large-scale processes the flow of data is so great that even small errors can create thousands or even millions of errors in a few hours that need to be dealt with quickly and efficiently.

Examples of such processes include call detail records flowing in from telecom networks to be priced and billed, high-volume interfaces between systems, sales order processes where it is common for the first transactions to come through before reference data have been set up, and complex case handling processes where a high proportion of cases are incorrectly processed in some way.

The basic level of support that a software tool can provide is the following:

- The ability to send items for repeated processing conveniently.
- Analysis and reporting of items needing attention and the results of attempted reprocessing.
- Initial classification of errors by type.
- A user friendly view of the data (e.g. showing customer name rather than just a customer identification code).

More advanced support automates the process of ERROR FILE REDUCTION BY CLUSTER by providing such features as these:

- The ability to study sample items and look for common characteristics.
- The ability to find other items with the same common characteristics, typically by writing queries (e.g. in SQL or some other query system).
- The ability to set up a programmed corrective action (e.g. using SQL).
- Online authorization of actions on sets of records, with the authorization captured and recorded.
- The opportunity to study the results of executing the programmed correction and to undo them if necessary, before committing to it.
- Automatic recording of the changes made and who was involved.

In summary, this kind of tool makes it possible to examine and correct high volumes of errors more quickly and easily, which in turn makes a satisfactory audit trail easier to implement. Therefore:

Acquire or develop a tool to examine and correct large volumes of errors resulting from smaller numbers of causes.

MASS CORRECTION TOOLS typically make use of ERROR FILE REDUCTION BY CLUSTER in some way.

60   Error file reduction by cluster

Example: The fundraising department of a charity might decide to clean up its mailing lists. After running various checks for anomalies it might find over a thousand names that probably need some kind of correction and then begin to investigate them and break them into clusters reflecting the work needed on each; for example, corporate donors versus individual donors, and potential duplicates versus addresses that do not match the postcode.

ERROR FILE REDUCTION BY CLUSTER is useful in any situation that requires investigating and correcting a large number of errors. This may be routine in a high-volume process, the result of a backlog, or it may arise in a RECOVERY/CLEANSING PROJECT. It is normally used in a MASS CORRECTION TOOL.

Investigating and resolving a large file of suspected errors is tough but necessary and sometimes remunerative work that needs to be done efficiently, using computer tools in the right way.

The task might be to resolve postings in a suspense file, or deal with unprocessed data from an interface, or perhaps investigate suspect items identified by anomaly and discrepancy searches. It might be routine work or, more likely, part of a project. It might be motivated by wasted time, lost money, customer service errors, or any other impact of poor data quality or incomplete processing.

Whatever the reason for needing to reduce an error file the work involved is usually long, tiring, and messy. It often involves making checks in the wider world, by telephone calls, correspondence, meetings and negotiations, as well as by looking at computer and paper records to work out what really happened and how to fix it.

If the work is not routine there will be debates about where the people to do the work will come from. The individuals chosen may feel unmotivated at times, particularly if they are not making rapid progress.

Computerization can make a great contribution but it is a mistake to rely too much on it and disasterous to imagine that software can be written that will automatically resolve every item. Perhaps it can, but the time and effort needed to get there by programmers/analysts and testers are usually high. The data involved and the task are messy and so hard to analyse. That's the nature of the problem.

It is best to work in an iterative way that makes best use of both user and programmer expertise, recognizes the value of experience with the data in building understanding, and leads to useful results quickly.

Error populations can usually be clustered into groups of varied sizes in such a way that within each group the items are very similar in their causes and remedies. An efficient approach requires identifying groups, prioritizing work on them, and then steadily working through the groups one by one making corrections in groups, if possible, and otherwise as soon as possible. Of course the order in which the groups are tackled may be revised many times as experience is gained.

To get an initial view of possible clusters it may help to use a statistical cluster analysis technique, but a simple alternative is to just sort the error cases by value (or some other measure of importance) then work down the list one by one investigating as best you can and looking for signs of repeating patterns.

If a potential cluster is suspected look at characteristics of known members to identify things that are distinctive about them and would allow other members to be searched for by eye or using a computer query of some kind. It may be that the boundaries of a cluster are unclear so a conservative definition may be needed to cut the risk of including members of other clusters by accident. Clusters may have sub-clusters, and so on.

Once you have a set of records thought to be in error in the same way the next step is to devise a process for investigating each item in that set specifically, setting out what is established by each type of evidence used. Ultimately someone will have to authorize action on those items and the consequences of getting it wrong could be severe.

When the investigation has been done the evidence can be summarized and presented for approval of the proposed action for individual items in the cluster or for the whole cluster in one go.

Clusters should be tackled in an order that brings the main benefits of the exercise as soon as possible. That means considering the value of resolving the errors and the ease of doing so.

In general, simple cases are better to start with and provide experience that leads to the ability to handle more complex cases.

The ideal person to do this work is someone who understands the business, the data, and the systems, and has the ability to write software and work with large spreadsheets. Failing that a multi-skilled team is needed where the user-side data experts work closely (ideally at adjacent desks) with programmers.

Software support helps when identifying members of clusters, rerunning anomaly and discrepancy searches, devising automatic correction routines, and streamlining investigations by pulling up related data automatically.

Over time a body of well-documented expertise should grow covering common issues and how to spot and correct them. Clarity should increase and the software tools should improve in power and ease of use.

Error file reduction requires superb record keeping to show what has been done, to store evidence, and record approvals given and action taken. It is helpful to have a well-designed administration system of some kind that can handle:

- Receiving new items for investigation.
- Resolving subsets of items.
- Storing records of work done and the evidence gained against groups of items and individual items.
- Sharing items between team members.
- Reporting progress, in terms of volume and value of work done, work outstanding, rate of progress, and extent of learning.

Typically, as error file reduction moves from being project work to being routine, more of it is automated.

In summary, ERROR FILE REDUCTION BY CLUSTER is usually the most efficient way to deal with large volumes of suspected errors. Therefore:

Combine human expertise and computer power to investigate and resolve errors in clusters of similar items.

There are no subsidiary control patterns to this one in this book.

Notes

1   Professor Raymond R. Panko of the University of Hawaii has made available a collection of data on spreadsheet errors. It is on his website at http://panko.shidler. hawaii.edu/SSR/index.htm.
2   Using beta distributions with audit sample evidence is a simple technique covered in most textbooks. A good source is Anthony Steele's (1992) *Audit Risk and Audit Evidence*. London: Academic Press.
3   Benford's law applies to the many sources that produce logarithmically distributed numbers, including electricity bills, street numbers, share prices, death rates, town populations, and lengths of rivers. The law refers to the distribution of first digits, which (for base 10 numbers) is: 1 (30.1%), 2 (17.6%), 3 (12.5%), 4 (9.7%), 5 (7.9%), 6 (6.7%), 7 (5.8%), 8 (5.1%), 9 (4.6%).
4   R is a statistical programming environment that is a freeware version of S-Plus and very popular among academics. Learning to use R is an investment but may be worth it. The basic R language has been extended by 'packages' of extra functionality contributed by users from around the world covering a staggering range of statistical and other functions. The R project for statistical computing can be found at http://www.r-project.org/.

Making Good Change Happen

11 *Triggering Good Behaviours*

Dealing with risk and uncertainty is not something that can be conveniently compartmentalized into one specialized activity. A unified, 'formal' corporate process under tight central control can be a useful addition but is unlikely to be more than a small part of the total approach, perhaps done primarily to meet external expectations.

The goal for anyone trying to inject better risk control into an organization (e.g. a risk control specialist, line manager, director), or into themselves, is to bring about pervasive changes to behaviour.

We should be prepared to consider *any* methods of bringing about those behaviour changes that might work.

Beyond coercion

To some extent it is possible to drive behaviour by laying down formal procedures, implementing systems, and providing tools. Beyond that we need to nurture helpful skills, beliefs, and preferences.

Successful nurturing helps in a number of practical ways:

- People are more likely to do good things without being told to each time.
- If following a laid-down procedure or using a system or tool requires some details to be worked out or problems to be solved then people are more likely to do that instead of allowing themselves to be stalled.
- If they work out details or solve problems they are more likely to do it in a way that is consistent with the overall design intention, using better solutions.

Without nurturing helpful skills, beliefs, and preferences some controls are difficult to implement successfully. For example, suppose you want to implement FLEXIBLE REQUIREMENTS within a process and introduce some procedures to support it. This still leaves people to decide what they will say in conversations about their requirements. The control is undermined if someone says: 'Right, so this document sets out our flexible requirements for this section of the project. But, if you ask me what that means, I'd say that if you can get this done by the end of November for a cost of less than two million that will be fine.'

Someone who understands the control and wants it to work would never say something like that. If they were worried that their statement of flexible requirements was not clear they would say instead: 'Right, so this document sets out our flexible requirements for this section of the project. If anything is not clear to you please feel free to raise it with me. I'm very happy to share the thinking behind this set of values and take any suggestions you have.'

Part III of this book begins in this chapter with ideas on how to make the tangible, formal parts of a control system as pervasive and influential as possible. Later chapters move on to how to influence personal skills and shift misconceptions, including those that exist because we think other people are less reasonable than they really are.

Using triggers for pervasive behaviour change

Much of human behaviour is driven from moment to moment by what is in front of us – whatever our good intentions, 'to do' lists, and day planners may say. It's human nature and almost certainly a product of the way we acquire and use knowledge.

Therefore, in this chapter I've divided possible influence methods into those that provide triggers to behaviour in real time, and those that do not. The methods that do not provide real-time triggers, such as training and policy documents, are traditional mainstays of risk control so I have only a few points to add. The other levers – what is in front of our faces (usually) on a computer screen and the behaviour of other people in meetings with us – can also be influenced to good effect and these other levers get more attention in this chapter.

The last part of the chapter goes through some common areas for change, suggesting what to try to change, and how.

Changing human behaviour is usually difficult, but many of the traditional mainstays of internal control suffer from a serious problem: they are out of sight and out of mind when the key behaviours are supposed to take place.

WRITTEN PROCEDURES, POLICIES, RULES AND EMAILS FROM ON HIGH

Written procedures are often criticized in management books but generally considered necessary at least for some things. In practice they tend to be more useful as design documents and references for people involved in designing processes, systems, and training. They rarely influence people who operate the processes and systems because they seldom bother to open them let alone read them carefully. Having said that, some do and generally find this makes them instant experts compared to their less well-read colleagues.

Policies and rules, whether held on a database somewhere or sent directly in an email from some senior executive, also tend to be forgotten quickly.

It may be that the documents do not set out the conditions that should cue recall of the action required and that people usually do not think to work out those conditions to compensate. Whatever the reason, the usual behaviour is to skim or ignore the rules then put them away, never to consult them again. When a situation arises that should trigger recall of the policy what is recalled instead is the behaviour that the person already uses, perhaps well learned, for dealing with that situation.

Written procedures and rules can work, but it is not easy. Typical weaknesses, in addition to being forgotten, are that the documents tend to get out of date, often contain a lot of puff and wasted space, are often idealistic rather than practical, and sometimes rely on diagrams whose clarity has been over-estimated.

Although the motivation may be to fulfil legal or regulatory requirements the practical effect is that often these documents read like a pre-emptive blame shifting move. They contain requirements few people can realistically be expected to follow fully but, nevertheless, shift responsibility for future problems from the issuer to the reader. The unfortunate effect is completed by sending people an email with a button so that recipients can confirm having read the document, understood its content, and accepted the 'responsibility'!

TRAINING

Training is good. People often need training, particularly where they have to use some new system and nothing can be achieved unless they have at least some basic knowledge.

Training is harder to make useful when people do not need it in order to do an adequate job and where there is a good chance that trainees have already worked out their own approaches that are as good as or better than those offered in the training.

Training people to manage risk and uncertainty more skilfully is an example of a situation where training is hard to make useful because people are already doing it to some extent. True, if you introduce a new computer system or some forms to support a risk management process then people need training to use it, but this need has been created by the introduction of the system or forms. It is on top of managing risk well.

For risk management training to be useful the content has to be superb and the delivery rigorous. It has to get people to recall new behaviours at the appropriate time instead of whatever they would have recalled without the training, perhaps weeks after the training event.

People need to understand the new knowledge, understand and agree with the reasons for using it, and rehearse using it in sufficiently realistic settings *several times* if it is to stick. This strongly implies that computer-aided instruction and on-the-job training are likely to be useful and that classroom training events which do not make good use of time should be avoided.

The subject matter of these courses is typically technical or at least intellectual rather than requiring personality adjustment. There is no need to spend time on personality questionnaires or games. Simply stay focused on the task, make rehearsals realistic, and do multiple rehearsals.

It is also likely to be worth following up the training periodically with some kind of refresher, and providing some kind of on-demand coaching/support.

Sources of real-time triggers

The things that appear in front of people and trigger their behaviour from moment to moment have good potential for *changing* that behaviour.

ON THE SCREEN OR OTHER DISPLAY IN FRONT OF US

In some jobs people are entirely driven by what is on the screen in front of them. It's as if the computer tells them what to do minute by minute throughout the day. Most people have more freedom than that but in offices even the most senior people today find that they spend a lot of time responding to whatever is on their computer screens.

Introducing a big new computer system that people have to use in order to get their jobs done is a way to coerce a large number of people to do exactly what they are told. Today it can be taken further than ever with traditional computer applications turning into 'workflow' systems that send people emails with work for them to do, and follow up to make sure it is done. The system can increasingly make use of large numbers of rules that trigger on-screen prompts. Many people in call centres don't even have a choice of words because a script is generated for them. Built in artificial intelligence means that thousands of people can be taking orders from an artificial boss!

Then there's office automation software i.e. word processors, spreadsheets, email programs, and presentation software. Not only have these programs replaced typewriters and calculation machines but their templates have replaced pre-printed stationery and taken things to a whole new level.

Document templates can be created for many more purposes because now it is easy to insert as much or as little text under each given heading as you like; there is no need for the form designer to give a fixed size box to fill in, though that is possible too.

Templates can also have computing functionality, particularly in spreadsheet programs like Microsoft's ubiquitous Excel. Functionality on a spreadsheet template that is useful but hard to set up increases the chance that people will actually use it. The functionality may be in the form of formulae, perhaps boosted by labour-saving macros.

Another way that the screen has taken over is that we repeat and reuse past work more than ever. It has always made sense to learn from past experiences and to reuse what can be reused. Copy and paste has made it possible to do this more literally and to a greater extent than ever before. The old joke asks: 'Why did the auditor cross the road?' Answer: 'Because they did it last year.' Today we should add that the auditor also documented the crossing of the road by changing the date on last year's document and clicking Save As.

Of course there are limits to all this. If people can defy a computer system then often they will. Some people now don't even look at many of the hundreds of emails they receive each day. Templates may be ignored or misused (wilfully or accidentally through misinterpretation).

Templates and reuse of old documents often conflict. Instead of using the latest template design people tend to work from an existing document. Even if use of template versions is closely monitored and strongly enforced it will often be worth considering adding a magic macro button that can suck in material from existing documents that conform to past template versions.

Formal programmes related to internal control and risk management usually rely heavily on computer screens, particularly spreadsheet templates and risk/control databases. If nothing else the system can be used to log when people have done some monthly, quarterly, or annual routine related to risk control, allowing laggards to be reminded and chased.

The usual downside with spreadsheets is that someone has the laborious job of collating several spreadsheets from different departments, selecting the most important items, and copying them onto a summary table. This is easily overcome by macro programming. The 'summarizer' spreadsheet can be made to open a series of risk register spreadsheets (perhaps given as a list of file names) and copy the interesting ones to a summary table, reporting faults as it goes.

A software package that provides a risk-and-controls database and related functionality should, in theory, be better all round but in practice there is a serious downside to consider. Implement the package and you are stuck with the way it works and how its developers later wish to develop it. Even if you develop something in-house you could be trapped if resources for changes in future are not available.

Why is being stuck with a package you like a problem? Because in future you may not like it so much. Risk control is still in its early stages of development and conceptual and practical breakthroughs are happening all the time. Perhaps since beginning to read this book you already have some ideas that you like and want to try out. It is easier to change a template you designed than to open negotiations with software developers.

OTHER PEOPLE IN MEETINGS AND ON TELEPHONE CALLS

Communication by screen includes email, instant messaging, texting, and paging, and so gradually shifts into telephone messages, telephone calls, and face-to-face meetings. Today, thanks to mobile telephones, answering machines, wireless networks, and open plan offices it is hard to get a moment's peace. We are pushed along by all those messages and conversations.

In meetings we have ideas, make decisions, give and receive signals about values, about intentions, about who is dominant, and how people feel about ideas and people. Informal and formal communication is going on constantly during meetings.

Typically, the more senior someone is in an organization the more of their time is spent in meetings. Leaders don't sit down, think hard, and make important decisions. Their diaries show us that they move from meeting to meeting being influenced, and exerting influence, as they go, gradually kicking strategy this way and that through their changing attitudes and responses to situations presented to them by others.

If our behaviour is to be used to promote improved management of risk and uncertainty then there are plenty of opportunities.

- Make new meetings/workshops: Influence the content by chairing them, setting the agenda, making presentations, selecting attendees, and asking questions.
- Change the content of existing meetings: Get risk control matters included in the agenda, especially if there is a standing agenda, and attend the meetings to contribute risk control related information and questions.
- Coach key people to conduct conversations differently: Ideal people to focus on for this include those who chair meetings, people who often speak at meetings, opinion formers, and people known to be sympathetic to the risk control cause, or to have beliefs that are consistent with the practices that need to be promoted. Work top down if possible so that people attending meetings see a good example to copy when they themselves run meetings. Aim to seed conversations with simple yet potent questions using effective words. For example:

  - *'Please talk me through the changes and challenges you are dealing with at the moment.' Follow up with: 'And how are you dealing with them at the moment?'*
  - *'Can you please explain the main areas of uncertainty related to this project?'*
  - *'What do these facts tell us about the risk controls we need to use?'*
  - *'What's the next surprise we are going to have?'*
  - *'Let's now think ahead to what might happen if we do that.'*
  - *'What other possibilities are there?'*
  - *'What data do we have, if any, to help us?'*

Some examples of implementation steps

So far in this chapter we've considered some ways to influence behaviour. Now it is time to look at how these can be put together in a coordinated way to implement some common controls. In general, the idea is to focus on lasting, tangible changes that will trigger behaviour as well as securing agreement to the principles. Even the most willing colleagues need reminders and help.

Here are three examples whose implementation involves a variety of techniques.

Implementing REPORTING WITH UNCERTAINTY

The pattern REPORTING WITH UNCERTAINTY requires that internal management reports include information about the uncertainty around the information they provide. For example, if financial information is unaudited and 23 per cent of the value shown depends on estimates that are guesswork then this needs to be explained clearly. Most management information is uncertain to some extent but typically this inconvenient fact is glossed over. REPORTING WITH UNCERTAINTY helps reduce the danger from this problem and is one of the best examples of 'embedded' risk control.

Assuming that people in a part of an organization are happy to implement the new requirement then things to do to implement it include the following:

- Formal agreement to the policy by a person or group with sufficient authority and power.
- Communication of the policy.
- Communication of guidance on how to comply with the policy. As a minimum people need to know what kinds of measurement uncertainty to consider and the acceptable techniques for showing measurement uncertainty and prediction intervals. They need to see examples of them, and know how much extra effort, if any, they are expected to make to improve information about uncertainty as opposed to simply expressing what they already know. Beyond that it could be helpful to show extracts from reports before and after design changes to comply with the policy.
- Communication of guidance on how to respond to information about measurement uncertainty and prediction intervals. Being paralysed by lack of reliable information is not an acceptable situation, but neither is it acceptable to ignore measurement uncertainty that could be reduced and would be worth reducing.
- Communication of guidance on how to respond to failure to comply with the policy. For example, the best response might be to ask for compliance in future but then, to avoid delay, go on to ask 'What can you tell us about the reliability of this information?'
- Personal meetings with chairpeople and meeting secretaries to make sure they at least are clear on how the policy is supposed to work, understand the guidance, and are ready and willing to carry it out.
- Direct intervention to amend key report formats, either by changing templates or by changing the design of the report at one point in time, knowing that each future report is created by amending the one before.
- Encouraging senior people to encourage others to question the reliability of information provided, in a constructive way rather than dismissively, and to ask sensitivity analysis questions like: 'How wrong would these numbers have to be for us to think of acting differently?' Encourage senior people to set a good example by doing so themselves.
- Including the skills of understanding, showing, and responding to measurement uncertainty in personal skills training provided to employees. For example, this might be by altering the content of a report writing course.
- Including the new policy as a meeting agenda item when the policy is introduced and as each new report is put forward for use.

All this needs to be done quickly and incrementally, probably using the Friendly Expansion strategy (see Chapter 15).

Implementing RISK WEIGHTING

The idea behind the RISK WEIGHTING control pattern is to set a policy on how risk is to be weighed in decisions and encourage employees to comply with the prescribed approach. Typically there will be more than one such policy.

Ideally this involves somehow expressing the value (negative or positive) of different levels of risk. A risk limit is, effectively, a crude form of this control where any risk below a threshold is given little or no weight, while any risk above the threshold is given a large negative weight. Other techniques give a smoother relationship between risk level and value to avoid dysfunctional behaviour around the threshold point.

RISK WEIGHTING comes into decision-making and performance measurement and is so pervasive (potentially) that a large part of implementing this control is deciding where to bother with it, or at least deciding where to start and then, later, when to stop.

Decisions that are taken frequently and have a large cumulative impact are an obvious target. Most large organizations have already set up formal processes for many of the decisions they take frequently.

For big, high-level decisions there will usually be a committee of senior executives who meet regularly to consider business cases and give formal approvals. The business cases are often prepared carefully according to a mandatory format (usually set up as a template in some office system software), often have financial estimates behind them (another template), and are often checked before the meeting to make sure that business case requirements have been met.

There are also smaller decisions that are taken, but so frequently that their cumulative impact is also huge. They are often taken entirely by software or by hundreds of employees, many times a day on information provided by a computer screen.

Other decisions are less frequent and less repetitive. They may have little or no existing formal processes and will often arise unexpectedly, never to be repeated. These are a less obvious target for RISK WEIGHTING but not entirely out of reach because they are heavily influenced by the personal skills of individuals.

If decisions are made on one basis but performance is measured and even rewarded on another then this could lead to problems. Consider tackling decisions and performance measurement for related activities at the same time or at least close together in time.

Another large part of the effort of implementation is designing detailed techniques for each situation where it is to be used. These need to cover the following items:

- How the weighting is expressed.
- How it us reviewed and updated.
- How it is communicated.
- How it is used in decisions.
- How its use is monitored and enforced/encouraged.

Some designs need to work for unquantified decisions, some with fully quantified decisions, and most with decisions that have a mixture of quantified and unquantified considerations.

Once there is agreement in principle to do RISK WEIGHTING for an activity or organizational unit there is plenty to get on with.

For existing formal decision-making processes:

• Agree the policy formally, perhaps in writing.
• Communicate the policy.
• Do the technical design for the risk-weighing technique and get agreement to use it.
• Elicit current risk weights (in whatever form is appropriate to the design) and put in place procedures for revising the weights in future.
• Communicate helpful guidance on how to comply with the policy and how to use any tools involved. This will usually include explaining revised business case requirements, suggestions on how to review a business case that conforms, and suggestions on how to respond when a business case does not comply correctly. This could include priming people to ask the right questions, such as 'What policies on weighing risk and uncertainty apply to this decision?'
• Alter business case templates and accompanying rules.
• Explain all this in extra detail to chair people and committee secretaries.
• Alter standing agendas.
• Revise the standard approval wording.

For existing programmed or software-supported routine decisions:

• Do the technical design for the risk-weighing technique and get agreement to use it.
• Elicit current risk weights (in whatever form is appropriate to the design) and put in place procedures for revising the weights in future.
• If software can be changed then change it to implement new ideas.
• If software behaviour can be controlled sufficiently by setting data parameters then change the data parameters.

For non-routine, informal decision-making:

• Identify erroneous zones i.e. situations where people currently make bad decisions because of inappropriately weighing risk. For example, if people have fixed targets to meet and also must work within a crude risk limit they may be tempted to take bad risks in order to boost performance when it is disappointing. (This is a product of a poor RISK WEIGHTING design but in some organizations it may be simpler to treat the symptom than the underlying design problem.)
• Invent scenarios that capture the essence of the problem situation and set scenario policies i.e. the behaviour you would like to see instead.
• Educate using the scenarios.

For related performance measurement:

- Design the risk-weighing technique and get agreement to use it.
- Modify procedures for data gathering and calculation.
- Modify systems/templates/spreadsheets.
- Where personal performance appraisals cover behaviour as well as results, include suitable items on behaviour in the face of uncertainty.
- Take steps to influence how people discuss behaviour under uncertainty in personal performance evaluation meetings.

Implementing FORECASTING WITH STATISTICAL EXTRAPOLATION

This control pattern uses statistics to cut the effort involved in forecasting, but it is not purely statistical. It only works if data and enough regularity are present but this is the case more often than most people think and when it does work the saving in effort can be considerable. This is more valuable if something is done with the forecasts, so it should usually be part of the REFORECASTING TO COMPLETION control.

Implementing this pattern requires some careful data analysis and design of tools, but it also requires effort to encourage people to make the most of their new tool.

People who have worked with targets before sometimes learn to play games with the system, such as manipulating expectations, special pleading over targets, and negotiating hard over numbers without ever thinking of them as more than aspirations. These behaviours can carry over into other management systems so that, instead of discussing alternative *action* plans and objectively responding to feedback from the reforecasting model, they continue trying to play games with numbers.

Consequently, once you have agreement in principle to explore FORECASTING WITH STATISTICAL EXTRAPOLATION there is a lot to do:

- Collect past actual data going back perhaps three years or more and create a system/spreadsheet that shows you what would have happened if you had relied on alternative statistical prediction rules over that time. For example, if you have a rule that needs 12 months of past data to make a prediction and you have three years of past actual data then you can simulate the results of forecasting for the last two years and measure the errors.
- Try alternative prediction rules, studying the pattern of errors each time to understand what sort of predictions work best. Start with very simple rules involving minimal mathematics. Empirical evidence[1] shows that these usually give predictions at least as good as those using complicated models and of course they are easier to do and for people to accept. If you think using more detailed data will help then try it, but don't be surprised if it makes no significant difference. If you can't keep the level of detail manageable you will need to go beyond spreadsheet technology and there is a risk that people will not be able to respond to a large number of very detailed forecasts anyway.

- Compare the accuracy of statistical forecasts with any forecasts actually made during the same period using whatever method is in place already. The aim is to find a better statistical rule, not a perfect rule.
- If the results of this initial exploration provide a rule good enough for people to agree to use FORECASTING WITH STATISTICAL EXTRAPOLATION then build the rule into a new forecasting model/spreadsheet that allows managers to make adjustments to the forecast by allowing for the impact of past blips and adding in the implications of actions they expect or plan for the future that will be different from usual.
- Use the initial study to estimate prediction intervals so that these can be shown with forecasts.
- Test the model and study how managers use it. Refine the model and write instructions for using it.
- Initiate new meetings, or alter existing meetings, so that people are encouraged to discuss action plans and use the reforecasting model to see quickly the estimated impact of alternative actions.
- As usual this means changing standing agendas, educating chairpeople and others attending.
- The guidance could cover use of the forecasting tool, reviewing forecasts (e.g. to ensure that actions are clear rather than just excuses to adjust numbers and manipulate expectations), and responding to inappropriate use of the tool.
- Establish some mechanism for monitoring use of the reforecasting tool.

Measurement and motivation

Adequate evidence of progress motivates more effort of the same kind, even if formal goals are not in place. As implementation proceeds it becomes increasingly important to measure progress and do so in increasingly satisfactory ways.

At first most people are sufficiently encouraged just to know that relevant things are happening. We don't expect immediate results. However, soon this becomes a more critical desire for evidence that the action is producing results. Finally, this turns into a desire for more convincing evidence that the results outweigh the costs of action.

Measurements of progress do not have to be perfect from the start and should not stay the same throughout. They need to be adequate and usually need to improve repeatedly as weaknesses of initial measurements are discovered and better ideas arise.

Note

1 A useful source is a website called Forecasting Principles, sponsored by the International Institute of Forecasters, and available at http://www.forecastingprinciples. com/.

12 Personal Education and Assessments

Most of the literature on risk control is about corporate processes and systems. By comparison, risk control as a personal skill, something that individual managers can learn about as they develop, is a new frontier.

What could managers learn beyond details of the risks and controls in their line of work (covered extensively in Part II of this book)? Learning how to use the company's risk management systems is really just continuing with the corporate process theme. Perhaps they could learn more about doing calculations with probabilities? Perhaps they could learn more about the psychology of thinking under uncertainty?

These would be good ideas under the right circumstances, but there is another possibility that applies to every organization at every level and gets to the heart of our difficulties with risk and uncertainty. This possibility is to develop the skills we use to respond to uncertainty in everyday situations, including conversations. It is the topic for this chapter.

Chapter 4 discussed situations where we tend to underestimate uncertainty, or at least act as if we have. It gave some high-profile examples of organizations that have collapsed or been badly damaged by this kind of behaviour and also explored the many situations that bring it out.

Although headline-making disasters are comparatively rare, the dangerous situations are extremely common and smaller losses and missed opportunities happen all the time.

We all manage risk and uncertainty with some degree of skill. Some people have good habits in these dangerous situations, some people have beliefs and preferences that should be a serious concern, and most people are a mixture.

Risk and Uncertainty Management Assessment (RUMA)

To understand more about how people think in situations involving risk and uncertainty I developed a survey tool called RUMA, which stands for Risk and Uncertainty Management Assessment.

A typical RUMA survey consists of descriptions of between three and six fictional scenarios, each of which is followed by a list of five or six actions that might be taken in the scenario. Each scenario is described in one or two paragraphs and each action is described in one or two sentences.

The respondent has to read each scenario then rate each action for how good they think it would be in the scenario, using the ratings 'Awful', 'Poor', 'Neutral',

'Good', or 'Great'. The respondent then says how certain they feel about the rating, using a percentage score. These answers are individual answers, never group answers.

The scenarios are drawn from a bank of over 20 scenarios. All are fictional, but most are based loosely on a real situation, which helps to keep them realistic. For example one of my favourites is based on evidence from the Holyrood building project public inquiry. Here is the text of the scenario and the actions.

BUILDING PROJECT

Imagine you are a senior government official who has been put in charge of a high-profile building project. So far the building is going according to schedule and the Minister (i.e. the senior politician involved) has taken almost no interest in the project apart from smiling press conference appearances. However, you have recently become aware that the company that is pre-fabricating sections of an elaborate glass roof have hit potentially serious technical difficulties with the design and are in dispute with the architects and construction managers. Angry letters are being exchanged between these three parties and you are being copied in as each positions itself as an innocent party. The true position is unclear. According to your plan there should still be enough time to complete the roof sections and install them on schedule. You have to decide what to tell the Minister, if anything, about the roof situation.

Potential actions:

- Tell the Minister nothing. The project is still on schedule and there is time to sort out the roof.
- Personally visit the roof-making company and have them show you the technical issues of which they complain.
- Tell the Minister immediately about the dispute and potential consequences, focusing on the worst outcomes. Prepare the Minister for the worst.
- Tell the Minister nothing until you have investigated the roof situation and have a course of action to recommend. Then, if your course of action requires Ministerial backing, explain the situation and ask for the decision.
- Give the Minister a brief presentation on all areas of risk and uncertainty related to the project, including the roof worries, and covering what you are doing to investigate and manage these, and the potential for Ministerial action or decision-making being required.

This is the classic 'do I tell my boss?' problem that most people experience from time to time. The temptation is always to say nothing and see if you can sort things out so you never have to give bad news. Psychologically it becomes a case of taking a risk to avoid a loss i.e. a risk of being caught out and a loss of face. This is a situation where many people are irrationally prone to bad risk taking. There are other traps too, as we will see later when looking at typical results from RUMA studies.

What RUMA studies have shown

RUMA is a relatively new development and in future a lot more will be discovered using this tool. So far the main observations from RUMA studies are as follows:

- The actions most strongly supported by most people are those that are open, honest, rational, and risk aware. (Of course, that doesn't necessarily mean that behaviour is the same as the answer given in the survey.)
- However, some actions with hidden dangers are also supported by many people.
- Even actions that most people would regard as a poor choice are supported by a minority of respondents.
- Sometimes, groups within an organization have preferences that reflect something about their organization or role in a way that leads them to favour, as a group, actions with hidden dangers.
- Where people support an action that most people do not support their level of certainty tends to be low.
- When respondents take the survey a second time after receiving feedback about their first ratings they are influenced by what their peers gave as ratings and by advice given, which may be illustrated by real case histories.
- There are large differences in approach between individuals.
- Most respondents are inconsistent in their responses, appearing to show high uncertainty awareness in some situations but low uncertainty awareness in others. This is probably because their ratings are influenced by many beliefs and most people have never systematically considered the risk angle.

To illustrate these points, Table 12.1 gives the results for the Building Project scenario given above. The numbers represent the percentage of the 141 respondents who chose each rating for each action.

Table 12.1   RUMA results for the project scenario

N=141	Awful	Poor	Neutral	Good	Great
Say nothing	40%	38%	12%	7%	3%
See for yourself	1%	4%	15%	47%	33%
Tell the worst	17%	36%	21%	20%	6%
Find a solution, then tell	4%	16%	12%	45%	23%
Tell everything	1%	3%	8%	38%	50%

The action of seeing the roof problem for yourself is separate from the other actions, which are alternatives to each other.

The best-supported action is to give a full presentation of all the major areas of uncertainty on the project, including the worrying roof situation. This is also the open, honest, rational, risk-aware action. At the opposite extreme, most people agree that saying nothing is a 'Poor' or 'Awful' choice.

This is consistent with the usual finding that people give greatest support to the open, honest, rational, risk-aware actions.

However, a clear majority also think it is a 'Good' or 'Great' idea to say nothing until a solution to the potential roof situation has been found and only then disclose to the Minister that there was something to worry about.

The hidden danger in this is that a solution will not be found and so disclosure will never occur.

People give a number of justifications for supporting this action. The main ones are these:

- Bosses want their people to bring them solutions, not problems.
- If you tell your boss about a potential problem the boss will interfere so it is best to do the actions you can first.
- In reality the best action is to have a go at finding a solution and then if you fail after a short time that is the time to disclose the potential problem. (This is not one of the actions on the list for this scenario.)

All these are dangerous lines of thinking. Bosses want to be kept informed of important matters, even if no action is required from them. Giving information is not the same as asking for help.

The idea of having a quick look for a solution before speaking up is particularly appealing but this is a psychological trap. Suppose you take a few days to consider the risk and still can't find a solution. How would you feel about giving your boss the worrying news now? Probably you would feel worse. Not only is there a bad situation, but it has been going on for longer and you held the news back. Surely it is wiser to hang on for another day longer, just long enough to get a reply back to your email, or for the suppliers to change their minds, or for some inspiration to strike you when you need it most?

Fortunately, prompt disclosure via a routine risk report is an easy option with no such dangers. If only people always opted for it.

The dangers in this situation are also indicated by the fact that, on average, one person in ten thinks saying nothing is a 'Good' or 'Great' action. This is not the same as saying that for *every* ten people one thinks saying nothing is a good idea. In most groups who work together nobody thinks this is a good idea, but in some groups it is more than 10 per cent and could be a lot more than 10 per cent.

People who take this line also tend to support actions in other scenarios that involve delegation by target setting.

Applying scenario-based testing and teaching

The principles behind RUMA are simply to:

1. use scenarios to define situations where erroneous thinking about risk and

uncertainty are common; then

2. use ratings of potential actions as a way to communicate views about how to act in those situations.

These same principles can be used in other forms.

We all manage risk to some degree of skill now, so working on personal skills is about raising that level rather than starting something new. Surveys can be used to see where people are now.

The scenarios alone are useful for capturing the essence of the problem situations in a way that allows people to talk about them.

This could lead to expressing policies or to educational events. It provides a way to understand what people currently think they should do and how they would react to alternative suggestions from other people.

It can also be used to assess an individual's skills, find people suitable for particular roles or projects, and find 'friends' likely to be good candidates for early use of new tools and techniques for risk control.

13 *Understanding Barriers to Improvement*

Previous chapters have pointed out the huge scope for increasing the value of risk control and explained many efficient control mechanisms that most organizations could and should make more use of. We can imagine organizations made up of people who skilfully manage risk and uncertainty using their own skills and also corporate mechanisms that are light, agile, smart, helpful, efficient, and continually improving.

If only getting to this situation was as simple as everyone reading this book and chanting in unison: 'Yes, that's what we all want to do so we will all make time for it and help in any way we can.'

Sadly, even if you are the most important person in an organization – in fact even if you are the *only* person in an organization – such easy progress is a remote possibility.

There will be barriers to improvement, some of them quite hard to deal with. This chapter surveys some of the most problematic barriers that are typically faced by anyone wanting to improve risk control. It also makes some suggestions on how to overcome or avoid those barriers, before later chapters go into more detail on some more of the important tactics for getting improvement to happen.

Low expertise and expectations

The more you learn about high performance control systems the more value it seems risk control can contribute. Conversely, if your knowledge of risk control is limited to the usual bureaucratic mechanisms and audit-focused projects then risk control seems much less exciting, your expectations of value will remain low, and you will not be motivated to learn more. Given competing priorities there's no reason why you should do any more than the bare minimum dictated by regulators.

Here are some tactics that could be used to attack this barrier to improvement:

- Pass on stories about gains made by others. Case studies and statistics are occasionally published that show real gains, at least in narrow projects. Encourage people to expect more.
- Promote measurement and reporting of net value added by risk control work. Do not miss easy opportunities to measure value provided by controls in your own organization.

- Promote personal skills and knowledge. Not many people want a deep understanding of segregation of duties, for example, but many of the intelligent control mechanisms are inherently more interesting to most managers. The more people know the more they will expect and the more they will be able to contribute. Chapter 12 looks at education and assessment of individual skills in more detail, while the whole of Part II is dedicated to design ideas that many managers would benefit from learning more about.

Uncertainty suppression

Chapter 4 introduced the idea of 'uncertainty suppression' and gave several examples of ways that we tend to behave as if we are more certain than we really are or should be. The forces behind uncertainty suppression mean that often people actively resist attempts to introduce technically desirable improvements to risk and uncertainty management.

For example, suppose an ambitious executive is driving a business idea towards approval and is determined to get his way. He's been talking up the benefits, talking down the costs, and feigning certainty for weeks. Then someone suggests introducing a new procedure that will help to ensure that new business proposals are evaluated objectively with full consideration of uncertainty. It even has specific steps to limit uncertainty suppression that will significantly weaken the business case he has been pushing. What is his rational response to this new idea? The rational response is to pretend to support the change while doing everything possible to ignore, evade, delay, and undermine it.

Tactics for overcoming this barrier include the following:

- Avoid upsetting existing politics. You could (1) choose a time when nobody important is trying to do something that would be embarrassed by the new controls, (2) announce a date of introduction that is far enough into the future to allow people to get their current dirty work finished, (3) introduce the controls to apply to new items only.
- Push through anyway. Maybe dirty work in the pipeline is exactly what you need to tackle and senior support is available to make it happen.
- Focus on controls that are hard to fake. This means controls where (1) it is hard to create evidence that the control's required action has been done when in fact it hasn't, and (2) if people do the required control action is it hard for them to avoid the beneficial effect (e.g. their own attitudes are changed even though they try to resist).

Which controls are hard to fake is a research topic at the moment and I don't think anyone really knows which they are. In Part II of this book I've tried to concentrate on controls that I believe are hard to fake. For example, HEALTHY CONVERSATIONS ABOUT CONTROL PERFORMANCE may seem like friendly conversations without much pressure involved but it is hard to discuss controls in the way required without actually doing them because of the need to come up with meaningful details and report them up the line.

Uncertainty suppression is institutionalized in most organizations because it is built into management mechanisms such as budgetary control against fixed targets. Therefore, another way to reduce uncertainty suppression is to replace these mechanisms with mechanisms that do the same job but without driving uncertainty suppression.

Gridlock

Very few controls are chosen and put in place by people who know what they are doing and have a *free choice*.

In my auditing and consulting experience I have been lucky enough to meet a number of risk-and-control managers in large organizations who are desperate to make a positive impact and bursting with good ideas. Unfortunately the programmes they actually implement tend to be almost identical to those implemented by others because, despite their expertise, they do not have a free choice.

Instead, people are hustled by urgent requirements to meet new regulations, forced to adopt mediocre practices by well-meaning auditors relying on simplistic but 'official' guidance, unable to get out of trying to make their predecessor's bad systems work instead of starting something new, and defeated by the limited knowledge and trust of senior executives. The kiss of death is in words like these: 'Look, why can't we just keep it simple and make a list of our top ten risks?' People working in international companies sometimes have to achieve consensus from all countries despite long-standing rivalries. All too often it comes down to a choice between poor risk control or no risk control at all.

This feeling of gridlock is not confined to risk control specialists. It often seems that everyone feels their hands are tied. Even members of committees drafting the 'official' guidance that contributes so strongly to gridlock feel their choices are limited by factors beyond their control. Everyone is working to get approval and agreement from others based on what those others *appear* to want.

Chapter 14 suggests tackling this gridlock problem by seeking incremental shifts in attitude and approach in as many organizational roles as possible. In Chapter 15 I suggest the Friendly Expansion strategy, which involves working first with people who are supportive, and only moving on to include others once early success has been achieved. Chapter 16 mentions research showing that most people have more rational ideas about risk and control than their language and some behaviour would suggest. Most people do not believe some key points of received wisdom but perhaps do not realize they are in a majority.

Another strategy I have seen used is to have an overall grand design in mind but wait for the organization to get motivated to do projects that can be used to build at least part of the grand design. For example, part of the grand design might be improved forecasting, but nothing can be done about it unless there is an urgent desire for improved forecasting at a senior level. Then, one day, something happens that seriously embarrasses senior executives and leads them to want improved forecasting, so now that part of the grand design can be put in place.

Audit and regulation focus

Audit is an important job and valuable. Many auditors are highly knowledgeable, hard working, and keen to make a worthwhile contribution.

Having said that, those same people would probably make an even greater positive contribution if their job was to use their expertise to design and implement high-performance control systems, using design methods rather than audit methods, considering all factors not just risk, and getting down into the technical details that make the difference between an inadequate control and a great one.

The world needs audit and auditors, but if there is a control problem it won't be solved by writing reports repeating the existence of the problem; someone has to fix the controls. Sadly, regulatory attempts to improve controls tend to lead to a lot more evaluation of controls (through auditing and certification) and only a little more controls development.

This book has focused on control mechanisms rather than audit as an antidote to over-auditing.

Weak or undeveloped techniques treated as proven

Not every suggestion for a risk control programme or control is a good one. Some are better than nothing, but only just. Some are worse than nothing. More often they have the potential to be good but need a lot of work and experimentation to achieve their potential.

Unfortunately we often feel obliged to pretend that our proposals are more solid and more proven than is really the case. This is classic uncertainty suppression but perhaps intensified by the pressure on risk control practitioners to appear thoroughly reliable and professional at all times, even when they are doing something nobody has ever done before.

The amount of innovation needed in risk control projects is much higher than most people realize and calls for appropriate project risk management techniques. Just applying normal project risk controls, only more strictly because the project seems hard to control, will usually do more harm than good. A more flexible, experimental approach is needed.

Chapter 15 looks at the problem of innovation in risk control projects and ways to manage it.

Unhelpful, limiting ideas

Some barriers are purely intellectual. Experts in risk control are the ones most likely to stand against progress as a result of intellectual objections, but some unhelpful ideas are so widely held that any large group is likely to contain at least some people who will have a strong objection to even well thought through improvements in risk control.

Limiting, unhelpful ideas promoted by people in positions of power are one of the reasons for the gridlock described above.

Chapter 16 is devoted to common ideas that can stand in the way of adopting good risk control ideas and practices, and suggesting ways to counter their limiting effects.

14 Key Roles and How Each Can Increase Value from Risk Control

This chapter is a plot. It's a blueprint for collusion. It's a cunning plan.

Realistically, not everyone in an organization is interested in risk control, still less in getting more value from it. But, some people *are* interested. If you are one of those people – and you're reading this book so it's a good bet – then find yourself among the roles here and read the suggestions for what to push for and what to push against. Then take a look at the other roles to get an insight into their preoccupations and some ideas for what to encourage them to support.

The roles of key players

The main players able to influence risk control in an organization that we will consider in this chapter are:

- *The board or a similar leadership committee.* Typically this will include some members who are executives and others who are part time non-executives there to provide the benefit of their wisdom and some independent challenge.
- *Risk control managers.* Most organizations have one or more groups of specialists to deal with various compliance and risk management tasks such as security, money laundering, Sarbanes-Oxley compliance, and business continuity. All these people are risk control managers. Although they are responsible for making things happen they usually find they have to do so by supporting line managers. For that reason many would prefer not to be called risk managers, but this is unavoidable.
- *Internal audit managers including the head of internal audit.* Internal audit stands apart from risk control managers generally because internal auditors should not, in theory, do anything other than conduct reviews and make reports saying what they found. They have no responsibility for bringing about improvements in anything other than their own work.
- *Line managers*, meaning of course the people who manage most of the real business of the organization.
- *IT managers.* Not much in large organizations today can be done without computers being involved in some way.

- *Everyone else in the organization.* Collectively this is the most important group, though individually each person usually has less influence on decisions that are taken.

Senior executives

If you are a senior executive then the odds are that you are in demand all the time, work long hours, have 50 or so projects on the go at any one time, and never quite have enough time to do anything as well as you would like.

Part of your problem is that everyone wants your support for whatever it is they think is important. Demands are imposed from outside your organization as well as from inside. They believe that consistent support from you will make the difference between success and failure for them, and they may be right.

Unfortunately, there are so many people who want this, and for so many different things, that it's hard to meet everyone's expectations. For many things you have just about time to sign a few documents and make encouraging and supportive statements in meetings, but that's about it.

Here are some suggestions on what to expect, press for, and encourage in the area of risk control.

- Expect risk control managers of all sorts to focus on business value, and money in particular, even as they are covering whatever regulatory demands concern them and you. Value first, every time.
- Expect projects to be justified by their net business value, quantified as far as possible, in nearly every case, even if the law means there is no choice but to go ahead.
- Expect costs and business benefits of risk control projects to be measured and reported.
- Insist that risk and control be tackled in a logical way, using appropriate mathematical ideas, and providing proper models of risk, not just worry-driven to-do lists i.e. risk registers. Insist on evidence of controls effectiveness from measurement of results, not just from certification or opinions on methods.
- Expect investment in people who improve controls to increase somewhat overall, but expenditure on people who just audit controls to stay the same or fall. Expect risk control specialists to be skilled and inventive.
- Expect all risk control programmes to deliver business benefits at frequent intervals (monthly or shorter) and do not tolerate projects that go on for months before anything useful arrives.
- Push to ensure that the need for controls design and implementation is anticipated and resources are directed in good time. If the impetus for control improvements is always remediation then something is wrong.
- Encourage education about risk and uncertainty so that people in your organization develop their personal skills as well as participating in formal processes.

Senior non-executives

If you are a senior non-executive then you are a part-time employee. Very part time. However, you have status, experience, and expertise and you are expected to use them. A lot of people look to you to provide some kind of challenge to the executives and in a way to be more focused on risk than they are, especially if you are on the audit committee.

The information to which you have access is vital to your effectiveness but a lot of people try hard to control the information you see. The management accounts shown at board meetings may not always be as clear or as informative as you would like, and at audit committees it is obvious that the whole event is being stage managed to ensure that nothing shocking ever happens and no actions result.

Not only should you be looking for the same things as the senior executives, but you should also expect to see evidence of risk and uncertainty being expertly managed by the executives, including during board meetings:

- Push for information that tells you, quantitatively, about the uncertainties in information you are given and expected to rely on. For example, if you are shown a forecast, where is the information that shows how accurate it is? What about error bands and analyses of past forecasting accuracy?
- When asked to participate in major decisions insist on being shown proper information about risks, with numbers. Always demand to know what the effect on the organization would be of things turning out in different ways, especially if projections show only one possible future. A business case that just shows a best guess of the results to expect, and with perhaps a list of risks and a sensitivity analysis of one factor at a time, is not enough.
- Push to ensure that the board's process for developing and monitoring strategies takes alternative futures into account properly, for example by scenario planning.
- Press for the board to be educated and coached in advanced risk and uncertainty management. Nobody is perfect.

In addition, and especially if you are on the audit committee:

- Look for a clean separation between audit, which should be strictly hands-off, and other work on risk, which should be hands on. It is never acceptable for auditors to review their own work or ideas.
- Expect improved assurance to come mainly from improved design of controls, so that they efficiently generate evidence of effectiveness, continuously, instead of the traditional reliance on internal audits.

Internal audit managers including the head of internal audit

As a senior internal auditor you have good access to senior executives, non executives, and much else besides. You know you should be strictly hands-off but, if your organization is small, people probably see you as the main expert on risk and controls and look to you for help on all related matters.

Your role calls for straight talking on occasions but still you are sensitive to politics and need to be diplomatic and careful at managing relationships. You probably have to fight for the resources you need and often feel that senior executives are not as supportive of control improvements as they should be.

When it comes to increasing value from risk control you are in an awkward position because many organizations would benefit from shifting your expert resources from hands-off reviews to hands-on design and implementation.

Moreover, the audit profession has been strongly promoting the non-mathematically influenced style of risk management for many years so steering your organization towards improvement is likely to involve some rethinking and a shift of position.

Happily, there are some things that you can encourage that promote value and are consistent with your interests:

- Push for the clearest possible split between pure, hands-off audit and actively improving controls in a hands-on way as a risk control manager might. Either put people in a separate team or monitor which role your people are in from one review to the next and keep reminding people of this.
- Promote the integrated risk control concept and especially the importance of intelligent internal controls. This is your licence to conduct reviews of management performance and to comment on the management of risk at every level.
- Educate your own internal auditors so that they are competent to review intelligent internal controls and so expand the scope of your work.
- Push hard for formal controls designs against which to audit. Most reviews involve an auditor asking a lot of questions to find out what controls are in place then thinking about whether they are enough. Ideally, they should receive a design document in good time showing what has been designed and should be in place. This makes audits more cost-effective.
- Push to see controls designs in advance of implementation so that you can comment at that early stage. Obviously this will also mean pushing for a process to be in place that identifies the need for control changes in good time and directs suitable resources to do them.
- Recommend control improvements that will provide continuous evidence of control performance in the form of statistics about error rates, backlogs, other aspects of quality and timeliness, etc.
- When it comes to the design of intelligent controls and what we used to call 'the risk management process', raise the bar by shifting to the logic of

the mathematically inspired tradition of risk management and relentlessly pointing out misconceptions, biases, and procedures that don't make sense. For example, review the clarity of risk register entries and report that, as is usual, almost none of them are clear enough to be useful.

Line managers

You are busy and important, getting on with the real business of the organization instead of wasting time on head-office paper pushing. You manage risk all the time, a lot more competently than some people think.

Governance, risk, and controls are not your biggest concerns most of the time. You are more interested in workload, capacity, people and their skills, customers, competition, marketing, service levels, and (like everyone else) internal politics.

Here are some things you probably won't mind pushing for whenever you get the chance:

- Fewer audits.
- Audits that lead to clever new ideas instead of obvious, simplistic bureaucracy. Intelligent internal controls that acknowledge the skills of the people using them are more likely to be helpful and effective, and to add real value.
- Better information about error rates, backlogs, IT reliability, and other measures of process health that you can use to monitor performance and improve it. You want to get more work done with less resource and doing that usually hinges on reducing waste, much of which is caused by not getting things right first time.
- Systems that provide the process health information.
- More expert help with controls design and implementation. Rather than have the controls experts just tell you things are not right and make some high-level recommendations, how about they get stuck into the detail and do something to help design and implement improvements? Having all the controls specialists sitting in internal audit is a problem because, strictly speaking, that means they are banned from helping directly.
- A more rigorous approach to overall risk management of the organization, not just risk registers and rough ratings. Many organizations have core activities that are carried out with considerable skill and sophistication and often this involves risk modelling and sophisticated decision-making under uncertainty. Only the more mathematically inspired approaches to thinking about risk can make wider use of this work.
- Serious management education about uncertainty and how to manage it. Most training courses on 'risk management' today are just telling you how to fill in the forms for some generic, low-tech risk management process that will not make you any better than you are now.

Your personal contribution to improving the way risk and uncertainty are managed is crucial. Consider your personal skills at managing people, communicating uncertain information, designing control systems, and so on.

IT managers

As a manager of information and communication technology you are very clear on the importance of focusing what you do on the real needs of your organization and doing what is valuable. At the same time you are beset with pressures, mostly fuelled by the sales and marketing people in computer companies, to keep up with technology and the latest technology management concepts. Are you agile? Is your architecture service-oriented? Are you maximizing the benefits of business process management? And so on, and on, and on.

You are also very aware of the cost of controls and the need for them – at least for some of them. Under the heading of computer security fall a frightening list of worries including disaster recovery, viruses, firewall penetration, disgruntled employees, fires, dodgy emails and controversy over email monitoring, the ever-growing storage problem, system availability, hardware failures, Sarbanes-Oxley, change control, security advisories, patches, project failures, capacity management, and so on.

Arguably it is your computer systems that provide most of the worthwhile controls in your organization. Most controls are there, not because the user community thought of them, but because one of your people wrote or bought the software that contains the control. If people in the business want better, more valuable risk control it's obvious who they will turn to.

Things you could support include these:

- Proactive high-level design and allocation of resources to controls design and implementation in good time. If others in the organization will not participate at least you can get started and do a lot of it without them.
- Have controls design and implementation specialists in your team and especially on your projects. Get expertise applied to risk and controls in the way system users will work and what the system will do to help them, as well as for more traditional IT security concerns like audit trails and access control.
- Make sure as many of your projects as possible are designed for incremental delivery of stuff that stakeholders value. Don't allow projects to work away for months without delivering something usable by someone. Ideally, expect something delivered every week or two weeks with lessons being learned that quickly from experience.
- Push for more sophisticated modelling and analysis of risks throughout your organization. In particular, argue for showing the full distribution of impacts from a risk rather than just probability and impact ratings. One problem with these simplistic ratings is that they throw away information about the extremes of impact. That means that extremely high impacts are understated, which is bad for business continuity, and very frequent low impacts are also understated, which is bad for virus protection and network security, which are under constant attack.
- Provide systems that report process health information such as error rates and backlogs.

Everyone else

Most of us fall into the 'everyone else' category, which means we are in the most important group. Whether your work brings you into contact with the risk control specialists or not, risk and control are still important in your life.

Uncertainty is a huge cause of strife and stress for most people at work. We are frequently put under pressure to promise and deliver consistent, predictable results as if the world was consistent and predictable. What so often stops us from achieving the results we hope for is that the unexpected happens, again, as usual. Conditions change, outside our control and more radically than anyone expected, something breaks, someone does something silly, conditions change again, and so on.

What we can all do to improve the way risk and uncertainty are handled is to learn to keep a more open mind about the future and learn to manage in a way that is consistent with that more open-minded view. We need to be able to recognize when we are being pressurized to suppress uncertainty and communicate in a way that keeps uncertainty in the open without undermining our credibility or causing paralysis from indecision.

In addition, let's all take every opportunity to press for risk control that delivers real business value, even when the work has to be done for purely regulatory reasons.

15 *Innovation and the Friendly Expansion Strategy*

Another reason that many risk control projects struggle is that they involve innovation but are managed as if they do not.

Projects which involve doing something that has never been done before, as far as you know, and will involve some invention and discovery along the way, present special problems. The more innovative the project the more easily it will shrug off attempts to impose normal project management disciplines. These projects are not to everyone's taste, which is just as well because if all projects in an organization were like this then chaos would soon result. These are not the projects any organization should have in large number, or make large investments in. These are the projects that often go wrong, that often end up somewhere unexpected, that create confusion and stress far beyond their (usually) small size, and yet that an organization needs to do from time to time to avoid falling behind. In short, you need them but volunteers may be in short supply.

Treating innovative projects as if they are normal, run-of-the-mill projects is a dangerous mistake.

For most people risk control is sober, responsible, cautious, assurance giving – and absolutely not innovative or experimental. It seems somehow wrong that risk control people might be trying to do new, unproven things. And yet that is what most risk control projects involve.

The early projects in companies to comply with Sarbanes-Oxley's Section 404 are an excellent example. Here were projects intended to provide reassurance. Perhaps people thought all audits were the same. The reality was that most early projects had little in the way of a plan, often no official resources (e.g. a budget allocation), were led by people who thought the work incompatible with their role (i.e. internal auditors), and were an adventurous leap into the unknown. Nothing quite like it had been done by companies before so people invented their approach, tried to get their auditors to say it was acceptable, and started with their fingers crossed while pretending they knew exactly what they were doing.

Companies took advice from audit and consulting companies, presumably because they offered audit experience, but this experience was not directly relevant to the review required. The big audit firms wrote guidance documents for companies but these were on the basis that companies would do the same as external auditors, only more of it. This was quite wrong and severely criticized by regulators a year or so later. The blind were leading the blind.

Soon there were people who could say they had the much sought after 'Sarbanes-Oxley experience' and had 'successfully' helped companies comply. But what they had was experience of doing the compliance projects in an inefficient way. Yes, the companies had complied but at a staggering and unnecessary cost.

In general it is much better to recognize the innovation involved in most risk control projects and manage those projects appropriately.

This chapter looks at the special characteristics of innovative risk control projects and how to make them successful. Just applying normal project management disciplines, but more strictly because these projects seem so hard to control, will do more harm than good

What to expect

Even when well managed, projects with lots of innovation usually involve:

- **High uncertainty:** This more than anything else defines the experience of innovative projects. The methods are uncertain. The likely results are uncertain. Attitudes are uncertain. Resources required and available are uncertain. (Often there is no 'budget' at the outset.) Objectives are uncertain. Yes, even objectives.

- **Shifting, often fuzzy objectives:** Objectives are uncertain even when great effort is made to clarify them. The problem is that we don't know what we will invent. It may turn out that we invent something that offers new advantages we did not suspect initially. It may be that, overall, this result is better than we originally hoped for, or worse, or just different. The answer is to think about objectives repeatedly, accepting and clarifying the uncertainties involved, and keep an open mind.

- **Endless problem solving:** Time and again our solution to one problem creates new problems elsewhere. Even when we are doing well there are still many shocking discoveries to make, many drawbacks, technical hitches, objections, political barriers, and so on and on. This is characteristic of innovation. An innovation takes time to permeate a society because everyone has to solve at least some problems in order to take advantage of it.

- **Lucky discoveries:** If you do these projects well you will find that the luck is not all bad. Keep your approach open to good luck and usually it will come along.

- **Unproductive meetings:** Many meetings on these projects seem unproductive but are not. Unfortunately, many others really are a waste of time. The problem is that not everyone understands these projects or how to contribute to them. Wheels spin pointlessly in pseudo-creative brainstorming, idiotic exercises with sticky notes and flip charts, and other substitutes for productive thought.

- **Uneven progress:** Will we have the problem half solved when we get halfway through the budget? Unlikely. These projects are more like scientific discovery than digging a ditch. You can work for weeks and achieve nothing, then, suddenly, it all comes together (or not).

- **Conceptual resistance:** Doing something new often triggers intellectual objections, mainly from people who are experts in the field. Non-experts usually have no difficulty with a new idea, if explained in plain language, because they don't have prior expectations or beliefs that conflict. In contrast, experts can completely miss a new idea even when explained very clearly. They think they understand, but actually hear what they expect, not what was said. For example, members of the Beyond Budgeting Round Table have told me that the main resistance to getting rid of budgetary control systems comes from internal auditors and finance people. People with other backgrounds, like sales, logistics, and production, have much less difficulty imagining a happy life without budgets.

- **Lack of consensus:** Since people involved in these projects are uncertain about so much it is not surprising that they agree on so little. A good starting point is to agree that things are uncertain and that the work should be done in a way that helps reduce unhelpful uncertainty without killing off opportunities, so that over time more agreement will be reached.

Who will succeed?

Before we look at the techniques and attitudes that promote success in innovative projects, here are some thoughts on the ideal people to include in the team. These projects call for powerful thinkers rather than diligent organizers. If the team doesn't have the right kind of intellectual horsepower to succeed then no amount of resource management is going to make a difference. What should we look for?

The ideal player is:

- **A clear thinker who can tolerate extreme uncertainty:** Since innovative projects create extreme uncertainty you have to be able to cope with it, and yet have the clarity to reduce it through insight and good strategies.
- **Highly inventive in the subject matter required:** This follows from the need for endless problem solving. Ask the ideal person if they have any ideas and they will have several promising ones almost immediately. Quantity of ideas without quality is not sufficient.
- **Multi-skilled:** Many innovations cut across disciplines and organizational boundaries. In risk control projects the ideal player knows controls (obviously), computer programming and IT generally, finance, computer packages, the business, cognitive ergonomics, other relevant psychology, and on top of that is an excellent persuader, writer, and speaker. Each knowledge gap means the person can be delayed by having to wait for someone else to cooperate. The greatest hazard in my experience is being told something silly by an IT specialist but not having the knowledge or self-confidence to realize what has happened. The next best thing to multi-talented individuals is a multi-talented team.
- **Willing to keep trying:** One of the most difficult aspects of these projects is the emotional impact of seeing one idea after another crushed by politics or new discoveries. The ideal person will often be the first to realize their idea needs to be replaced. This takes considerable drive and self-confidence.

- **Driven to make things better:** It's no good if people on the project are easily put off by feeble flak like 'If it's not broken don't fix it', 'We don't want to reinvent the wheel' or the ever-popular 'We know our business'. The driven innovator knows the objective is to improve, not to fix, that wheel technology has never stopped developing, and that people can always know more about their business than they do now.

- **Able to tolerate being in a minority:** Innovators need to be comfortable with having most people thinking one thing while they are thinking another. It is vital to be totally immersed in the work the project is changing, to understand past behaviour and beliefs, and yet to avoid becoming drawn into the existing way of thinking and unable to see beyond it. This is even more difficult when things are uncertain because it is human nature in this situation to look at what others are doing and copy.

- **Brings ideas from a different field:** Cross-fertilization can be very useful. An industry employing hundreds of thousands, even millions of people can still be insular and unaware of just how narrow its thinking is.

Useful techniques

Here are techniques and tactics that are useful in highly innovative projects:

- **Discuss uncertainties early on, and keep coming back to them:** Since uncertainty is so high it helps to get it out in the open, acknowledge it, and let it shape your approach to the project. It is a big mistake to pretend you are less uncertain than you really are, and almost as bad not to make the effort to increase awareness of uncertainties. List them, categorize them, talk about them, discuss how you hope to learn more over time. In successive iterations of this discussion your analysis may become more organized and scientific.

- **Value experience gained:** A common mistake is to think innovation is the same as 'blue sky thinking' i.e. an exercise in imagination unfettered by real-life constraints. Long, abstract discussions conducted in meeting rooms or 'off site' venues inevitably spin round in confusion within this data free zone. It can be helpful to shake off old habits, but a better way of doing this is to look very carefully at reality and let it provide the clues. A superb example was shown on UK television in the series 'Better by Design', in which two product designers, Richard Seymour and Dick Powell, were challenged to redesign everyday objects and make them better. Richard and Dick are astonishingly talented and produced some outstanding ideas on this programme, some of which have subsequently been turned into successful products by major companies. So, how do they start their search for improvement? They look closely at what products are like now. When the challenge was to redesign the toilet they looked at toilets, sat on them, uncovered medical advice on how to sit on toilets, went to an exhibition of toilets in Japan, and talked to people about their experiences with toilets. In short, they immersed themselves in the current experience of using toilets! While they did so ideas for improvements sparked from them and people they talked to. These were not designs, just ideas, elements, possibilities.

Another kind of experience that is vital on innovative projects is the learning we get from trying something and looking to see what happens.

- **Early, incremental deliveries:** The sooner we *deliver* some kind of improvement, even if it is small or narrow, the quicker we will learn. Learning by trying something out is more powerful and reliable than learning by theory alone. The principles of 'skunkworks', as pioneered at Lockheed Martin when developing spy planes such as the SR71 (Blackbird) and its predecessor the U2, include making something that flies as soon as possible. This is so that the design can be evolved with the benefit of testing experience. Techniques for designing and managing projects with many frequent deliveries of improvements, and where the overall project is evolving, have been set out brilliantly by Tom Gilb in his method 'Evo'.[1]

- **A benefits delivery pipeline:** If you are to deliver beneficial change in increments from an early stage then you need to set things up to allow that to be done efficiently. Risk control projects often involve designing a process or some reports for people to use. You need some 'users' who are interested enough to try out your new inventions, give feedback, and perhaps become sales people for your ideas. Typically these users won't know in advance what they will like and find useful. They may have some ideas about that but not necessarily any better than yours. Your approach will be to get them to try things and react naturally, not as critics but as the users they are.

- **Measure results:** A key element of Evo is measurement of improvements. This is usually done in very simple, practical ways, and rarely turned into net present value terms. How long does it take to enter a sale? How many mistakes do people make per hundred deliveries? Simple measures such as these are good enough for most purposes.

- **Do not commit large resources:** If you conduct the project as a series of small deliveries that are valuable to stakeholders then the commitment of resources at each delivery will be small. It is usually a mistake to let people spend a lot of time and money without delivering something.

- **Repeatedly rethink the benefits:** Benefits *evolve*. In innovative projects this happens even if you don't try, but it is less painful if you know what to expect. Also, if you understand benefits evolution and repeatedly discuss the latest thinking on possible benefits throughout your project you are more likely to notice new, emerging benefits. Holding yourself rigidly accountable to the benefits dreamt of at the start is not helpful. Of course there is the danger of being tricked by imaginative and shifting benefit stories into supporting a project that ultimately achieves nothing useful. If you are seeing frequent deliveries of measured improvements then there is little danger of this.

- **Project the future with ranges, not best guesses:** To keep uncertainty explicit and set realistic expectations, state views about future benefits and costs using ranges, ideally probabilistic ranges.

- **Try multiple experiments in parallel:** When you are not sure what will work it makes sense to try things and see. The fastest way to do this is often to try several ideas in parallel. Another idea along these lines is to run separate project teams with low budgets rather than put all your resources in one team that may get stuck down an unproductive avenue. Two separate projects each costing £100,000, with the same brief, may well produce a better result than a single project costing £500,000.

- **Breadth first:** Problem solving and design are a form of search. We are searching a very large 'problem space' and that size is the big problem. If you are lucky enough to look in a good place early on then success follows quickly. If you don't get lucky you may never find a satisfactory design. Obviously we would like to improve our odds and the way to do that is to sift through a lot of information related to the topic looking for deductions that will constrain the solution and so narrow the search. For example, you may realize early on that only a solution that is acceptable to a particular person will be accepted, or that it has to cost no more than a certain figure, or that the colour should be a warm colour, or that the solution will probably have to be on a cycle more frequent than annual to stand a chance. These little deductions soon build up to a useful basis for searching efficiently. Often you can search for a long time then find something that constrains the solution so tightly that the decision on what to do is made immediately.

How to sabotage innovative projects

If your ambition is to make sure an innovative project is a *failure* then here is what you should do. The following techniques are so easy that even people who want successful projects occasionally do them, not understanding the damage they do.

First, insist on consensus as to exactly what the project will deliver, when, and with what resources. Do not under any circumstances accept any uncertainty in this and do not allow any work to proceed until firm commitment and unanimous agreement have been achieved. If agreement is ever achieved then make it as hard as possible to change anything and frown on opportunism. In the unlikely event that this fails to kill the project develop a formal project plan with large phases of work that make sure nothing is actually delivered until the very end. Set out the project with logical sounding headings like 'analysis' and 'solutions development'. Anything will do as long as it doesn't involve trying something out in practice.

If, like a hardy weed, the project struggles on then your problem might be that there are some strong innovators on the team. If so you must do everything you can to drive them away or prevent them from contributing. Now is the time to set up some brainstorming meetings. Flip charts, sticky notes, breaking into groups, feeding back 'conclusions' – you know the kind of thing. Make sure everyone is treated the same, no matter how obvious the differences in relevant design skill. Make sure nobody has time to think new ideas through properly and that anybody who does have well-thought-through proposals sees them put onto the flip chart along with the others, misinterpreted, mixed, and mangled into useless oblivion.

If, despite all your precautions, someone actually does come up with a promising idea do not worry. They are playing into your hands. Simply welcome the idea, praise it, and focus all resources and thinking on it and it alone. Sooner or later the idea will hit problems and when it does that narrow focus will mean it is stuck. Tackling the problem from several directions at once, or searching for even easier ways in, would give a much better chance of success so make sure people don't get up to those tricks.

The key to effective sabotage is to present what you are doing as sensible, good management. Make it sound 'logical'. Stay calm, take notes, say supportive things, and you can be sure of getting away with it.

On the other hand, if you want success then make sure none of those sabotage tactics are used, even with good intentions.

The Friendly Expansion strategy

This strategy is useful where you have some risk control improvement that needs to be applied throughout an organization or at least wherever it is worthwhile. The procedure is this:

1. **Start with 'friends':** Apply the improvement in a limited part of the organization where the conditions are favourable and the people concerned are friendly towards the idea.
2. **Get some experience:** Use the initial work as an opportunity to gain experience with the tool or approach. Get ideas from the triallists. Watch what they like and what causes them problems.
3. **Improve the ideas/tools/etc.:** Improve the tools/approach in the light of experience.
4. **Get some evidence of value:** Gather evidence of the costs and benefits of the idea, carefully noting what should be expected in future bearing in mind what has been learned.
5. **Move out a bit and repeat:** Extend use of the idea to a bit more of the organization and repeat the above process.

Gradually, people who oppose the idea will have less and less to complain about and will find themselves in a vanishing minority. Another possible outcome is that you will find you have expanded the idea to all areas that can benefit from it.

An alternative to Friendly Expansion is to design something centrally and then launch a global roll-out, hoping that the initial design is good enough to be worthwhile and that objections can be overcome or ignored.

Many risk control programmes driven by external regulation end up being delivered as a waterfall project rather than incrementally, and are hustled along by externally imposed necessity powerful enough to overcome even legitimate objections.

In contrast, risk control programmes without external pressure sometimes start out as an attempt to carry everyone along at the same time but end up being Friendly Expansion because some people simply do not cooperate.

It is usually better to aim for Friendly Expansion from the start, within an incremental project.

'Friends' can be identified in a number of ways. For example:

- Just present your plans and watch reactions.
- Make educated guesses based on their circumstances and recent experiences.
- Get recommendations.
- Use a survey to find out what individuals and groups believe.

Some organizations that use Friendly Expansion make the mistake of using the same department or team as the first stage every time. This might be the most competent team of managers, or perhaps the smallest department with the fewest problems to solve.

This can lead to some resentment and reduces the credibility of early evidence of effectiveness.

However, for most people Friendly Expansion is either their chosen approach to rolling out new ideas or the approach that is forced on them by the initial unwillingness of some groups.

In some ways the innovation that risk control projects so often require is a problem, and yet it is also the solution to that problem. The better we are at recognizing flaws in our designs and switching rapidly to better designs the easier it is to spread those designs across more of an organization.

Note

1 Gilb, T. (2005) *Competitive Engineering: A Handbook for Systems Engineering, Requirements Engineering, and Software Engineering using Planguage.* London: Butterworth-Heinemann.

16 *Helpful Alternatives to Unhelpful Ideas*

This book describes an approach to risk control that emphasizes ideas like creativity, value, distributed use of multiple methods, and human skill alongside corporate processes. In this chapter I will consider some of the unhelpful ideas that can delay progress, for example by making people feel they cannot put numbers on risk, or have to do risk control one way and no other.

These unhelpful ideas are linked to each other, encourage poor practices, and block better practices. We need to understand them, recognize the problems they cause, and know how to counter them.

Contrasting practices

Here is a caricature of an organization that is approaching risk control in the spirit advocated in this book:

> *The organization's vision is that its people learn to manage risk and control better and that their increasingly skilled behaviour is supported by a range of appropriate and ever-improving processes, most of which are decentralized.*
>
> *Typically, these involve going from unstructured analyses and designs to increasingly well-structured views based on explicit models. They begin early and continue throughout projects and other activities. Time and skill go into controls design activities.*
>
> *Numbers and pictures are used to clarify risk perceptions and make rational decisions about controls, taking into consideration economic, cultural, and strategic factors as well as risk.*
>
> *The approach is continuously improved using data and open, honest conversations. A by-product of this is continuous monitoring of the performance and contribution of risk control.*
>
> *All management information is presented along with uncertainty shown in one of a number of approved ways, so it is never forgotten. Board members see all risk, but structured at a level and in a way that makes sense for them, and informed in part by analyses from others in the organization.*

This is natural, pervasive, hard to ignore, open to alternatives, and difficult to dislike. Over time we should expect to see substantial changes to behaviour and processes resulting in increased value.

Now consider a contrasting caricature.

The organization's vision is that all risk control is driven by a single mechanism that generates controls and is known as the risk management system. It is one giant process stretching throughout the company and is identical in every respect wherever it operates. Its crude mechanics are prescribed and must be followed.

Workshops were once held at which people called out risks which were listed on a risk register as they were suggested and then rated for their probability of occurrence and impact if they occurred, both on a scale of None – Low – Medium – High.

The risks were then displayed on a probability-impact matrix coloured red, yellow, and green, and any risks on a yellow or red square needed control actions to be planned and taken until they moved to green. Controls were selected from the four Ts (Terminate, Transfer, Tolerate, or Treat) with no explicit design work at all and no further learning about risks planned.

This was the only consideration in deciding if a control was worthwhile and risk is treated as the only source of control requirements.

Subsequently, progress with risk has been assessed using a self-certification database that asks hundreds of individuals to confirm that they have operated their allotted controls during a period and that things are under control. The status of risk has been reported on special risk reports, separately from other management information, and considered in meetings dedicated to risk and control. The board has concerned itself only with the top ten risks.

On projects, risk analysis begins once the project has clear objectives and a basic plan, but ends during feasibility work because it is believed that at that point the risks should all be fully understood.

With this combination of techniques I would expect to find that the risk register database is a mass of ill-defined, overlapping risks with potential gaps (but too messy to assess); that more advanced forms of risk-thinking have carried on in secret or been driven out; that few good new ideas for control system improvements have been generated; that risk assessments would be inaccurate if they were not meaningless; that areas for improvement have been quietly covered up; and that life goes on as usual with risk control sitting in a dusty box, unloved in a forgotten corner.

Six strategies to promote better practices

Having better, more exciting ideas for control mechanisms is a big part of improving value from risk control. However, it is not the full story.

I believe that unhelpful and incorrect ideas are part of the reason why organizations sometimes implement practices similar to those in the second caricature. Many of these beliefs come from textbook theory, but not all.

However, the link between beliefs and actions is not straightforward. There are inconsistencies between beliefs and between behaviours and beliefs. Theories about risk and uncertainty are often controversial and hard to understand.

After decades of largely futile arguments I have concluded that debates in risk control, like politics, are usually too complicated and fraught with misconceptions to be resolved by conversation. Therefore, directly tackling those unhelpful beliefs should usually be a strategy of last resort.

However, there are several other strategies to try first, usually relying on the fact that most people are rational and intelligent if given the right conditions.

FIRST STRATEGY: JUST DESCRIBE THE DESIGN

The first strategy to consider should be simply to describe the design of control you have in mind. This cuts the risk of activating any unhelpful ideas that might be present.

Probably the main reason that people employ any of the unhappy practices in the second caricature is that they are not aware of better alternatives. Explaining alternatives is enough with many people for them to want to do something better instead.

Sometimes the new practices you are suggesting will be more consistent with a person's beliefs than their current practices so there is a chance that they will see your design and immediately feel happy with it.

For example, it is common in guidance on risk management to talk of 'identifying' risks and to make no comment on what makes a good breakdown of risk and how to create one. This is accepted by many people and reflected in the practices sometimes adopted by organizations.

However, there is a puzzle. The word 'identifying' implies that the risks exist already rather than being chosen subsets of the uncertainty attached to our thinking about the world. If risks exist already then there is no choice about how to divide our uncertainty into risks, which is also implied by the lack of guidance on how to make choices.

All this implies that people who talk and act this way believe that risks are givens and so there is only one way to write a correct/valid list of risks in a given situation and with a given set of objectives (if you ignore alternative descriptions and orders). But, in fact, nearly everyone[1] believes that alternative lists *are* possible and some will be more useful than others. They believe this for a variety of good reasons.

In this example beliefs and actions are not consistent and it is actions that are lagging behind, so introducing a new set of actions may be all that is needed.

Another example concerns audit evidence on the effectiveness of controls. The received wisdom, repeated in textbooks, training courses, and regulations, is that controls effectiveness is evaluated by doing two things:

1. establishing that the design of the controls is such that if they were operated as designed the system would be effective; and
2. testing that individual controls have operated as intended.

However, other forms of evidence are also relevant, such as data on the actual level of inherent risk and process health statistics. These powerful forms of evidence do not appear in the standard theory and yet almost everyone instinctively understands that they are relevant to evaluating controls effectiveness.

Once again beliefs are ahead of actions, but in this case there is an explicit, established body of theory that, if people think of it, could stand in the way. This is a reason for not mentioning that theory and just letting common sense take over.

SECOND STRATEGY: PUT THE DESIGN IN A HELPFUL CONTEXT

Sometimes beliefs in one context are inconsistent with beliefs in another. For example, some people, when asked to give a probability number for an event that has not happened before, feel very uncomfortable and believe they cannot do it because they don't know the probability. And yet, in the context of betting on the outcome of sports events, those same people are able to evaluate odds and place bets. In principle this is the same task, but in a different context.

This leads to the second strategy, which is to mention a context that will help people select the appropriate theory from alternatives they have in their minds.

When it comes to putting numbers on probabilities it is a good idea to liken it to betting on sports because this helps people get in touch with their beliefs about situations where there is high uncertainty but numbers are still used, and to good effect. It is a mistake to refer to school-book situations like tossing a coin or dealing cards from a well-shuffled deck. For most people these examples cue ideas that are quite different. Business situations are much more like betting on horse races than betting on dice.

A variation on this second strategy is to point to other behaviours that people already perform that reflect supportive theory.

THIRD STRATEGY: MENTION SUPPORTIVE BELIEFS

Many good designs for controls are based on simple observations and beliefs that most people agree with but that are inconsistent with theory behind some competing controls.

If people are interested in the theory behind a design then another way to avoid activating unhelpful beliefs is to explain that theory, but avoid mentioning competing theories.

For example, the observation that risk control requirements vary enormously between different applications of control-generating controls implies that the controls used to generate controls in different applications will probably need to be different in some ways. No problem there, and who could disagree? However, if you start instead by saying that standardization of controls is not all it's cracked up to be then theories about standardization will awaken and the conversation can soon be sidetracked into a maze of misconceptions about standardization, communication of risks, and building risk analyses at different organizational levels.

Similarly, the observation that people at different levels of an organization look at things from a different perspective implies that the ideal analysis of risk at each level will also be different (e.g. different levels of detail, different concerns, different models). Again, this is common sense. However, if you start instead with criticism of the idea of rolling up risks from one level for presentation to the next then the debate can quickly get bogged down in the assumption that the only thing different about the perspective at different levels is the amount of detail shown.

FOURTH STRATEGY: ASK QUESTIONS TO FIRM UP WEAK THEORY

On many issues related to risk and uncertainty most people do not have an opinion. They may be going along with some poor practice because they have been told it is expected without ever questioning seriously whether it makes sense. Not everyone needs to be an expert so there is little wrong with this.

It also gives us another way to get people thinking from helpful beliefs instead of incorrect or irrelevant theories. We can just ask them to think carefully and choose from a range of alternatives.

For example, according to most guidance and textbooks on risk management and internal control the purpose of these activities is to ensure that organizations achieve their objectives (which are givens, even though they may need some clarification). Indeed risk management and internal control can be designed on that limited basis, but if you have an idea for managing risk and uncertainty during the *shaping* of objectives then you need to argue otherwise.

Most non-specialists do not have a clear view on what they think risk control is for but you can help them form a view by giving them a free choice between options such as these:

- *Achieve original objectives*: The role of risk/uncertainty management is to help the organization achieve the objectives/targets it set at the start of a year or a project. Uncertainty/risk management has no role in setting or revising those objectives.

- *Achieve given objectives*: The role of risk/uncertainty management is to help the organization achieve its objectives/targets, though these may change during a year or project. Uncertainty/risk management has no role in setting or revising those objectives/targets.
- *Perform well*: The role of risk/uncertainty management is to help the organization perform well, and that includes helping to set and revise objectives/targets.

Most people[2] choose the last option, perform well, and hardly anyone is tempted by the first, which is the literal interpretation of the textbook answer. So, in this case, there is no need to give arguments in favour of going beyond the traditional textbook view because, given a free choice, that's what most people decide for themselves.

Here's another example. People often write and talk about risk as if risks are almost the same as physical objects: singular things with their own existence much like an apple, orange, or number 85 bus. They talk of 'identifying' risks (like identifying a rare bird perhaps), do little to define the boundaries of a risk and separate it from others, and think it appropriate to rate the impact if the risk happened as if that impact has just one possible level.

Does this make sense? Does anyone genuinely believe that risks are like physical objects in these ways? Probably not, and this might be another situation where it is worth giving people a free choice between options such as:

- *Risks are external objects*: Risks are a fact of nature, part of the world around us, and as such they exist already for us to discover, have their own natural definitions, and exist no matter how much information we have.
- *Risks are given uncertainties*: Risks are a product of our uncertainties, and these arise from lack of knowledge as well as the inherent practical difficulty of predicting the world. However, we have no choice about how risks are defined.
- *Risks are uncertainties we can define*: Risks are a product of our uncertainties, and these arise from lack of knowledge as well as the inherent practical difficulty of predicting the world. We can choose how we structure our uncertainty into risks.

I do not know what the popular answer would be but strongly suspect that the first, and most unhelpful, option would not be popular when subjected to concentrated thought.

FIFTH STRATEGY: DIRECT COMPARISON

Suppose that, despite giving a positive rationale for a design and mentioning contexts in which that rationale is familiar to people, there is still resistance from someone on unfounded theoretical grounds. What then?

Or, suppose someone is arguing for a design and has given a rationale that includes misconceptions that could also block another, better design. What can be done?

Quite often these debates are not about whose idea is the one that should be implemented, but whose idea is even fit to be evaluated against the others with a view to implementation.

In this situation a reasonable approach is usually to argue for fair consideration of the alternative design options available. This might be done by pointing out that a design has worked elsewhere, or is liked by some reasonable people, or has been worked out carefully, or is worthy of consideration for some other reason. Often it involves pointing out that the thinking behind it is different but still a legitimate alternative opinion.

For example, someone who believes that 'risk appetite' is an inbuilt part of corporate personality may be reluctant to consider techniques for weighing risk in decisions that do not involve a risk appetite statement or similar system of thresholds. For them risk appetite exists naturally in the form of an upper limit and must be articulated if meaningful risk management is to be done. From this point of view working with a risk appetite is logically essential.

However, for others 'risk appetite' is a synonym of 'risk limit' and means a system of limits that is as much an invention as budgetary control (and works in basically the same way). From this point of view working on risk appetite is not essential and other techniques can be considered.[3]

Controls designed from both perspectives deserve consideration. This is perhaps best done by looking at what would happen if the alternative control procedures were implemented because this approach side-steps the theoretical difference.

Another example concerns probability impact matrices (PIMs). These are two dimensional grids where one axis represents the probability of a risk happening and the other dimension represents some measure of the impact of the risk if it does happen.

PIMs have become so common and are so often promoted in books and regulations that some people have come to the point where they see PIMs as the *only* way to characterize risks, even arguing that other techniques are just PIMs in disguise, which they are not.

If you have an alternative to PIMs that you would like to try then the first stage is simply to get acceptance that alternatives could exist and that they could be at least as acceptable to users as PIMs. My research has shown that well-designed alternatives put up against PIMs in a fair trial are about equally acceptable to users, despite the greater familiarity of PIMs. I found that cumulative probability statements are about as acceptable to users as PIMs. Cumulative probabilities were more popular with risk experts. New graphical forms of cumulative probability statements may achieve even higher usability but that research still needs to be done.

SIXTH STRATEGY: CONTRADICTION

The last resort is to engage in direct argument.

Good arguments exist to refute many unhelpful and incorrect ideas that block improved risk control but using them is not easy.

Common problem areas

Here are some common practical problem areas with suggestions on beliefs that may be contributing to them, and ideas on how to tackle them.

MESSY RISK REGISTERS

Risk registers are a very common way to format information about risks and controls but many have become a confusing mess of ill-defined items where the extent of unintended gaps and overlaps is impossible to determine.

This is the typical result of trying to analyse risk without having a model to which uncertainty attaches, but many people are unaware that using models is a valid alternative. I also suspect that another reason for not bothering more with clear definitions of risk items and not trying harder to progress towards structured models is a cluster of hazy, half-conscious beliefs about risks based on the notion that they are like physical objects.

The cluster of beliefs looks something like this: risks are like physical objects. They exist already. They have their own obvious, natural boundaries (like an orange has a skin) that separate them from each other. Therefore, beyond putting risks into categories, there is no need for structuring or decision-making about how to structure them. Nor is there a need to write down clear definitions of risks. As long as a good enough name is used other people will know what was intended.

As I suggested earlier, and illustrated with research, these beliefs are reflected in language and in the content of guidance but most people, if asked directly if they agree with them, will say they do not. Therefore just inviting people to think carefully for themselves about the true nature of risk/uncertainty should be helpful.

If we knew everything would we ever face risk or uncertainty? Some believe that at least some aspects of the world are inherently impossible to predict. In other words, randomness is real. However, this is at the sub-atomic, quantum level and the debate is almost impossible to follow unless you understand the mathematics and principles of quantum physics very deeply.

In everyday life the reason we don't know what will happen is just that we don't know enough and even if we did we could not use all that information.

Even if we can't agree on whether risk is purely a matter of ignorance it is certainly true that ignorance is the big part of it and something we can often work to reduce.

If you say 'area of uncertainty' instead of 'risk' it tends to help people to think differently about risk. It is a reminder that ignorance is a key part of the problem and that the areas listed are one choice out of many, each area needing clear definition.

SYSTEMATIC UNDERSTATEMENT OF RISK LEVELS

Underestimating risk is nearly always a problem because of our tendency to view the future with mental blinkers. The techniques we use to make estimates should help to counter that bias. Unfortunately, some common techniques actually make things worse.

The problem, again, is those probability impact matrices. The probability of some event happening is fairly well defined, but the impact needs care. What is the impact of 'Loss of market share' or 'Injury due to accident' or 'Client initiated design changes'? Obviously it depends on how much market share is lost, how many injuries there are and how severe each one is, and how many client changes there are and how far reaching.

An event is really a set of outcomes, each with a (probably uncertain) impact associated. Therefore the 'impact' of such a set needs to be specified properly. One good interpretation is that it is what mathematicians call the 'expected' impact, which is the probability weighted average of all the possible outcomes.

When weighing risk in decisions it is usually necessary to summarize the risk down to one value, perhaps as a number, so the weakness here is just summarizing too early, while we are still considering all the consequences and potential responses.

However, there is another, much more serious problem and this is where the systematic understatement of risk levels comes in. Most instructions to people when making impact judgements with PIMs do not mention the need to reach some kind of average. They just ask for 'the impact' as if there is only one to consider. Consequently, we just think of whatever comes to mind first and judge that. All other outcomes get left behind.

For example, if the risk is 'Loss of market share' and this has been judged to be a risk with low impact then the possibility of losing a lot gets removed from consideration completely, even if it is possible, though less likely, than a small loss.

Why are the instructions worded as they are and why do we accept them without question? Again, the main reason is probably that the technique has been recommended and the job is just to get on with it.

However, the technique implies that risks are singular things with only one impact. That is why there is no need to explain what to do about risks with multiple potential impacts.

As with the idea that risks are like physical things, this is a belief that only needs to be thought about clearly and put up against other ideas to be dispelled. It is obvious that each risk relates to multiple possible futures and so needs to be characterized with that in mind. The instructions must be changed or a different method used.

LOW QUANTITY AND QUALITY OF NEW CONTROL IDEAS

The main reason that people struggle to come up with good new ideas for controls is lack of knowledge of control techniques. Simply learning about good alternatives should help most people to produce more valuable ideas for their own purposes.

However, there seems to be more to it than that. The major guidance documents on internal control and risk management have very little material on the design of controls which suggests an underlying belief that design is either not important or too easy to need attention. If mentioned at all it is portrayed as a simple matter of selecting from a small number of obvious options.

This belief that design is trivial may be a legacy of the audit influence on risk control, but wherever it has come from it is now entrenched in several influential documents. Most old school risk management processes are some variation on the picture shown in Figure 16.1, with boxes representing activities and arrows representing data flows or the main direction of inferences.

As you can see the word 'design' does not appear at all and we have to assume it is taken care of somewhere in the 'Plan risk responses' box. COSO's influential framework for internal control is typical in that design is not mentioned at all, even though the framework clearly sets out to be comprehensive.

In the daily life of risk control specialists a lot of time and energy goes into design work, and shopping around for existing designs, because it is complex and important. Ultimately the value of any risk control exercise is limited by the value of the best controls that anyone can think of.

If Figure 16.1 is redrawn to give space to activities in proportion to their importance and resource consumption it ends up looking more like Figure 16.2, in which 'Plan risk responses' has been replaced by a cluster of new boxes, which are tinted here to highlight them.

In Figure 16.2 design and planning are separated, design is top down, and there is research into design options (which includes shopping).

Clearly, controls design is not a trivial matter. It requires skill, time, and supportive processes and tools. There's always a way to improve if we want to.

The second strategy – that of introducing a helpful context – can be used to encourage a more energetic interest in good design. While few people are expert professional designers, most of us have some understanding of creative design and problem solving, and recognize it as part of some activities. Mention controls design in the same sentence as architecture, systems development, and the design of consumer products.

Another reason for weak ideas is a tendency to think that risk is the only source of requirements on controls. (Alternatively, this may be stated as control objectives, though they are just the flip side of risks.) Look at many methods for

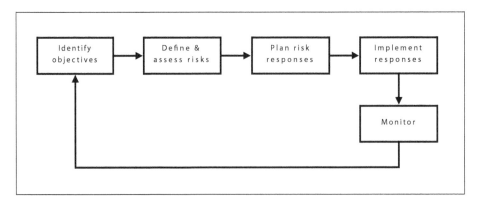

Figure 16.1   Risk management process with no design of controls

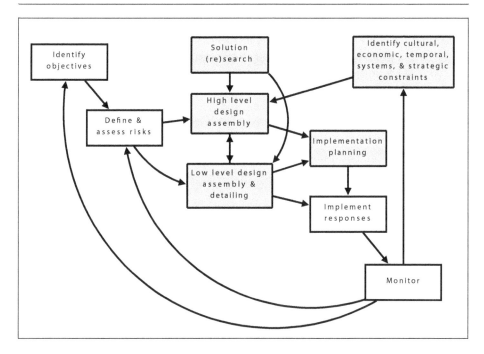

Figure 16.2   Risk management process with design of controls expanded

generating controls and the layouts and procedures progress from risks to controls with no explicit consideration of any other factors that might influence the design of controls. This may be another legacy of the audit influence.

These methods make it too easy to think of a control that would address a risk and then think the job is done, even though the control idea would be costly, take too long to implement, and conflicts with the organization's culture. The more other factors are taken into consideration the more challenging and rewarding design becomes.

A third reason for weak ideas is the belief that individual controls either work or they do not. This is prevalent in auditing and has become part of the lore of reviews under Section 404 of the Sarbanes-Oxley Act. It encourages people to think that one control per risk is ideal and that two controls for one risk represents duplication.

One way to tackle this is to refer to the well-established principle that no control system provides a guarantee, and illustrate this by mentioning collusion and human error. Similarly, no individual control is totally reliable but we can do better using multi-layered designs. Often it is more efficient to fix minor deficiencies in the performance of one control by adding another layer than by gold plating one control.

RELUCTANCE TO USE NUMBERS

Quantification is one of the most controversial topics in risk control. Skill with numbers and mathematical techniques varies so much from one person to another that what is obvious to one person is baffling to another. While one person is busy mastering Lebesgue integrals another may feel that multiplication using a calculator is the height of mathematical sophistication and best avoided if possible.

To some extent, debates about how far to take quantification are really debates about how much mathematical skill is to be required of people and how much that skill is to be rewarded. In some jobs mathematical skill is highly rewarded but in most work settings the majority prefer to see mathematical skill as a bad thing, suggesting lack of social skills and inadequate practical knowledge.

Risk control can be done better using the right mathematical techniques, if you have the skill, and almost always is better done using numbers regardless of skill. Some of the reasons that people reject numbers are based on misconceptions.

My research on this agrees with others. It shows that people generally find numerical descriptions of risk more informative and want to receive them. The problem is more with *giving* descriptions in numerical terms.

One reaction is to say 'I can't put a number on the probability because I don't know what it is'. This can probably be traced back to our experiences of probability in school, which are usually based on situations involving tossing coins, throwing dice, and drawing coloured balls 'at random' from large bags.

In these settings prediction is made impossible by design, so that the best that can be done is to work with the proportion of heads, or sixes, or red balls that would be expected if you repeated the experiment a vast number of times. For convenience the proportions are assumed to be known without requiring any research. For example, the coin is described as 'fair' which means by definition that the probability of heads is the same as tails and is 0.5.

Situations where the long-run relative frequencies of different outcomes are not known in this way are not discussed, which is a pity because they are much more common in everyday life.

Philosophers are still thrashing this out but from a practical point of view betting on sport shows that people can and do work with risk numbers for situations where long-run relative frequencies are not given, and that people who do this with more skill do better (e.g. keep more money) than others.

It works; we just can't agree on why.

As suggested earlier in this chapter it is helpful to use betting on sports as a context to cue relevant beliefs about putting numbers on risk and to avoid mentioning dice.

Experiments with prediction markets suggest that, in future, organizations may be able to harness the views of employees on defined risks of interest by subsidizing betting on probabilities of different outcomes. The technology exists and performance can be excellent in the right circumstances. The setting helps people get over their theoretical worries.

When asked to give probabilities many people feel that giving an exact number suggests they have more knowledge than they really do. There are several ways to deal with this including asking for ranges and using separate ratings of confidence.

Another alternative is to allow freely chosen words or phrases such as 'fairly certain', 'possible', and 'unlikely' or to provide a menu of such phrases so that people can express whatever view they have without using numbers directly. (People do not have consistent meanings for these phrases across different situations, so it is not the most reliable technique.)

One technique that does not solve the problem is to make people select words on a scale such as 'high, medium, low' where the range is divided into non-overlapping buckets. Contrary to most perceptions, this technique still requires accurate knowledge of probabilities because it requires people to make choices near the fixed boundaries of the buckets.

The logic of this is hard to follow and explain so in practice it is best just to describe a design with numbers that allows people to express their doubts honestly.

DISAPPOINTING LEVELS OF EMBEDDING

Most people believe that embedding is a good thing and recognize embedding when they see it. For example, which of these is a better example of successful embedding of risk control?

- Scenario planning is used to think about possible futures and develop plans.
- Plans are made then lists of risks are written and possible control actions considered.

Most people see the first approach as more embedded.

Unfortunately, what often happens is that procedures invented to meet regulatory requirements for assurance are made more frequent, delegated further, and by familiarity become seen as business as usual, from which it is a short step to describing them as 'embedded'.

As usual the main reason for this is probably lack of alternative ideas, but there can also be unhelpful beliefs lurking beneath the surface. There seems to be a tendency to see risks as a special category of thing with a separate existence rather than as uncertainty attached to other knowledge.

For example, occasionally organizations try to merge their risk register with a list of their critical success factors (or objectives, or metrics). The source documents will have been developed separately but are surprisingly similar. One might say 'CSF 21: low churn' while the other says 'Risk of high churn'. In the merged document these two will usually appear as separate items, though under the same heading.

An embedded way to look at this is to say that churn is something the organization is interested in and wants to reduce, but it is uncertain what future churn will be. The risk is an attribute of the construct of churn and inseparable from it.

An appropriate way to deal with this belief is usually to describe control designs and introduce supportive theory. People already recognize and appreciate proper embedding when they see it and just need to hear practical proposals for action.

Notes

1 Roughly 85 per cent of people in a poll I conducted in 2007.
2 In my survey of 30 people interested in risk and/or performance management, 20 preferred 'Perform well', five went for 'Achieve given objectives', two chose 'Achieve original objectives', and two chose 'Other'.
3 It seems that even individual attitudes to risk are not what they sometimes seem. In one experiment differences in willingness to perform risky behaviours were linked to different perceptions of risks and rewards, not differences in risk taking propensity. Weber, E.U., Blais, A-R., and Betz, N.E. (2002) 'A domain-specific risk-attitude scale: measuring risk perceptions and risk behaviours', *Journal of Behavioural Decision Making,* 14 (4).

17 *The Seven Frontiers*

This final chapter is a happy ending. It is true that practical and conceptual progress in risk control has often been painfully slow, but there has been progress and there will be more. These are the seven frontiers on which I expect to see further progress in the coming decade.

Frontier 1: More controls design and less audit and remediation

As mentioned in Chapter 2, a war is going on; a war between the quality movement, the previously dominant approach to process reliability (and efficiency), and the internal controls movement, which is gradually gaining ground. Perhaps this trend has something to do with the change in employment from manufacturing towards services, and financial services in particular.

It surely has little to do with technical merit. Although the internal control perspective has the advantage of risk-thinking and explicit consideration of fraud risks, it is still far behind the quality movement on measurement and design engineering.

However, as quality and internal control gradually swap ideas, and as more and more money is spent on controls, people are beginning to spend more of that money on people whose job is to design and implement better controls.

Another driver is the deluge of 'remediation' produced by projects to comply with Section 404 of the Sarbanes-Oxley Act 2002. Some companies and their auditors have listed thousands of control remediation actions and too many of these have been poorly thought out. I predict a backlash that includes putting competent people in charge of controls improvement.

Also, it is becoming increasingly clear that the key to low-cost compliance with Section 404 is to design control systems that efficiently generate and capture evidence of effectiveness as they operate. This, perhaps more than anything, should be a reason to focus on skilled controls design.

Frontier 2: Corporate risk management getting closer to internal control

Over the last couple of decades the definitions of both 'risk management' and 'internal control' have become ever broader and now I see no worthwhile distinction between them. In Chapter 3, I presented an integrated view that pulls the two together into a simpler whole.

However, risk managers and internal controls managers tend to have different backgrounds and preoccupations. Risk managers tend to be concerned with big, non-recurring risk events and often have insurance or engineering backgrounds. Internal controls people are more concerned with smaller, recurring, internal risk events and tend to have audit or accounting backgrounds.

Already this difference is breaking down and I have met operational risk managers in banking who seem almost equally interested in both routine and non-routine risks, and whose background no longer seems to have much influence on their approach.

There is also a technical reason for internal control and risk management coming even closer together.

While risk managers tend to be better at getting involved in the big business issues and talking with senior management about things that really concern them, the internal controls community is getting better and better at running a 'system'. The trend is towards documenting risks and controls in detail and using confirmations and self-assessment to make sure every last control is complied with all the time.

Gradually people are seeing that the grinding power of the 'system' approach can also be applied to the risks that management, even senior management, take. I have coined the phrase 'intelligent controls' to refer to things that managers can do to manage uncertainty more effectively. Scenario planning, for example, is an intelligent control and a company can make a policy of using it, just as it would make a policy for doing bank reconciliations.

Frontier 3: Better quantification

It's ironic that internal controls thinking, despite being a movement led by the big audit firms (of accountants), has paid almost no attention to quantifying risks or the benefits of controls in a credible, mathematically competent, and data-supported way. Most assessments don't get past 'high-medium-low.'

This is a huge contrast to the quality movement, with its vast array of statistical process control techniques and its emphasis on measurement and on results.

However, as organizations spend more and more on internal controls they reach a point where intuition is no longer enough and reassurances that the work is worthwhile need to be backed up with facts.

Again, operational risk management in banks may be the leading edge of a trend towards better data gathering and quantification. Many banks have done a lot of work to measure operational risk. Some have also begun to look for statistically important relationships between potential drivers of operational risk and the events that result. Gradually intuition is giving way to a more scientific approach.

Frontier 4: Behaviour change beyond risk registers

The objectives of a risk register are to have better risk management and to confirm by the risk-to-control mapping that the main risks are covered. When risk managers begin introducing risk management systems in an organization this is typically where they start.

Once that particular system is running smoothly they often get involved with initiatives to improve controls, such as injecting risk assessments into projects, working out procedures for business case approval, and developing policies for resilient sourcing.

They do this because, in practice, having a nice-looking risk register is no guarantee that risk is being managed well. If managers still pretend to be more certain than they really are (or should be) to get their way, if people hold back bad news in the hope that things will turn out right in the end, if risk management procedures for bids are seen as an obstacle to be gamed until the right answer comes out, and if the company still staggers from one 'unexpected' crisis to another then it doesn't matter what the risk register looks like; risk and uncertainty are being mismanaged.

It is common sense that a risk management programme should cause managers to manage risk better and that means they should behave differently (and not just to the extent of filling in the risk register).

This individual progression from risk registers to directly improving behaviour may be the way that the risk management profession as a whole progresses.

Perhaps we will also see risk managers turning their attention to ways of influencing managers' behaviour directly, such as by education programmes that explore cognitive biases, social factors influencing risk perception and communication, and skills for communicating uncertain information without losing face.

Frontier 5: Risk management that targets psychological factors

I often talk about the psychology of uncertainty and how it leads to bad planning and decisions. This is something people find very interesting and everyone can think of examples from their own experiences of occasions when someone suppressed uncertainty about something, usually with unfortunate results.

Here's another example to add to those already given in this book. At a company whose business involves bidding for large contracts, a system was introduced that worked out minimum bid prices. This system asked sales people for information about risk factors and used this as a significant part of the calculation. Unfortunately, when the system gave a price the sales people did not like some would delete risk factors until they got a number they preferred.

This kind of thing is astonishingly common and so I think we can expect to see increasing interest in ways to counter it. At the moment it is often mentioned informally but in future it could and should become an accepted part of risk management (and internal control) theory.

Frontier 6: Risk and performance management merging through a causal model

Go into a typical large organization and ask for their risk register and their scorecard or something similar that states their major goals and measures of progress. Now compare the two and you will notice that they are remarkably similar.

Very often something stated as a 'critical success factor' perhaps on the scorecard, has a similar item in the risk register that is just the potential failure to achieve what is stated in the critical success factor. Where you find a critical success factor that does not have a matching risk you have to wonder why not, and conversely where there is a risk without a matching critical success factor and the risk does not refer to some external condition, you have to wonder why the critical success factor is missing.

This is hardly surprising as risk analyses are very often driven from statements of objectives. What is surprising, however, is that there are two separate documents looked after by two separate teams. One group is trying to come up with actions that will make something happen. The other is trying to come up with actions that will make sure it does not fail to happen.

Obviously some kind of integration looks promising.

The current leading thinking in performance management is that measures of performance should be based on a causal model of how the organization and its environment work. This model links levers management can pull to the results ultimately achieved. Kaplan and Norton, the original Balanced Scorecard gurus, call this a Strategy Map.

CAUSAL MODELS could be used to generate the Strategy Map and risk analysis in one exercise.

Frontier 7: Technical risk register reforms

My final frontier used to be more of a plea than a prediction, but now at last there are signs that the glaring problems with many risk registers are becoming clear to more and more people and there is growing interest in reforms.

Typically this will mean moving towards more mathematically inspired approaches.

Finally

Imagine the effect of making progress on all seven frontiers of risk control. Imagine systematic implementation of hard-hitting controls, with measured benefits, profound behaviour change leading to wiser management at all levels, techniques that are both simple and effective, and the satisfying feeling of having efficient controls carefully designed and implemented in good time.

Of course that won't happen in one go. Take it little by little, looking for small but tangible improvements all the time.

Let's enjoy this Wild West, the frontier territory of risk control, with its many opportunities for innovation, while it lasts.

Index